Catastrophic Consequences

Catastrophic Consequences

Civil Wars and American Interests

STEVEN R. DAVID

The Johns Hopkins University Press
Baltimore

© 2008 The Johns Hopkins University Press
All rights reserved. Published 2008
Printed in the United States of America on acid-free paper

2   4   6   8   9   7   5   3   1

The Johns Hopkins University Press
2715 North Charles Street
Baltimore, Maryland 21218-4363
www.press.jhu.edu

Library of Congress Cataloging-in-Publication Data
David, Steven R.
Catastrophic consequences : civil wars and American interests /
Steven R. David.
p.   cm.
Includes bibliographical references and index.
ISBN-13: 978-0-8018-8988-2 (hardcover : alk. paper)
ISBN-13: 978-0-8018-8989-9 (pbk. : alk. paper)
ISBN-10: 0-8018-8988-X (hardcover : alk. paper)
ISBN-10: 0-8018-8989-8 (pbk. : alk. paper)
1. United States—Foreign relations—21st century. 2. United States—
Economic conditions—21st century. 3. Civil war—Saudi Arabia—
Economic aspects. 4. Civil war—Pakistan—Economic aspects.
5. Civil war—Mexico—Economic aspects. 6. Civil war—
China—Economic aspects. I. Title.
JZ1480.A5D38 2008
303.6′4—dc22   2007052590

A catalog record for this book is available
from the British Library.

Special discounts are available for bulk purchases of this book.
For more information, please contact Special Sales at
410-516-6936 or specialsales@press.jhu.edu.

The Johns Hopkins University Press uses environmentally friendly book
materials, including recycled text paper that is composed of at least
30 percent post-consumer waste, whenever possible. All of our
book papers are acid-free, and our jackets and covers are
printed on paper with recycled content.

For Sarah, Julia, and Katie

Contents

Preface   *ix*

1 A New Kind of Threat   1

2 Saudi Arabia: *Oil Fields Ablaze*   21

3 Pakistan: *Loose Nukes*   50

4 Mexico: A *Flood of Refugees*   82

5 China: *Collapse of a Great Power*   115

6 The Coming Storm   147

Notes   173
Index   197

Preface

This volume grew out of my experiences — and frustrations — in teaching the introductory course in international relations at the Johns Hopkins University over the past 25 years. As in many classes on international relations, I focused on the core issues of war and peace, especially among great powers. Drawing from Thucydides, Morgenthau, and Waltz, I carefully explained the theories of why countries went to war with one another, and then considered those theories in the context of great power conflicts such as the Peloponnesian War, the wars of German unification, World War I, and World War II. These theories also were employed to explain why wars did not happen, notably the happy failure of the United States to come to blows with the Soviet Union in what became known as the Cold War.

Although the class proved popular, I became increasingly disenchanted with its emphasis on the causes and prevention of war among major powers. After all, the last great power conflict, World War II, occurred over 60 years ago, and despite occasional concerns expressed about China, the prospect of another great power war appeared increasingly remote. Nuclear weapons, the spread of democracy, and globalization had convinced most heads of state that the costs of war far exceeded any benefits. It was clear to me that the United States and most other countries had less to fear from outside attack than at any time since the emergence of modern states in the seventeenth century. Focusing on issues of war and peace among great powers no longer seemed to make much sense.

All the more so because the United States confronted real threats to its security and economic well-being not considered by traditional international relations theory. What the United States worries about today are governments collapsing allowing nuclear weapons to fall into the hands of extremist groups, of civil conflicts engulfing key trading partners and oil exporters, of violent instability pushing otherwise prudent regimes to undertake diversionary wars, and of chaos on its southern border flooding America with refugees, drugs, and disorder. Understanding how to address these very real threats rather than focusing on the dangers of a bygone age became the focus of this book.

It quickly became apparent to me that these new threats shared two characteristics. First, unlike traditional threats focused on international relations, they are largely *unintended*. Second, the most likely way most of these threats would be unleashed would be through civil wars or some other form of widespread domestic instability undermining the governments that kept these potential dangers in check. Addressing these threats required identifying those countries where civil war was plausible and, if it occurred, would threaten vital American interests and then determining what, if anything, could be done about the potential dangers raised by these conflicts.

Four countries emerged as most worrisome: Saudi Arabia, Pakistan, Mexico, and China. For reasons explained in the book — each country will be detailed in its own chapter — all run the risk of being torn apart by civil conflict in the coming years. The threats unleashed by these conflicts differ with each country. For Saudi Arabia, it is the loss of oil; for Pakistan, the loss of control over its nuclear weapons; Mexico poses the multiple dangers of floods of refugees and illegal drugs, spillover of violence, and the plight of millions of Americans living and traveling in a war-torn country; China threatens to do severe damage to the American economy while endangering the security of key American allies. For each of these cases, the prospect of civil war heightens the *probability* that these threats will come about and increases the *harm* that would result to American interests if they do.

Trying to determine how to deal with the problems unleashed by these potential civil wars proved as daunting as assessing the dangers they presented. The usual tools states employed to guard against threats — deterrence, prevention, defense, and preemption — are not likely to be effective against the inadvertent harm sprung by civil conflicts. Insights on how to proceed came to me not from the literature of international relations, but rather by considering the response to another form of unstoppable threat, namely, preparations undertaken to deal with natural catastrophes such as hurricanes and earthquakes. I briefly consider this approach in my conclusion.

My book takes an untraditional look at what menaces the United States and what can be done about it. It reflects a world where interstate war is becoming all but obsolete, but where wars within countries continue unabated, where the greatest danger comes not from leaders meaning to hurt America but from governments that lose control over what goes on within their borders. I propose a new way of thinking about threats to American interests that I hope will be of value to both scholars and policymakers.

Many friends and colleagues helped make this book possible. Portions of the manuscript were read by Aaron Friedberg, Kellee Tsai, Robert Freedman, Thomas Thornton, Steve Yetiv, Peter Marber, and Daniel Markey. Daniel Deudney helped me sort out key arguments and suggested the title. Jon Links, of the Bloomberg School of Public Health, provided much-needed assistance on employing the natural catastrophe model for political events. I benefited from several exchanges with Scott Sagan regarding Pakistani nuclear weapons. Students in my graduate seminar — Michael Danzer, Wesley Fredericks, Sunil Vaswani, Thomas Williams, and Evan Tucker — all provided useful feedback on earlier versions of the manuscript. Sunil Vaswani, Thomas Williams, and Mary Otterbein helped in preparing the manuscript for publication. Since not all of those who provided suggestions for this book agree with its arguments, final responsibility for the views expressed rest with myself. I owe a debt of gratitude to Henry Tom of the Johns Hopkins University Press, who expertly and expeditiously guided the book through the editorial process. Finally, I am forever grateful to my wife, Maureen, and my three daughters, Sarah, Julia, and Katie, for impressing on me the primacy of domestic politics.

Catastrophic Consequences

CHAPTER ONE

A New Kind of Threat

Historical events have given lie to the conventional wisdom on civil wars: that they are internal matters which great powers may simply ignore. Since the end of the Cold War, the United States has again and again found itself in the middle of civil conflicts, including in Iraq, Afghanistan, Somalia, and the Balkans. The attention paid by the United States to these civil conflicts should come as no surprise. Only recently have major powers refrained from involvement in civil wars. Traditionally, just the opposite has been the case. And with good reason: revolutions in France, Russia, China, and Iran sparked profound changes in the international system that remain with us today. During the Cold War, internal conflicts in Korea and Vietnam drew the United States into costly interventions, while domestic strife in El Salvador and Nicaragua dominated American foreign policy in the 1980s. For the Soviet Union, internal wars provided the source for both one of Moscow's greatest victories (Cuba) and one of its most costly defeats (Afghanistan).

Since the collapse of the USSR (brought on in part by the Afghan disaster) and the end of the Cold War, new questions must be asked about civil wars and American interests. Proxy fights between Russia and America are no longer likely. The domino effect is no longer a concern. Though wars within states continue to greatly outnumber those fought between them, some now argue that the United States should ignore internal squabbles. These civil wars, they contend, are the domestic affairs of poor, weak countries, not important enough to merit American involvement. Getting enmeshed in complicated disputes and age-old hatreds will sap American resources — and for no good reason.[1]

There is something to this view. Most civil wars do not directly threaten the

United States or its allies. While the great majority of post–Cold War internal conflicts have raised humanitarian concerns, few have seriously affected American security or economic interests. This, however, was largely a matter of luck. The United States should recognize a vital and sobering truth: that civil wars can pose deadly threats to America. These threats are not the traditional dangers of state-to-state aggression, such as outside attack or invasion, but are equally serious. Though largely ignored by scholars and policymakers, who remain fixated on the idea of interstate conflict, civil wars and other forms of domestic violence in other countries have emerged as one of the principal perils to American vital interests.

The role of civil wars in endangering American interests has been largely overlooked, because aggression from other countries has traditionally been seen as the most important threat against the United States and its allies. Scholars have become so focused on the dangers great powers pose to one another that some have concluded that the study of international relations is simply the study of great power conflict.[2] Those who believe great powers are likely to be peaceful in their dealings with each other tend to be optimistic about the course of international relations, while those who believe great powers are likely to go to war with one another are pessimistic.[3] This focus on great power war is not surprising. Throughout history, great powers have been concerned with issues of peace and security, and the biggest threat to the peace and security of great powers has come from other great powers. To threaten a powerful state, you needed to be a powerful state. Only great powers had the military forces, the economic might, and the organizational skill to threaten other powerful countries. And threaten them they did, in war after bloody war. From the emergence of modern nation-states in 1648 to World War II, the great powers of Europe engaged in countless conflicts, leading many to conclude that war among powerful states is merely the natural order of things. But great power conflict came to an abrupt end in the aftermath of World War II. From 1945 to the present, the world has seen the longest period of extended peace among the great powers in recorded history. Great powers simply do not go to war with each other any more, and there is every indication that what historian John Lewis Gaddis has called the "long peace" will endure.[4]

What does the United States worry about if not an attack by another great power? It worries about central governments weakening and collapsing, with weapons of mass destruction falling into the hands of terrorist groups or detonated by accident or without government authorization. America worries about internal wars destroying the ability of countries to export critical natural resources or purchase American treasury bonds and goods necessary to keep the American economy functioning. America is anxious about foreign leaders pursuing reckless policies to divert attention away from domestic strife. The United States fears widespread instability on its border, unleashing floods of refugees and threatening the safety of hundreds of thousands of American citizens living and traveling abroad. America is also concerned about the humanitarian disasters that civil wars leave in their wake, although they are not a threat to vital interests.

What these threats have in common is that they are largely *unintended* by the leaders of the countries from which they originate. Being unintended, the spillover effects of instability are not easily deterred. American policymakers have traditionally influenced foreign leaders through a simple formula: make the costs of defying America greater than the benefits. This has largely worked because the United States is so strong. In terms of military power, there are no countries or groups that can challenge America's might. When economic strength and cultural attributes are added, it is clear that the United States has an array of instruments that would make any potential antagonist think twice before threatening America. Deterrence, however, is not effective when governments are not behind the threats that America seeks to counter. If deterrence will not work, the United States may choose to rely upon actual self-defense or preemption instead. Unlike deterrence, however, these strategies can be enormously difficult to carry out and in some cases are impossible. By weakening government control, civil wars unleash threats that strike at the very heart of America's existence while eliminating America's ability to deter those threats, traditionally America's best protection against those who wish it ill.

Understanding the central importance of civil wars in endangering American interests requires first recognizing why international war and other deliberate decisions to harm the United States are not the problems they once were. It is then necessary to understand why civil wars and domestic conflicts more generally show no signs of going away. As will be seen, when civil conflicts occur in a country whose stability is of vital concern to the United States, American interests are threatened as much as by willful attacks. Because threats unleashed by civil wars are mostly not deliberate, they pose challenges fundamentally different from what American policymakers have addressed in the past, calling into question our traditional understanding of international relations and the best ways for America to ensure its security in the post–Cold War world.

THE DECLINE OF INTERNATIONAL WAR

For the first time in its history, the principal threats to the United States do not stem from the decisions of other governments. For reasons that are not difficult to fathom, the United States presently faces little, if any, danger from attack from other countries. The United States is the foremost military power of its time. Even after major cutbacks following the end of the Cold War, the United States still has thousands of nuclear warheads deployed in submarines, in underground silos, and long-range aircraft. It would be impossible for any adversary to destroy or disable all these weapons in a first strike. Any country launching a nuclear attack against the United States must recognize that it would suffer devastating retaliation. Since world leaders are rational in the sense that they are sensitive to costs, and because no interest is worth bringing about one's own destruction, it is highly unlikely that the United States would ever become the victim of a deliberate nuclear attack ordered by the government of another country.[5]

Nor does the United States have to worry about a conventional assault. The United States has the strongest armed forces in the world, with some estimating that the American defense budget is equal to that of the rest of the world's put together. No country has the logistical means and military might to challenge America's supremacy. While China is sometimes mentioned as a superpower adversary, Beijing is still far behind the United States in its ability to project force and in the technological sophistication of its weaponry.[6] Even if a leader becomes convinced that the United States could be militarily vanquished, the fear that the prospect of an American defeat would provoke nuclear retaliation would be enough to overturn any decision to go to war.

American power is not the only reason the United States need not worry about threats from other states. Because interstate war in general has become so rare, the security of American allies and the maintenance of American interests throughout the world are not threatened by attacks from other countries to the extent they have been in the past. The dramatic decline in international war is perhaps the most profound transformation in international relations since the emergence of modern states in the seventeenth century. War between states used to be a common occurrence. Between 1816 and 2002, there were 199 international wars (including colonial wars and "wars of liberation").[7] In the post–Cold War era from the 1990s through 2006, there have been only three clear-cut cases of international wars: Iraq's invasion of Kuwait in 1990 and the two American interventions against Iraq (1991, 2003) that followed. Excepting Iraq, therefore, international war has been absent from the globe for over a decade and a half, and in some years there have been no cases of international war at all.[8]

The reasons for international peace are many, and they are likely to persist. Nuclear weapons aid peace because attacking a nuclear-armed state is widely, if not yet universally, understood to be suicidal. Territory, a prime reason for war, has diminished in importance as agriculture has declined as a source of wealth. Long-range missiles, too, have usually lessened the strategic significance of holding on to specific parcels of land. Conquering other populations yields little benefit in a time when a country's economic well-being is increasingly dependent on a skilled, free citizenry. The triumph of the holy trinity of classical liberalism — democracy, trade, and international institutions — has also helped to reduce interstate war as ever more national elites recognize that armed conflict makes prosperity impossible and their own political fortunes tenuous. Put simply, nearly all agree that the costs of war between states have risen while the benefits have declined.[9]

These forces for peace have created what political scientist Karl Deutsch has termed "a security community" — a group of countries among which war is inconceivable.[10] The most highly developed states of the world, including the United States, Japan, and Western Europe, make up the security community in the post–Cold War era. For the first time in history, the strongest countries are not threatening each other with armed conflict. What is often ignored, however, is that weaker powers outside any security community also benefit from the causes of international peace. Although some have not reached the point where war is no longer an option, they too have less to fear from attack by their neighbors. This is true even for traditional rivals. The last major war between Israel and the Arab states was in 1973, between India and Pakistan in 1971. In the developing world as in the West, interstate war is on the decline.

To be sure, as the 2003 American intervention in Iraq demonstrates, international war has not yet become obsolete. Tensions between North and South Korea, China and Taiwan, India and Pakistan, and throughout the Middle East could still lead to warfare. And yet, the "security community" envisioned by Karl Deutsch does appear to have taken hold and spread beyond the great powers. While no one force for peace is definitive, taken together, they have created a post–Cold War world where conflicts between nations, while still possible, have become rare. Inasmuch as these forces for peace show few signs of disappearing or weakening, the prospects of peace between states are as bright as they have ever been. With the dawning of the post–Cold War era, the fear of attack from other countries that has driven international relations for centuries no longer stands at the center of American concerns.

THE PRIMACY OF CIVIL WAR

While international war has all but vanished as a threat to American interests, warfare *within* countries shows no signs of going away. Before discussing the prevalence and persistence of these conflicts, it is necessary to clarify what is meant by civil wars. Even more than international war, civil war is an elusive concept. For social scientists, civil wars are armed conflicts occurring principally in one country in which there are at least 1,000 battlefield-related deaths in a year with at least 100 of those deaths occurring on each side. Inasmuch as 1,000 battlefield deaths would overlook many violent disputes, some analysts prefer the term "civil conflicts," in which only 25 battlefield-related deaths need to occur in a year. Some definitions go beyond the number of casualties to require that there be a struggle for state power in which one of the combatants is the existing government for a civil war to occur. Others maintain fighting reaches the level of civil war only when uniformed armies clash in conventional battles to determine who will rule the country.[11]

Whatever the accepted definition might be, no one disputes that civil wars come in many different forms. The most basic distinction is between ethnic and ideological conflicts. In ideological conflicts, such as in Vietnam, groups compete by trying to persuade a population that its future is best left in their hands. Ideas are critical in such wars as you try to win the "hearts and minds" of potential supporters. In ethnic conflicts, such as in Rwanda, allegiance is determined by DNA. There is no process of persuasion, no effort to bring outsiders to your cause, only a contest over which ethnic group can impose its will on the others.[12] Civil wars also differ as to scale and organization. Some, like the American Civil War, involve large conventional armies clashing on battlefields in a manner similar to major interstate wars. Others, such as in Sierra Leone, are little more than small roving bands of hooligans terrorizing the populace. Some civil wars are driven by the desire of a group to secede from the state without seeking the removal of the regime or the destruction of the state itself, as seen in the Eritrean-Ethiopian civil war that lasted decades until Eritrean independence in 1991 or the Biafran war in Nigeria in the late 1960s. Other civil wars stem from a desire to topple and seize the government, as in the Russian Civil War of 1918–1920 or the Greek Civil War of 1946–1949. Finally civil wars differ as to the degree of external involvement. Some civil wars (Nepal's, for example) have had relatively little foreign participation, while others (Congo) are veritable international fields of battle. As might be expected, the more intransigent and ambitious the goals of the belligerents, the more bloody and long-lasting a civil war is liable to be. And the more long lasting it is the more likely there will be foreign involvement.

The concept of "political violence" goes beyond civil war and includes such diverse phenomena as revolutions, insurrections, insurgencies, terrorism, and coups. In his 1970 classic, *Why Men Rebel*, Ted Robert Gurr divides political violence into three forms: turmoil (spontaneous, unorganized violence, such as riots and local rebellions), conspiracy (organized political violence that does not involve large numbers of participants, such as assassinations and coups), and internal war (organized political violence with widespread involvement whose aim is to topple the government).[13] This study is concerned with the full range of activities considered to be political violence provided that they challenge the ability of a government to maintain order within its borders. From the perspective of American interests, it is less the specific form of political violence that matters than it is the loss of control, which unleashes the threats that endanger vital American concerns. As such, I use terms like "civil war," "internal conflict," and "domestic violence" interchangeably, given the common threat they pose to societal stability and governmental rule.

However defined, civil wars have always been more numerous than international wars, a dominance that has grown over time. From 1816 to 2002, civil wars made up only slightly more than half of all wars.[14] With the end of the Cold War, international wars, as noted, have dropped precipitously, but internal conflicts still abound. It is true that in absolute terms civil conflicts have declined as wars related to decolonization have ended and the superpowers no longer back clients in the Third World as part of their Cold War competition. Nevertheless, fully 95% of armed conflicts from 1995 to 2005 occurred within countries rather than between them.[15] Since the end of the Cold War, over one-third of all countries have endured serious civil conflict.[16] Those that may have escaped internal violence are still in danger of succumbing to civil war in the future. According to the political scientists Monty Marshall and Ted Gurr, fully 31 out of 161 countries surveyed have a high risk of being vulnerable to civil conflict, while an additional 51 countries have a moderate risk. All told, therefore, half of the world's states can credibly be seen as being at risk of falling victim to civil war or some other form of major internal disorder.[17]

Making matters worse, once civil wars begin, they are notoriously difficult to stop. Civil wars typically last much longer than wars between countries. They are far more likely to be halted by one side winning a military victory than by a negotiated settlement. Unlike state-to-state conflict, where the belligerents can retreat back to their respective countries once the war is over, in a civil war the opposing sides must somehow live together in a single country despite the profound differences that drove them apart. As such, civil wars have a disturbing tendency to flare up again after a peace settlement has been reached.[18] Insofar as organized violence is a problem, it is largely a problem that occurs inside a country's borders.

Aside from being so prevalent and chronic, civil wars show no signs of going away. The forces for peace that almost completely halted wars between states largely do not apply to civil wars. The reassuring logic of nuclear deterrence does not hold in civil wars, where mixed populations may preclude clearly delineated targets upon which one can threaten murderous retaliation. While there have been no civil wars that have engulfed entire nuclear weapons states, widespread domestic strife in such nuclear powers as China, Pakistan, India, Israel, South Africa, and Russia does not provide much encouragement about the peace-inducing effects of nuclear arms.

Nor does the recognition that war does not pay offer much hope of halting civil conflicts. The intifadas waged against Israel in the late 1980s and first years of the twenty-first century erupted with the full knowledge of the Palestinian people that they would bring economic ruin in their wake. No one suggests that democracy prevents war within countries as it appears to do between countries. Civil wars or major internal violence in democracies like the United States, India, and Israel give lie to the notion of a "democratic peace" when the fighting is confined to one country. While global norms against conflict do some good in inhibiting wars between countries, they are largely ineffectual with regard to internal wars. When Saddam Hussein gassed Iraqi Kurds in 1988, it produced scant international protest. Saddam Hussein's invasion of Kuwait in 1990, however, provoked a grand multinational intervention, led by the United States, that reversed his aggression. The lesson is clear: if you want to go to war, confine it to your country. Nor does globalization seriously inhibit civil conflict. Just as the benefits of globalization are uneven across countries, exacerbating international tensions, so are they uneven within countries, making worse existing domestic conflicts. The notion that people have internalized norms of nonviolence and peaceful resolutions of disputes does not apply for many civil conflicts, where brutality and needless bloodshed are commonplace.

Most important, the causes of civil war show no signs of going away. Civil war, even more than international war, can be caused by a staggering array of possible factors ranging from the collapse of central governments to the sheer joy of violence.[19] Of the many alleged reasons for civil war, three stand out. First, for civil war to erupt there needs to be an intense grievance held by a substantial portion of the population. If you are not fighting mad about something, you are not likely to fight. Second, people need to believe they have the *right* to engage in violence. This right may stem from the belief that the government is illegitimate, or that other groups in the state are not part of the broader community whether they are formally citizens or not.[20] Finally, people need to believe they will gain from violence before initiating civil strife. The belief that you can win through armed struggle goes a long way toward ensuring that armed struggle will commence. Determining where future civil conflict will erupt, therefore, is relatively straightforward. Where there are intense grievances held by groups who believe they have a right to rebel and that they will be victorious, civil war is likely. Where even one of these factors is absent, the chances that civil war will erupt are slim.[21]

The characteristics of countries throughout the world, especially (but not exclusively) in the developing countries of Asia, Africa, Latin America, and the Middle East, provide fertile ground for the causes of internal war. Intense grievances abound in the developing world.[22] The over 30 countries classified by the United Nations as "least developed," including Yemen, Haiti, and Chad, have life expectancies of only around 50 years, with fully half the people being unable to read and write. Almost a fifth of the world's population lives on under $1 a day, the great majority of whom are in developing countries.[23] Poverty is not in itself a cause of civil war, but is a contributing factor, as evidenced by the prevalence of internal conflict in poor countries.[24]

What's worse, the world is filled with incompetent and corrupt regimes that are unable or unwilling to better the lives of their people. For many countries, the government is not even present in wide areas of the state, much less available to solve problems or provide security. Regimes frequently favor certain groups based on region, religion, or ethnicity, infuriating those who are not part of the chosen few. A major reason for civil conflict erupting in Iraq following the American intervention was the belief that a Shia-dominated government would not give a fair shake to the Sunnis, who, when they were in power, discriminated against the Shia. Many governments have inflicted brutalities on their people, a legacy that is rarely forgotten. Massive unemployment, the absence of public education, and lack of political participation have fostered the growth of extremist ideologies filled with hatred. Some are ethnic based, such as the hypernationalism of the Hutus in Rwanda; others are driven by religious fervor, such as the emergence of Al Qaeda. Whatever their source, these ideologies are likely to be violent and destabilizing, at times leading to civil war.

In many countries, people have a strong belief that they have a right to rebel because they do not support their government's right to rule over them. The lack of legitimacy that is epidemic in the developing world is not difficult to understand. Most of the states in the developing world are less than 60 years old. It took the European states several centuries before they achieved legitimate governments; it is understandable if the less-developed countries take more than several decades to reach the same level.[25] Most governments in the developing world are not democracies.[26] They have not been selected in free and fair elections in which most of the people are allowed to vote. Because the people did not choose their government, they feel no moral obligation to follow its dictates. Without democracy as a legitimizing force, many regimes rely on extremist ideology or religion to justify their rule. This works so long as their citizens accept the ideological or religious vision of the regime. If they do not, if they reject its ideology or question the religious commitment of the leadership, the government loses its authority. The performance of a government can also undermine its legitimacy. If the regime cannot attend to the basic needs of its people, a situation that is rife among the less-developed countries, groups will have little trouble in justifying a right to rebel. The absence of institutions to channel conflict and respond to grievances is the norm in the developing world, and as Samuel Huntington pointed out nearly 40 years ago, is a major source of internal conflict.[27]

Many countries lack a sense of community, further weakening any sense of legitimacy. Rather than coherent states with a strong sense of national identity, they are artificial creations of colonial powers, countries created by outside countries where none had existed previously. These countries are legal entities, in the sense that they have international recognition and a seat in the United Nations. Nevertheless, they have no common tradition or ideals to bind them together. The ruling government may hold sway over little more than the capital city. As such, there is very little identification with the state. Instead, loyalty is owed to one's ethnic, religious, or regional group. You are a Kurd, Shia, or Sunni rather than being an Iraqi; an Ibo or Hausa instead of a Nigerian. Since the great majority of developing states are made up of many different groups, the stage is set for intergroup conflict. Since these "other" groups are not part of your community, you have every right to make war on them, as they do on you.[28]

Conditions within the less-developed countries often convince insurgents they can be successful in meeting their goals, thus encouraging the resort to violence. Governments in the developing world tend to be weak, in that they cannot achieve what they seek to accomplish. Their weakness stems in part from their being independent for such a short time. They have not had the years to develop the traditions and experience that would enable them to command obedience from their citizenry. Unlike the Europeans, governments in developing states have come of age in an environment marked by international interference, demands for mass participation, and concern for human rights, making their efforts to govern far more difficult.[29] Developing states often lack trained personnel to staff the bureaucracy and legislature, further hampering efforts to get things done.[30] Corruption, inefficiency, and ineptitude characterize the regimes of many of these new, struggling regimes in the developing world.

The very absence of war between countries has had the unfortunate side effect of contributing to the weakness of governments, especially those in the developing world. As the sociologist Charles Tilly has argued, war is a central reason for the creation of strong countries. States confronted with war had to mobilize popular support and impose taxes if they were to survive. States able to do this persevered and prospered. Those that could not meet these challenges disappeared. Europe had roughly 500 independent entities in the year 1500. By 1900, that number had shrunk to around 20. The brutal evolutionary process that destroyed so much nevertheless left the survivors strong and resilient.[31]

Among many of the developing states, however, this process did not take place. The combination of the lack of interstate war and the international norm of supporting the preservation of formal states has meant that very few countries need fear for their existence. Countries, for the most part, do not disappear, but they survive as states in name only. Their governments are unable to tax their people, nor can they mobilize their populations for support. Because of the absence of an external threat, there is little incentive for leaders to establish the social control necessary for a strong state to emerge.[32] As the political scientist Michael Desch has argued, while developed countries can meet the "burden" of peace by falling back on strengths they acquired when they faced external threats, a benign international environment exacerbates existing fault lines within younger states that never had to deal with a serious outside threat, making them even less able to cope with domestic challenges when they emerge.[33] Civil conflicts abound in these countries because insurgents have a reasonable belief that they can win against the weak regimes they confront.

Challenging these weak regimes takes a surprisingly small number of rebels. As the political scientist John Mueller argues, what we tend to think of as full-fledged civil conflicts often stem from the actions of a handful of malcontents. It takes leaders to whip up passions, but at the end of the day they only need to recruit a fanatical core of followers to commit mass mayhem. Mueller estimates that the civil war in Colombia is fueled by less than 6,000 rebels, while the Chechen conflict in Russia is driven by some 3,000 insurgents. Even the Rwandan genocide, which killed some 800,000 Tutsis and moderate Hutus in three months, was undertaken by less than 10% of the Hutu population. Many of these "insurgents" perpetuating civil violence are not politically motivated but are simply common criminals and sociopaths, challenging the government either for personal profit or because they are testosterone-driven young males who enjoy the thrill of killing. Their armed struggle is frequently sustained by the presence of valuable natural resources, such as diamonds, that pay for a continuing supply of arms, food, and recruits. It is reassuring that the majority of civil conflicts are not fought by mass armies involving most of a country's population. Nevertheless, since it takes just a few to disrupt an entire state, the threshold to bring about widespread domestic violence is frighteningly low.[34]

Although civil conflict is more likely to occur in countries that are considered part of the developing world, no state is immune. States once considered part of the developing world, such as South Korea, Taiwan, Brazil, and Costa Rica, face few prospects of civil conflict. On the other hand, countries once seen as part of the developed world, such as Russia and the former Yugoslavia, have experienced much internal strife. Just as countries move in and out of "developing" status, so too does their risk for civil conflict vary over time. Wherever the causes of civil war exist, wherever angry groups believe they have a right to commit violence that will advance their goals, the prospects for civil conflict will flourish.

International relations theory tells us that wars occur between countries because, in the absence of a world government, there is nothing to stop them. Today, weak and ineffective governments in many countries have created a situation in which civil conflicts occur because there is nothing to stop *them*. In the international arena, incentives for peace have made the lack of world governance all but irrelevant in halting interstate war. Within countries, however, the weakness of factors promoting peace and the persistence of aggrieved populations ruled by illegitimate governments in inherently weak states suggest civil wars will continue. International relations theory thus has it backward: instead of living in a world of international anarchy and domestic order, we have international order and domestic anarchy.[35]

WHY WORRY

Just because civil wars and domestic strife are likely to persist does not mean that they will threaten American interests. For as long as the United States has existed, civil conflict has raged throughout the world, raising the question of why such conflicts should arouse American concerns now. The United States needs to be worried because in the post–Cold War world America's security and economic well-being depend upon order being maintained in certain key states. If order is not maintained, the effects of civil wars are likely to spill over to other countries, at times threatening vital American interests. Dire threats to the United States, therefore, stem not from the deliberate decisions of heads of state to attack American interests. Rather, the greatest dangers faced by the United States in the twenty-first century occur when leaders in certain countries *lose* control of what goes on within their borders. By weakening governmental control, civil conflicts in certain countries not only endanger the interests of their own states, they threaten America as well.

Of the many dangers to the United States that would be unleashed by civil conflict, several stand out. The greatest is the use of weapons of mass destruction against American allies or the United States itself. Weapons of mass destruction typically comprise nuclear, biological, radiological, and chemical arms. Of this group, nuclear weapons are by far the most worrisome because only they are able to produce sudden destruction on a scale never before witnessed in the history of mankind. It only takes a single nuclear bomb to destroy a city along with millions of its inhabitants. With the spread of nuclear weapons and fissionable materials to countries throughout the world, there is an alarming possibility that this destructive capability will fall into the wrong hands. Once extremist groups gain control of nuclear arms, delivery against the United States or its allies would be frighteningly easy.[36]

Biological weapons are nearly as worrisome as their nuclear counterparts. Biological weapons are living organisms that kill or maim. Some, like smallpox, are highly contagious, while others, such as anthrax, are frequently deadly. Under the right conditions, biological weapons can kill hundreds of thousands.[37] Even when the level of fatalities is not high, biological weapons produce a staggering psychological impact. Only five people were killed in the post-9/11 anthrax attacks in the United States, but offices of the Capitol were closed for months, mail service was drastically curtailed, and there was a heightened level of fear throughout America. If biological warfare does not rise to being a weapon of mass destruction, it will, at the very least, succeed in being a weapon of mass *disruption* wherever it is deployed.[38]

Only slightly less alarming are radiological weapons, so-called dirty bombs. By attaching radioactive material, such as cobalt or americium, to a conventional explosive, large areas can be contaminated for years. One shudders to think of the effect of a dirty bomb in New York's Times Square or the Mall in Washington, DC.[39] Finally, there are chemical weapons, such as poison gas. It is not clear that chemical weapons are any more lethal than conventional arms, but like biological and radiological weapons, they have a powerful psychological effect. Unlike nuclear or possibly biological weapons, chemical arms do not pose an existential threat to the United States or other great powers. But if used against the United States directly, American forces abroad, or American allies, they could be a cataclysmic challenge to Washington's sense of security.[40]

Weapons of mass destruction allow the very weak, for the first time in history, to inflict catastrophic damage on the very strong. No longer is it necessary to be a great power to threaten a great power. The mere possession of a single nuclear bomb, or possibly a vial filled with germs, elevates a primitive country or ragtag group to a mortal threat against the mightiest of nations. So long as these weapons are within the firm control of strong states, however, America and other countries can rest comfortably. Just as deterrence kept the peace between the United States and the Soviet Union during the Cold War, so too can it be counted upon to keep the peace between the United States and the new proliferators.

Problems arise when the government loses control over its weapons of mass destruction, most alarmingly when it loses control over its nuclear arsenal. At this point, deterrence collapses and the likelihood of these arms being used against the United States and others soars. Civil war or major domestic disorder is a prime means by which governmental control over its arsenal can become compromised. At the very least, nuclear accidents become more likely. The primitive designs of nuclear arms, especially in developing states, make them vulnerable to detonation if they get caught up in the firefights of civil conflict. Accidental detonations could produce a humanitarian disaster, or worse, could provoke a nuclear war if the explosion was misread as an enemy attack. Civil war also increases the chances of unauthorized launchings of nuclear arms. The command and control of the nuclear forces of many countries is suspect. Especially in the context of domestic violence, the ability of governments to prevent lower-ranking subordinates from launching weapons may be undermined. A colonel seething with hatred might take advantage of the chaos of civil war to initiate an attack against a regional rival, perhaps provoking a major nuclear war. Even a limited strike would hurt American interests by eroding the taboo against using nuclear weapons and possibly causing many innocent deaths. For any of these horrors, the comfortable reassurances of deterrence do not apply. By letting loose weapons that had previously been under the control of responsible governments, civil wars raise the possibility of a nuclear attack that would seriously threaten American interests.

Deterrence will also be of little use if weapons of mass destruction fall into the hands of terrorist groups, such as Al Qaeda. Deterrence rests on the assumption that adversaries can be persuaded not to do something they are capable of doing by the threat of unacceptable punishment. Terrorist groups cannot be dissuaded from their deadly agendas, because their location is largely unknown. Since they are not countries, they have no "return address," complicating any threat of retaliation. Moreover, many of the adherents of terror groups embrace death. Perhaps they truly believe that death in a noble cause will transport them to Paradise, or they may believe intently the justness of their cause merits the sacrifice of their lives. Whatever the reason, it is difficult if not impossible to find a punishment that is unacceptable to an antagonist who welcomes martyrdom.[41]

While terrorist groups have been around a long time, the emergence of organizations like Al Qaeda present an unprecedented challenge to the United States. Instead of concentrating on attacking American military forces or launching limited strikes against American interests, these groups seek to kill as many Americans as they can. The view that some groups seek to commit mass carnage was not widely accepted before September 11, 2001. Prior to 9/11 scholars puzzled over why terrorists had not launched more murderous attacks. To be sure, bombings and hijackings took their toll, but casualties tended to be relatively modest. For some scholars, the level of casualties was kept down not because these groups lacked the capability to wreak more harm, but because they *chose* not to engage in mass killings since it would not serve their long-term goals. Killing large numbers of innocent people would not topple governments, win worldwide sympathy, or gain them the independence they sought. As one terrorism expert, Brian Jenkins, famously remarked, "Terrorists want a lot of people *watching*, not a lot of people *dead*."[42]

The events of 9/11 have not proven kind to these views. The murder of 3,000 innocents, most of them Americans, made it clear that at least some groups seek to kill as many Americans as they can. To remove any doubt, Al Qaeda has declared that it is entitled to kill millions of Americans in response to U.S. policies in Palestine, Iraq, and elsewhere.[43] This debate over the plausibility of megaterrorism is over. Once some groups are able to kill large numbers of Americans, they will do so. The key to stopping them is not persuading them they are wrong, or that they will suffer if they attack the United States, but denying them the means by which they can carry out their murderous designs.

The problem, however, is that especially in the post–Cold War world, the means to wreak catastrophic harm are all too available. The spread of nuclear weapons and fissionable material as well as other weapons of mass destruction to countries in the developing world, such as Pakistan, India, North Korea, and Iran, presents opportunities for transfer to extremist groups that previously did not exist. Civil war is not the only way these weapons can find themselves in the hands of those who would do America harm. Theft and voluntary transfer of arms remain ominous possibilities. But when civil war occurs in countries where extremist groups abound, there is an alarming possibility that these groups will take advantage of the chaos and violence to seize nuclear arms. By facilitating the transfer of nuclear weapons and other weapons of mass destruction into the hands of those who will unhesitatingly use them against American cities, civil wars could play a central role in jeopardizing the most vital of U.S. interests.

American dependence on imported natural resources is another development that makes the prospect of civil wars in some countries so dangerous. Civil wars can destroy resources the United States needs to maintain its way of life. While the United States imports a wide range of raw materials necessary to keep its economy functioning, oil stands alone in its importance. The United States and most of the rest of the world are dependent on imported oil. This reliance has increased over the years to the point where over 60% of American oil needs are supplied by other countries, with American allies even more dependent. Some argue this dependence is not cause for worry since even hostile regimes will need to sell their oil to reap any benefits. Indeed, the mullahs of Iran and Libya's Muammar Khadaffi (when he was radically anti-American) did not hesitate to make their oil available to the highest bidder. Oil exporters, it is argued, will also refrain from charging too high prices, so as not to depress demand or instigate searches for alternatives.

All these reassurances, however, are undermined should civil war strike a key oil-producing state. If civil war breaks out in an oil-exporting country, the oil fields are likely to become a key target. If the fields and their supporting infrastructure are destroyed, oil will not be *able* to be pumped or transported, regardless of the wishes of the government. Civil conflict can disrupt oil exports even if the fields remain intact by destroying port facilities and pipelines and interfering with shipping. Moreover, civil war may place into power groups who do not care about profit, preferring to leave the oil — and its corrupting influences — in the ground. The United States simply cannot rely on the logic of profit-maximizing leaders to provide it with oil at a reasonable cost if those leaders become enmeshed in civil war.

Aside from natural resources, civil wars endanger the American economy when they threaten countries whose investment and trade policies are vital to America's economic well-being. Over one-quarter of America's national debt is held by foreigners, with Japan and China two of the principal creditors. If either country stopped buying American treasury notes, the United States would find it exceedingly difficult to finance its growing budget deficit, plunging the American economy into recession or even depression. While there has always been concern that outside countries would halt or dramatically reduce their purchase of treasury securities, these fears have been allayed by the knowledge that to do so would hurt them as badly (or more so) than it would the United States. If, however, civil war *prevented* the purchase of American bonds, economic incentives would play no role. The loss of trade with critical partners would further exacerbate America's woes. Seen in this light, the United States continues to face a threat from great powers, only today the threat is economic and the source is domestic instability rather than military attack.

The United States, like any country, seeks to control who and what comes across its borders. Whether it is the fear of terrorists, the desire to halt illegal drugs, fear for American border communities, or concerns over illegal immigrants, Washington has a vital interest in protecting its frontiers. Civil strife threatens this interest when it occurs in countries located close to the United States, where the effects of violence are not confined to the country where it takes place, but spill over to affect America as well. Civil wars are also implicated in the welfare of American citizens outside the United States and protecting American borders. At any given time, millions of Americans live and travel abroad. Their safety is a vital interest of the United States, at times prompting American military action to rescue citizens trapped in foreign countries. While widespread violence anywhere can threaten American lives, the United States has a special interest in those countries where large numbers of Americans would be placed at risk.

Each of these threats is made worse by the prospect of outside great powers meddling in civil conflicts to the detriment of the United States. While the era of great power war may well be over, great power competition lives on. Precisely because international war is so costly and risky, the prospect of a state advancing its interests through the manipulation of civil conflict is especially attractive. During the Cold War, the Soviet Union backed civil wars in Korea and Vietnam to weaken the United States, while Washington supported a range of insurgencies in places such as Nicaragua and Afghanistan to hurt the Soviets. In the post–Cold War era, while Iran would never attack the United States directly, this has not stopped Tehran from backing Shia insurgents in Iraq's civil war, often resulting in the deaths of American soldiers.[44] Most civil wars already involve outside powers who provide arms, advisers, and sanctuaries to the belligerents. If civil conflict erupts in a country of importance to the United States, it is likely that other states would get involved, especially if their role could be hidden. It is possible to imagine, for example, Iran fanning the flames of a Saudi civil war, driving up the price of oil (thus enhancing Iranian profits) while weakening the American economy, or perhaps China exacerbating Mexican unrest to divert American resources away from challenging Beijing's bid for supremacy in Asia. Whatever the precise scenario, a civil war erupting in a critical country could serve as a magnet for outside powers to interfere in ways that will often be inimical to American interests.

WHERE TO WORRY

The potential of domestic conflict to threaten vital American interests raises the question of which civil wars the United States needs to worry about. Many civil wars will not arouse American concerns. They will take place in countries of little importance to the United States, have little international effect, and can be safely ignored. How then can the United States determine which civil wars it should be concerned with? Two criteria must guide policymakers in answering this question. First, is the *likelihood* of civil war in any particular country. American interests would be endangered by a war in Canada, but the prospect is so improbable it is not a cause for concern. Second is the *impact* of a civil war on the United States; would it threaten vital American interests? Future conflict in Chad may be plausible, but it would have such a negligible impact on the United States that it does not justify much attention aside from humanitarian concerns.[45]

Which countries, then, warrant American attention? There are many states where there is a reasonable prospect for civil war, which if it occurred, could harm American interests. They include major powers such as Russia; countries with important resources such as Venezuela and Nigeria; rogue states such as North Korea; and important regional powers such as Turkey, Israel, Egypt, India, and Indonesia. In none of these countries, however, is the combination of high stakes and likelihood of civil war sufficiently alarming at present to warrant extraordinary American concern.

Only four places, in fact, meet the criteria of engaging critical American interests where the outbreak of civil war or major domestic disorder is a realistic possibility: Saudi Arabia, Pakistan, China, and Mexico. Saudi Arabia is the world's biggest oil producer and the sole country with the ability to make up shortfalls in production elsewhere by increasing its own output. It is the only country whose removal from the world oil market would in itself wreak catastrophic damage on the economies of the United States and the rest of the industrialized world. Saudi Arabia is also a country brimming with the potential for civil war. Terrorist groups linked to Al Qaeda have committed brazen attacks in its major cities. The royal family is weakened by internal splits, allegations of corruption, charges that it is insufficiently Islamic, and anger at its ties with the United States. Despite the high price of oil, the Saudi economy is in deep trouble, with high unemployment among a restive, young, and growing population. If domestic strife erupts, the oil fields would be a likely and vulnerable target.

The prospect of civil war in Pakistan may pose the greatest threat to American security in the post–Cold War era. Pakistan possesses a significant arsenal of nuclear weapons along with the fissionable materials to make many more. Pakistan is the home of countless Islamist groups who would like nothing better than to use weapons of mass destruction against the United States or its allies. If Pakistan becomes engulfed in civil conflict, the possibility that nuclear weapons would fall into the hands of one of these extremist groups becomes frighteningly high. This is all the more alarming because Pakistan is so likely to fall victim to civil war. Separatist movements are active in three out of four of its provinces, Islamists have penetrated the armed forces, Al Qaeda and the Taliban openly challenge governmental rule, prodemocracy demonstrators rail against increasingly dictatorial governance, and what stability the military regime offers can be blown away with a single bullet or bomb. Pakistan's history has been one of coups, rebellion, and civil war. If its future at all resembles its past, Pakistan will continue to be torn apart by internal strife, only now, as a nuclear weapons state, the effects of such civil conflict will range far beyond South Asia to perhaps embroil America as well.

It is a fortuitous development that Mexico does not possess nuclear weapons, because in almost every other way its descent into civil war threatens vital American interests. Mexico is home to hundreds of thousands of Americans and is America's third largest trading partner (after Canada and China). Mexico is also the largest source of illegal immigrants and drugs to the United States, problems that could dramatically worsen if Mexico succumbs to civil strife. How might civil war develop? The narcotics industry has worked its way into the fabric of Mexican society to the extent that it is now one of Mexico's largest sources of hard currency. As in Colombia, drug dealers threaten to take over the state, either formally or behind the scenes. Meanwhile economic problems abound, especially in the poverty-stricken south, crime is rampant, and Mexico's oil — necessary to keep the economy afloat — is running dry. Despite being democratically elected, Mexico's divided governments composed of lame-duck legislators serving lame-duck presidents are much better at producing gridlock than effective responses. As Mexico's hotly disputed 2006 election showed, the society is deeply polarized and roughly equally divided between rich and poor, north and south. The United States would not be able to ignore the outbreak of civil war or large-scale violence in its southern neighbor. During the Mexican Revolution of 1910, fighting threatened to spill over the border often enough that the United States had to deploy most of its armed forces to contain the conflict. Nearly a century later, ties between the two countries have become dramatically closer, and so too are the harmful effects that would be produced by Mexican instability.

China is the second biggest holder of American treasury bonds and the second largest trading partner of the United States. China is also a key market for American allies, including Taiwan, South Korea, and Japan. All of this could make the collapse of the Chinese economy in the wake of civil conflict catastrophic for America. The loss of Chinese investment in the American bond market would force Washington to jack up interest rates that could dampen growth, cause a major decline in stock prices, collapse the housing market, devalue the dollar, and generally wreak economic havoc in the United States. The benefits of American trade with China would disappear as companies that relied upon China for exports (e.g., Wal-Mart) would lose jobs and American consumers would be denied the inexpensive goods they have come to expect. The spread of Chinese instability could reverberate throughout Asia, perhaps undermining governments and producing a confrontation with the United States. An unstable China might be tempted to attack Taiwan or fall victim to the "loose nukes" nightmare that so bedevils Pakistan.

All this matters because the unraveling of China is eminently thinkable. Despite its booming economy, China is a fragile society whose order could be undermined at any time. China's many sources of instability include a leadership whose legitimacy derives from a Communist ideology that no one takes seriously; rising urban unemployment as state-owned enterprises give way to private control; an exploding countryside where violent protests against poverty and inequality grow each year; an antiquated banking system whose record of bad debts would embarrass the most risk-prone loan shark; growing unrest from ethnic minorities, including a restive Islamic population; and increasing crime produced by tens of millions of rootless young men with no prospects of work or marriage. Chinese history is characterized by governments losing the "mandate of heaven," with rebellion and civil war in its wake. The same could happen today, only now the effects would go well beyond China itself.

During the Cold War, an enormous amount of military, economic, and scholarly effort went into deterring a Soviet invasion of Western Europe. America did not then hesitate to protect itself. The prospect of internal war erupting in key states is now more likely than was that of Soviet troops pouring into West Germany, and the consequences would be just as catastrophic. With the Cold War over and domestic conflicts virtually the only form of organized violence still being fought, scholars and policymakers need to shift gears and recognize that not all threats to American interests are deliberate, purposeful acts of a coherent enemy that can be deterred with the right policy. As the following chapters show, civil wars could inadvertently unleash catastrophic harms that transform global politics and endanger vital American interests. The United States eventually won the Cold War by preparing to defeat a wide range of potential threats to its security and economic well-being. Nothing less will be necessary to defeat the equally pressing threats posed by civil wars in key countries.

CHAPTER TWO

Saudi Arabia

Oil Fields Ablaze

For a complicated country, there is much that is certain about Saudi Arabia. It is certain that the United States and the rest of the industrialized world will remain dependent on Saudi oil in the coming years. America already imports most of its oil, and its European allies and Japan are even more reliant on foreign sources. Much of that oil comes from the Persian Gulf, and most of the Persian Gulf oil comes from Saudi Arabia. All signs suggest that this dependence will only grow in the future. America's thirst for oil is expected to skyrocket in the next few decades. China, which had exported oil in the early 1990s now has become the world's third largest importer of petroleum (after the United States and Japan). Other countries, such as India and South Korea, are also buying much more foreign oil as their economies modernize and domestic sources of energy dry up. The few new fields being discovered are not keeping up with the increased demand and the potential of recent finds does not begin to match what Saudi Arabia is known to possess.

It is also certain that depending on Saudi Arabia to meet the world's oil needs is extraordinarily risky. To be sure, the Saudi leadership recognizes that it must sell its oil in order to keep the country's economy afloat and (not incidentally) to remain in power. If Saudi Arabia is wracked by internal instability, however, the profit-maximizing inclinations of its leaders do not matter. Each stage of the Saudi oil industry from extraction to refining to transport is vulnerable to attacks by domestic enemies, attacks that could halt oil production for several months or even longer. Saudi Arabia is bursting with groups furious at the royal family, including Al Qaeda, disaffected Shias, and members of the ever growing royal family itself. Hesitations about confronting a legitimate government scarcely exist in Saudi Arabia, as many have already dismissed the royal family's right to rule given its failure to follow Islamic guidelines. Although the Saudi security services have achieved some success in suppressing antigovernmental terrorism, they reflect the problems of a divided, pampered society and would be no match against a determined foe. So long as the oil money continues to flow into Saudi coffers, there is hope that the kingdom can remain intact. If revenues falter, however, Saudi Arabia could fall victim to prolonged domestic violence, crippling its ability to fuel the economies of the oil-importing countries, including the United States.

Grasping the danger that the unraveling of Saudi Arabia holds requires first understanding the central role the kingdom plays in the worldwide oil market and to the American economy. The wide range of threats to the stability of Saudi Arabia are then considered followed by a brief discussion of how civil war might actually begin. As will be seen, it is difficult to imagine a more likely threat to the prosperity of the world community and to the United States than is found in the prospect of civil conflict tearing apart Saudi Arabia.

IMPORTANCE OF SAUDI OIL

Saudi Arabia is the most important oil-producing country in the world. It is the only country whose removal from the oil market would in itself produce catastrophic consequences for the United States and much of the rest of the oil-importing world. Saudi Arabia is indispensable because it exports more oil than anyone else, typically around 10 million barrels per day. It will continue to be the world's biggest exporter for the foreseeable future because no other country comes close to Saudi Arabia's capacity to produce oil. Saudi Arabia sits on 25% of the world's oil reserves, which is more than twice what Iraq has, five times that of Russia, and ten times that of the United States. Saudi oil is also very cheap to produce. On average, it costs only about $2 to extract a barrel of Saudi oil, compared to seven times that much for new oil outside of the kingdom. Saudi oil is especially attractive because it comes in five different grades — as compared to one or two grades for most other countries — enabling it to meet the diverse energy needs of virtually every country. The ease with which Saudi Arabia can produce and export oil explains why it accounts for fully 12% of the world's production — a share that is projected to rise to 30% by 2020. The importance of Saudi Arabia to the world oil market is heightened further because of its location in the Persian Gulf, which contains fully two-thirds of the world's oil. If unrest in Saudi Arabia spreads to other countries in the Gulf, an already dire situation would become catastrophic.[1]

Saudi Arabia is also crucial to the oil market (and thus to the global economy) because it is the only "swing" producer in the world. Saudi Arabia alone has the spare capacity to increase oil production quickly to meet a spike in demand or shortfall elsewhere. The Saudis can ramp up production because they keep oil fields in reserve that can, if needed, produce an extra 2 million barrels per day while all other oil exporters are producing at their limit. Saudi Arabia's position as the only country with appreciable spare capacity is relatively recent. In 1985, the Organization of Petroleum Exporting Countries (OPEC) had 15 million barrels in spare capacity, or about 8% of the world demand, compared to today, when virtually all the spare capacity is in Saudi hands. The margin to meet the increased need for oil or to cope with shortages has thus been reduced and dangerously concentrated in one country. The Saudis historically have used their swing capacity in a constructive manner to cope with supply interruptions. They quickly stepped up production and prevented any major price hikes or panic during the Iran-Iraq War of the 1980s, when oil sales were sharply curtailed from both belligerents; the 1991 Gulf War, when production from Iraq and Kuwait was lost; and in 2003, when civil unrest in Venezuela and Nigeria cut exports.[2] Given the potential instability of these and other oil-producing countries, future shortages are inevitable. When they do arise, the importing states will have no choice but to once again turn to Saudi Arabia to make up the difference.

Saudi Arabia is likely to be the world's only swing producer for years to come. No existing fields have any hope of rivaling its capacity and no new sources of oil are likely to emerge that could replace what Saudi Arabia produces. Prospects for lessening the need of Saudi oil are especially dim because investment in new oil and gas production is falling about 15% short of what is needed to even keep up with world demand.[3] New fields are not being actively sought because energy companies are worried that prices will collapse in the wake of future oil gluts, as they did in 1998 (when oil fell to $10 a barrel), nor do they want to keep existing fields in reserve because of the costs involved in maintaining nonproductive assets. Saudi Arabia, on the other hand, can afford to keep oil wells idle because the state owns the fields and does not have to justify the lack of profits to resentful stockholders (as would be the case in most other countries in the world, including the United States and Russia). Oil projects take two to ten years to get running, so even if companies change their mind about new investments, there will still be a shortfall for at least the near future. While supplies are diminishing around the globe, the Saudis plan on ramping up production to 15 million barrels a day so that when the next oil crunch comes the world will have no choice but to turn to Saudi Arabia.[4]

There is good reason to believe that a crunch will indeed be coming. World oil demand is expected to grow from around 80 million barrels of oil a day (in 2004) to 121 million barrels by 2025.[5] Much of the increase is fueled by the United States, with its growing economy and addiction to SUVs. By 2025, the United States is expected to consume 30 million barrels per day of oil, up from around 20 million barrels in 2006.[6] The skyrocketing demand for oil will also come from the rapidly growing Asian economies. The People's Republic of China exported oil as late as 1993, but as domestic sources became depleted and its economy heated up, Beijing has been forced to turn to foreign suppliers to meet its oil needs. China now imports half of its oil, or about 3 million barrels per day, a figure that is certain to rise as China's economy grows and its citizens trade in bicycles for automobiles. Already, in the past ten years, China's oil use has risen by 80% and it will soon become the second largest user of petroleum (after the United States). Other Asian countries, such as India, Japan, and South Korea, are also expected to dramatically increase their oil imports, as are many countries in Europe.[7] As globalization enhances worldwide economic growth, so will grow the demand for oil. With each rise of one percentage point in the global growth rate requiring 500,000 new barrels of oil, the thirst for oil becomes virtually limitless. Russia, the Caspian Sea, other Persian Gulf States, and West Africa lack the reserves and/or capability to meet this increased demand. Only the Saudis are in a position to meet these escalating needs.[8]

The loss of Saudi oil, or a good portion of it, to the world market would be particularly devastating to the United States. At the time of the 1973 Arab oil embargo, the United States imported roughly one-third of its oil. By 2006, after decades of drawing upon dwindling domestic sources, combined with rapidly rising consumption, America imported some 60% of its oil. To be sure, the United States purchases only about 15% of its oil from Saudi Arabia, but that figure understates American dependence on Saudi oil. What matters is not where a given country gets its oil, but the total amount of oil available for purchase. Saudi Arabia is so critical because it makes up such a large share of the world market. The loss of that oil, even for a few months, would produce a mad scramble by importing countries to compensate for the oil they could no longer purchase from Saudi Arabia by seeking other sources, none of which has the capacity to increase production to make up for a Saudi shortfall.[9]

The economic consequences of such a scramble would be catastrophic for the United States and other oil-importing countries. It is impossible to determine precisely what those consequences would be, since they involve questions of how much Saudi oil would be off the market and for how long. Whether other sources of oil would be affected would also play an important role in determining its effect. Nevertheless, there is no question that any appreciable loss of Saudi oil, or even the threat of such loss, would have harmful effects for the American economy because oil is central to so much of what Americans need. Whether it be gasoline to power cars, plastics for consumer goods, or the creation of petrochemical fertilizers to grow food, oil is essential to the American economy. The United States underwent three recessions following oil shortfalls and their resulting price hikes in 1974, 1980, and 1991.[10] The loss of a substantial amount of Saudi oil for greater lengths of time could throw the American economy into another recession, or perhaps a depression. The mere concern of hostile disruption raised the price of a barrel of oil approximately $8 in 2004 and a *failed* 2006 attack on Saudi Arabia's Abqaiq oil complex caused an immediate $2 increase.[11] The actual loss of Saudi oil for a few months would produce far harsher effects, raising the cost of oil to unconscionable levels.

Since it is estimated that for every $10 increase in the price of oil the American economy loses a half point of growth, paying so much for a barrel of oil could cause the United States to experience a decline in GDP for the first time since the Great Depression. Inflation, which rose to 11% after the 1973 embargo and 13% in the aftermath of the Iran-Iraq War, would likely rise again. The stock market would almost certainly take a huge hit, as it did after the 1973 embargo, when it lost almost half its value in just over 21 months.[12] Unemployment would surely increase, as it did following each of the five major oil disruptions since 1970.

Most alarmingly, there is little the United States could do to compensate for the loss of Saudi oil. The International Energy Agency (IEA) commits its members to share oil in the event of a shortfall, but if there is a global shortage there simply will not be enough oil to go around. The United States maintains a strategic reserve, but it has only enough oil for a couple of months and its maximum extraction rate of 4.1 million barrels per day will not be enough to meet American needs in the face of a worldwide dearth of oil supplies.[13] With alternative suppliers lacking the excess production capacity to make up for any deficit, the withdrawal of Saudi oil (or a good portion of it) would cause a panicked rush for remaining supplies. While it is true that in time the United States might come up with alternative sources of energy and begin to take conservation seriously, the damage and shock inflicted on America in the short term would be staggering, delaying any recovery and likely doing irreparable harm to the economy of the United States and other oil-importing countries.

CUTTING OFF SAUDI OIL

How might the supply of Saudi oil be cut off? One possible way is for the Saudi royal family to choose to launch an embargo, as it did in October 1973. At that time, in the midst of the October War between Israel and Egypt and Syria, the Arab oil ministers agreed to an embargo, slicing production by 5% a month and all exports to the United States (and the Netherlands) until Israel withdrew from territories it occupied since the 1967 war. Although actual production cuts amounted to no more than 10% of supplies, panic set in as soon as the embargo was announced. Oil prices went up sixfold virtually overnight (to over $17 a barrel) and long lines sprang up at gasoline stations throughout the United States. The North Atlantic Treaty Organization (NATO) was thrown into turmoil, as European countries, led by France, sought to distance themselves from Washington. Billions of dollars poured into the Arab oil-exporting countries (particularly Saudi Arabia) from the West. Finally, on March 18, following American efforts for a settlement between Israel and its neighbors (but without Israel withdrawing from the occupied territories), the Arab governments agreed to end the embargo.[14]

Despite the huge transfers of wealth to Saudi Arabia that occurred as a result of the embargo, it ultimately did far more harm than good to the royal family, making it unlikely they would ever again decide to cut off oil to the United States. The embargo sparked worldwide inflation, raising the prices of goods (particularly weapons) that the Saudis imported from the West. The disruption in supply and soaring cost of oil pushed importing countries to seek energy supplies outside of Saudi Arabia and other Arab exporting countries, much to the dismay of the Saudi government. The importing countries (including the United States) found new sources of supply, put more money into developing alternative fuels, and began earnest efforts at conservation. The Saudis also found themselves losing market share to countries willing to break the embargo (such as Iran) and with the establishment of the IEA, the Saudis (and other oil exporters) recognized that they could no longer target an embargo against a single country, given the requirement of oil-importing states to share all available supplies. Moreover, by weakening the United States, the 1973 embargo hurt the country that served as the strongest protector of the royal family. With few friends and many enemies throughout the world, Saudi Arabia could ill afford to alienate its most critical ally.[15]

Most important, another embargo is unlikely because the Saudi regime recognizes that in order to benefit from oil, it must sell it. The royal family has made a critical bargain with the Saudi people. In exchange for free (or near free) goods and services, the royal family gains the support — or at least the acquiescence — of its citizens. If oil revenues are halted, even for a short period of time, the royal family will be unable to provide for its subjects in the manner to which they have become accustomed. Because such a path threatens their hold on power, it is highly improbable that the Saudis will forgo the revenues they earn from oil exports. The Saudi leadership will not commit suicide in order to hurt others. Even in the wake of ever increasing American support for Israel since 1973, no new Saudi oil embargo has been launched or even threatened.

If the royal family will not willingly stop oil production, how then might Saudi oil be curtailed? One possibility is that the present regime will be toppled and replaced by a government that refuses to produce oil for export. This is not as far-fetched as it may sound. What appears to be logical in the Western world — maximizing profits — does not necessarily make sense for those from other cultures and backgrounds. Throughout Saudi Arabia's history, there have been those agitating for a return to the purer times of the Prophet Muhammad in the seventh century. They have enjoyed substantial support in Saudi Arabia, where many decry the corruption and alien influences brought in by modern innovations. One of these groups took over the Grand Mosque of Mecca in 1979, declaring that once in control of Saudi Arabia, they would cease the production of oil for sale outside the country.[16] The founder of Al Qaeda, Osama bin Laden, who has actively sought to topple the Saudi regime, remarked that the price of oil needed to be dramatically raised.[17] Should groups like this seize power, a not inconceivable event, they could well choose not to produce the oil that the United States and the world so desperately need or jack up the price so much as to wreck their economies. The path to power of such a radical group would almost certainly be the violent overthrow of the present regime.

ATTACKING THE OIL FIELDS

An even more likely prospect that would deny Saudi oil to the rest of the world is the destruction of the oil fields themselves as part of a wider internal conflict. The oil fields might be destroyed inadvertently in the course of fighting, or they could be destroyed on purpose to deprive the royal family of its resources, or by the losing side as an act of vandalism similar to Saddam Hussein's 1991 torching of the Kuwaiti fields. However the oil fields might be destroyed the outcome would be that the Saudi government would not *choose* to stop exporting oil — it would no longer have the *capability* to do so. Arguments that one need not fear a cutoff of Saudi oil because petroleum-exporting states will have to sell their oil to reap the benefits or that embargoes would incur more costs than gains for the regimes mounting them have no meaning when it is physically impossible to extract the oil or get it to the world market.

At first glance, stopping all or most of Saudi oil production appears virtually impossible. Saudi Arabia has about 100 oil and gas fields, with over 1,500 wells. While about half the oil reserves are concentrated in just eight fields, they cover large amounts of territory. The largest field, Ghawar, alone is 150 miles long and 25 miles wide.[18] Destroying all the wells in such a vast area would be extraordinarily difficult and even if the wells could be set on fire, rapid repairs could have them back in operation in a short time. Despite these challenges, Saudi oil production can easily be halted or disrupted. The key is not in attempting to destroy the oil wells, but rather on focusing on key choke points whose destruction would stop production for months or more. Destroying or damaging these choke points is well within the capabilities of a determined insurgent group.

What are these choke points that are so critical to Saudi oil production? Several stand out because they are vulnerable to attack and, if destroyed, would seriously impede Saudi oil output for a long time. First, there is the Abqaiq oil complex, through which nearly two-thirds of Saudi oil (about 7 million barrels) passes each day. As former CIA official Robert Baer argues, the keys to this site are the ten stabilizing towers where sulfur is removed from petroleum, making the oil into a useable resource for energy. The sulfur is eliminated by injecting hydrogen into the oil inside the stabilizing towers. This causes the sulfur in the oil to be converted to hydrogen sulfide gas, which rises to the top of the tower, where it remains until it can be safely removed. If the top of the tower is damaged, perhaps by sabotage or rocket-propelled grenades, the hydrogen sulfide gas would be released into the atmosphere, where it produces harmful effects. Once exposed to the open air, hydrogen sulfide forms sulfur dioxide, a corrosive acid. The sulfur dioxide will settle on various pipes, valves, and pump stations, eating away at the vital fabric of oil production capability. Even more horrifying, the gas would kill those in the immediate area, sicken those farther away, and most probably create mass panic among the oil workers. A sizeable attack could slow production from almost 7 million to only 1 million barrels a day for two months. After four months, the Abqaiq complex would still be operating at less than 40% of its capacity, meaning that the Saudis would be producing 4 million barrels a day *less* than they had previously. This shortage is equal to the OPEC production cutback during the 1973 oil embargo.[19]

The importance of Abqaiq was underscored in February 2006, when suicide bombers attempted to drive two cars filled with explosives into the Abqaiq com-

pound.[20] Although the attack, believed to be mounted by Al Qaeda, did not succeed in doing any appreciable damage, it demonstrated that militants have targeted key installations like Abqaiq as part of their campaign to topple the Saudi
regime and cripple the West.

Pipelines are another critical weakness in the Saudi oil system. Once the oil is
pumped out of the ground, it moves through over 11,000 miles of pipe, much of
it aboveground. While replacement parts exist, repeatedly destroying large sections of the pipeline at several points can seriously impede the export of oil, as
Iraqi insurgents demonstrated following the toppling of Saddam Hussein's regime. Even more efficient than blowing up pipelines is to disable some of the approximately 50 pumping stations that are scattered throughout the kingdom. Oil
goes nowhere unless it is pumped. The pumping station at Abqaiq processes
nearly 2 million barrels a day. Destroy it, and you've significantly impaired the
movement of oil.[21]

Saudi oil terminals would also be attractive targets for anyone seeking to cripple oil production. Saudi Arabia's main oil terminals include the world's largest
offshore facility at Ras Tanura, Ras al-Ju'aymah on the Persian Gulf, and Yanbu
on the Red Sea. Taken together these facilities are capable of processing over 14
million barrels of oil per day.[22] Each of these terminals is vulnerable to attack,
with the Ju'aymah terminal especially worrisome. This terminal is a tinderbox,
with tanks filled with oil and natural gas. An attack on the terminal that destroyed
some vital equipment (such as the mooring buoys), or that ignited oil fires, could
cripple exports for seven months.[23]

Most alarming would be the use of weapons of mass destruction, especially nuclear weapons, against the oil fields. Osama bin Laden has declared that it "is a
duty to acquire" nuclear arms and it is known that Al Qaeda has made several attempts to do so.[24] If Al Qaeda or some other enemy of the Saudi regime was able
to destroy the oil fields with a nuclear device, the result would be an economic
and security panic that would be unprecedented in world history. A more likely
possibility is attacking the oil fields with chemical, biological, or radiological
weapons. Although not nearly as destructive as nuclear arms, these weapons create mass fear and chaos when they are used. As such, they are ideal for use against
the oil fields, which depend on foreign workers. While chemical, biological, and
radiological weapons may not kill many people, if they can bring about the mass
exodus of oil workers, they will stop oil production dead in its tracks.

Chemical weapons, perhaps in the form of a choking gas or a deadly liquid,
could blanket the area of the oil fields. Dispersal of chemical weapons might be
carried out by aircraft, missiles, artillery shells, and even individuals with spray

tanks. For unprotected workers, the effects would range from choking to convulsions to death. Biological agents, living organisms that reproduce and spread, also could be unleashed on the oil fields. Anthrax, a lethal disease caused by bacteria, and smallpox, a deadly infection caused by a virus, might be employed. Once a group gains possession of deadly germs, spreading them should not pose much of a problem. Anthrax might be spread in powdered form through office ventilators or crop duster aircraft. Smallpox could be disseminated through infected individuals coughing and wheezing their way through crowded areas. It would only take a few infected people to cause mass panic, emptying the oil fields of workers.

Equally devastating would be the use of radiological weapons, or "dirty bombs." Dirty bombs are relatively easy to make, requiring only the expertise to put together a conventional explosive and securing radioactive material. Sources of radioactive material are found in many places, including laboratories, food irradiation plants, and oil-drilling facilities. Although the blast would kill some, the more significant harm caused by dirty bombs is their contamination of a large area. Exploding a single piece of radioactive cobalt (measuring about a foot long and one inch in diameter) from a food irradiation plant would contaminate an area of 1,000 kilometers, substantially increasing the rate of cancer throughout the infected region. The use of the radioactive material americium would be less harmful, but since americium is commonly used in oil wells it might be a more likely weapon of choice for an attack if other radioactive materials are not available. In the wake of the detonation of a dirty bomb, workers may choose to remain in the oil fields, especially if paid much more, but the resulting panic and uncertainty would send massive tremors through the oil markets. It is feared that Al Qaeda may already have built a dirty bomb, making this threat not as remote as some would hope.[25]

There is little doubt that Saudi oil is critical to the economic health of the United States (and much of the rest of the world) and that its production can be destroyed by determined attackers. This raises the critical issue of whether conditions exist in Saudi Arabia that would lead to such assaults. For Saudi Arabia to be prone to the kind of civil unrest that would threaten the oil fields, three conditions need to be met. First, groups in Saudi Arabia would have to be sufficiently angry at the government to consider using violence to advance their interests. Second, these groups would need to believe that they had the *right* to violently oppose the regime. Finally, these groups would have to believe that by resorting to violence they had a reasonable chance of being successful. Unfortunately for Saudi Arabia, the United States, and much of the rest of the world, these conditions flourish in the kingdom and are worsening. The result is a Saudi Arabia that could explode into violent conflict at any time, destroying the oil fields and much of the world's economy in its wake.

GRIEVANCES

Of the many grievances felt by the Saudi people, perhaps the most surprising are those that stem from weaknesses in the economy. On one level, the economy is performing well. Thanks to a third oil boom in the last 30 years, the difficulties Saudis experienced in the 1990s appear to be a distant memory. With oil prices hovering over $60 a barrel in 2005, the Saudis earned over $150 billion in oil sales, producing a budget surplus. Foreign reserves have risen to $177 billion from just $70 billion in 1970. Per capita gross domestic product is expected to reach $13,600, compared to around $8,000 throughout much of the 1990s. The government has been able to raise public salaries for the first time in decades, has developed ambitious programs to build roads and schools, and is attempting to reduce its dependence on foreign workers through a policy of Saudization. High oil prices apparently have been very good for the Saudi economy.[26]

The problem with this seemingly rosy picture is that Saudi Arabia's dependence on oil — some 95% of export earnings, 80% of state revenues, and 40% of Saudi Arabia's gross development product comes from the sale of oil — hurts more than it helps.[27] As a "rentier" state — a country that depends on natural resources for a large portion of its income — the Saudi government does not have to earn the support of its population. A government not used to meeting the needs of its citizens is not likely to be tough enough to meet challenges when they arise. Moreover, the Saudi people lack the motivation to develop the education, training, and skills that would enable them to compete in a globalized economy, which could lead to problems in the future. As detailed by economists Jeffrey Sachs and Andrew Warner, countries with great wealth in natural resources grow more slowly than other states. They tend to have less entrepreneurial activity, more government corruption, and less emphasis on developing a robust export sector.[28] So long as the natural resources provide the wealth the country needs, there is no crisis. Once the funds stop rolling in, however, the population will learn that it is ill equipped to confront the competitive pressures of the "real" world, leading to anger and resentment.

Saudi Arabia's dependence on oil also hurts because of "boom/bust" cycles that disrupt normal growth. After the huge increases in the price of oil following the 1973 oil embargo, Saudi Arabia embarked on a massive spending campaign, only to come up short when the price of oil fell drastically in the 1980s and 1990s.

During these decades Saudi Arabia produced over twenty years of budget deficits. Its per capita GDP declined 40% from its peak in the 1980s to the first years of the twenty-first century, only to rebound as oil prices once again rose.[29] Even with the huge oil price increases, Saudi Arabia's per capita oil export revenues have declined by 80% (from $22,589 in 1980 to $4,564 in 2004) due to rapid population growth and a drop in real oil export revenues.[30] This roller coaster pattern contributes mightily to a sense of economic grievance. Saudis get jobs when the price of oil is high, only to lose them when the price drops. Rebellions most often occur not in times of crushing poverty, but when rising expectations are not met.[31] The dashed hopes that have become a familiar part of the Saudi world worsen grievances and lay the grounds for violent instability.

Even when oil revenues are flush, the Saudi regime engenders opposition by the way it distributes wealth. The Saudi government has become essentially a provider of goods to a demanding Saudi population, forever angering those who believe they are not receiving their fair share. Shiites in the east, the merchants in the Hejaz, and those living in the Asir, Jizan, and Najran provinces in the southwest of the country are just some examples of powerful groups who are aggrieved by what they believe is the relatively paltry assistance they have received from the Saudi government. So long as wealth is allocated strictly from the top, rather than generated from the Saudi population, there will always be those who believe they are not receiving their due and who will take out their resentments against the government.[32]

Problems besetting the Saudi society and economy are worsening. With one of the highest birth rates in the world, the Saudi population is soaring. Half the population is under 18, three-quarters were born after 1975, and the World Bank predicts that the total population will grow from almost 22 million in 2000 to over 46 million in 2030.[33] Much of the population is flocking to the cities, overwhelming meager services, creating fetid slums, and contributing to an exploding growth in crime.[34] The educational system, run by the religious clerics, barely prepares Saudis for working in their own country, much less meeting the demands of international competition. With just 13% of the Saudis working in the private sector and the government only able to provide work for 10% of Saudis entering the job force each year, a massive unemployment problem has emerged. While official figures place unemployment at 10%, most economists say it is at least 30% for Saudis younger than 35. Some 175,000 high school graduates enter the market each year, most of whom cannot find the jobs they are seeking. What emerges is a large group of young men with little to do and expectations of living the easy life — not a formula for stability.[35]

Meeting the needs of this expanded population will not be easy, even given Saudis' oil wealth. The Saudis already spent $26 billion in backing Iraq against Iran during the 1980s and $55 billion (along with other Persian Gulf countries) to support the United States in the first Gulf War. Repairs to the physical infrastructure of the society, especially electrical and water services, will cost over $100 billion. Meanwhile, the Saudis continue to provide a wide range of services to its citizens, including free schooling and medical care, with virtually no taxation. An obvious solution to spending more than you earn is to either reduce expenditures or increase taxes, but the Saudi government is unable to do either. They cannot reduce services for their citizens because their hold on power is dependent upon their performance, namely, giving to the people what they have come to expect. They cannot raise taxes, because the Saudi population won't stand for it. The result is unmet needs when the price of oil falls and lots of unhappy citizens. The situation will not likely improve soon. Saudi efforts at developing a private sector outside of oil are not likely to bear fruit. Their educational system continues to churn out Koranic scholars instead of civil engineers. No efforts at population control are being made. For a government whose very survival depends on maintaining the good life for its people, another price collapse could well threaten the very existence of the regime.[36]

The Saudi government is not only threatened by grievances from disgruntled citizens, it is also challenged by anger from within the regime itself. At the top of the Saudi government is the king, who rules through consensus with other members of the royal family. So long as everyone more or less agrees with the king's policies, difficulties are manageable. Achieving consensus within the royal family, however, has never been easy and is getting harder with time. The sheer size of the royal family is one problem, with no one even knowing just how large it has become. One estimate says there are 30,000 members, who will increase to over 60,000 in a single generation,[37] while another guess puts the number of princes at 5,000, growing to 20,000 by 2020. With the number of princes doubling every 25 years, securing agreement on key issues will become increasingly problematic.[38] Grumbling among the Saudi populace regarding the corruption of the royal family has become a constant in Saudi politics. Supporting tens of thousands of additional "royals" in a manner to which they have become accustomed will surely promote additional turmoil both within the royal family itself and among the Saudi populace when hard economic times come.

Aside from sheer numbers, the issue of succession divides the royal family. When the king dies or becomes incapacitated, the top echelons of the royal family need to decide who will replace him. This procedure works so long as the

Saudi elite are in basic agreement as to who should rule, as was the case when Prince Abdullah became king in 2005 following the death of King Fahd. Problems arise when there are divisions in the royal family about how to proceed. A key issue relates to the tribal nature of the royal family. The top echelon of the royal family is split between those of the Sudairi clan (the sons of Saudi founder King Saud's Sudairi wife, Hassa) and the sons of Saud's other 22 wives. The seven sons of Hassa include such prominent officials as the late King Fahd, Prince Sultan (the minister of defense), and Prince Nayef (the minister of interior).[39] Opposed to this group are the non-Sudairi sons, including King Abdullah. By splitting the royal family in two, clan-based disputes make cooperation more difficult and could produce a succession crisis when power needs to be passed to the next generation of princes.

Divisions in the royal family are exacerbated by deep differences in their approaches to religion. As political scientist Michael Doran has argued, two camps have emerged in the Saudi royal family over the growing role of the religious establishment in Saudi politics. The religious clerics and Prince Nayef support an even greater role for religion in Saudi affairs. They endorse a concept called *Tawhid*, or extreme monotheism, which draws from the Saudi founding faith of Wahhabism. They argue that many who claim to be monotheists are really polytheists and idolaters, including Christians, Jews, Shiites, and even some Sunnis. The United States is the chief enemy of the kingdom, according to this group, because its culture corrupts Saudi society from within. The opposing group, led by King Abdullah, supports *Taqarub*, or rapprochement. It believes in cooperation within the Muslim community and even between Muslims and non-Muslims. It seeks a diminished role for religion in Saudi life and is more favorably disposed to the United States.[40] The presence of two rival factions in the royal family who disagree over fundamental issues suggests deep problems in the governance of Saudi Arabia. It appears that the united face the royal family likes to show to the world is, in fact, a facade. If the royal family unravels, the glue that keeps Saudi Arabia together will disappear, setting the stage for civil strife.

Dissension in the royal family is exacerbated by divisions in the armed forces. As with many developing states, the ruling regime in Saudi Arabia is more worried about threats from within the country than from other states. The Saudi regime has structured its military forces in a way that degrades its effectiveness against outside attack in order to better insulate the regime from coups d'etat. The creation of the Saudi National Guard fulfills this mission. The purpose of the National Guard is not to defend the country against external invasion, but to serve as a counterweight to the regular army. Both the regular army and the National

Guard are formidable forces, each with around 100,000 men and substantial quantities of armored equipment. The army and National Guard, however, do few joint operations and draw from different segments of the population (the Guard is more overtly tribal in makeup).[41] They have different command structures and serve under the leadership of different members of the royal family. This does indeed make a coup more difficult, as the coup makers would have to overcome the resistance of the soldiers of the rival service. By dividing the military into competing factions under different leaders, however, the Saudi regime increases the possibility that the armed forces, acting out of some political, religious, or tribal grievance will be drawn into a larger rebellion.

Resentments among the Saudi Shiite population also threaten to explode into violence. No one knows exactly how many Saudi Shiites there are, though most estimates place them at between 5% and 10% of the Saudi population, comprising some 2 million people.[42] The Shia population is of particular concern because it is concentrated in the oil-rich Eastern Province, where it makes up more than half the population and where some cities and towns are exclusively Shiite.[43] Shiites are treated as second-class citizens in Saudi Arabia. They are denied any meaningful political role, their communities receive far less government assistance than other Saudis, they do not enjoy religious freedom, and they maintain very little social contact or intermarriage with Sunnis.

The Wahhabis (an extreme Sunni sect that makes up the religious leadership of Saudi Arabia) despise the Shiites, asserting they are not "true" Muslims. The Shiite veneration of the Prophet's son-in-law, Ali, is seen as an insult to Muhammad and a blasphemous practice of polytheism.[44] Wahhabis also are suspicious that Shiites are in league with Iran, which has a majority Shiite population. These concerns heightened following Ayatollah Khomeini's ascension to power in 1979, when riots erupted in several Saudi Shiite cities resulting in at least 21 Shiite deaths. Since the Shiites live where the oil is, their actions against the government are especially sensitive, as demonstrated by two explosions in a petrochemical complex in 1987 that were traced to Shia groups.[45] While the Shia probably lack the power to create an insurgent movement of their own, they are likely to exploit challenges to the Saudi regime when they arise. It is noteworthy that the 1979 Shiite riots broke out while Saudi attention was focused on suppressing an extremist *Sunni* uprising at Mecca's Grand Mosque. If violence again wracks Saudi Arabia, the ruling regime will have to keep at least one eye on its disaffected Shia population.

Tribal dissatisfaction is another source of instability in the kingdom. Saudi Arabia may look like a homogenous country from the outside, but is in fact an em-

pire made up of distinct regions with tribes who make up more than half the
Saudi population. Many of these tribesmen resent the rule of the Al-Saud family,
whom they see as different from themselves, and particularly object to the Wahhabis telling them how to worship and live. Making matters worse are memories
of brutal massacres committed by the Al-Sauds as part of the formation of the
Saudi state in the early twentieth century.

The specific grievances against the Al-Saud family vary with region and tribe.
The relatively liberal merchants of the Hejaz, in western Saudi Arabia, chafe
under puritanical Wahhabi precepts. The Asiri tribes, bordering Yemen, are
deeply religious but are angered at prohibitions against following their own version
of Islam. In the northern Al Jouf region, where tribes maintain close ties with
Iraq, there is intense rage against the Saudi government for allowing American
troops into their region in preparation for the 2003 invasion of Iraq. Some of the
tribal anger is expressed against the United States. Fully 12 of the 15 Saudi hijackers on 9/11 came from Hejazi and Asiri tribes, while Saudis from the Al Jouf region regularly pour into Iraq to battle American troops. Beginning in December
2002, the United States began requiring Saudi visa applicants to list their tribe's
name, in recognition that tribal animosities represent a security threat to both
America and the Saudi regime. Rebellions and civil disturbances rooted in tribal
grievances have periodically wracked the kingdom, including major riots erupting in the Al Jouf region in April 2002. Through coercion and bribery, the Saudi
regime will try to keep the tribes in check. Nevertheless, few like to be ruled by
those they consider to be strangers, especially when that rule is seen as repressive
and discriminatory. So long as Saudis identify primarily with their tribe or region
rather than their country, the potential for civil conflict is kept very much alive.[46]

The hypocrisy of the Saudi leadership is a never-ending source of grievances
throughout Saudi society. Hypocrisy is particularly frowned upon in Islam, which
should make the Saudi regime especially nervous. While claiming to rule under
the precepts of Wahhabism, many in the royal family are known to engage in all
kinds of licentious behavior when safe from the prying eyes of the public. Stories
of Saudi princes gambling, drinking, and womanizing are spread across the country, making it clear that their adherence to Islam, much less Wahhabism, is a
sham. Moreover, a key component of Wahhabism is hostility to the West, and especially to the Western religions of Judaism and Christianity, which are seen as
mortal enemies of Islam. And yet, the Saudi leadership cultivates intimate ties
with the United States, which keeps it in power. The hypocrisy of the royal family is equaled only by the Wahhabi leadership. In exchange for their official positions and perks, the Wahhabi clerics turn a blind eye to Al-Saud's corruption and

ties to the West. This double standard, or lack of any standards, is a source of rage for many Saudis, much of which is seized upon by Islamist militants such as Osama bin Laden to target the regime.[47]

The Saudi regime has had the luxury of never having to earn the loyalty of its subjects. Instead, it has relied upon the mixed blessing of oil to coopt or bribe away potential foes. Even its oil wealth, however, has not made an appreciable dent on the pressing economic and societal problems that have been allowed to fester, nor has it appeased large numbers of Saudis both within and outside the government who are angry at the royal family's policies and behavior. Having failed to accumulate a stock of goodwill, the Saudi leadership will have little to fall back upon when hard times come.

RIGHT TO ATTACK

If the growing but still inchoate grievances that permeate Saudi Arabia are to be transformed into armed rebellion, the opponents of the Saudi regime will have to be galvanized by the belief that they have a *right* to topple the royal family. For that to happen, the Saudi regime must be seen as illegitimate, a perception that can only come about when there is a widespread belief that the royal family does not represent "true" Islam. Religion is central to the survivability of Saudi Arabia because it provides the basis for governmental rule. The purpose of the Saudi government is to ensure that Islam is practiced correctly, meaning a strict adherence to Islamic principles. The Saudi government is also charged with safeguarding the two holiest cities in Islam: Mecca, site of the Grand Mosque, which is the spiritual center of Islam, and Medina, where the Prophet Muhammad was born. The Saudi constitution is the Koran and its laws all originate with the Sharia — the Islamic legal code. If the government is seen as carrying out its Islamic duties properly, it will be obeyed. If not, rebellion is not only permitted, it is demanded.

Understanding how religion is central to Saudi legitimacy requires going back to the founding of the first Saudi state in the 1700s and tracing some of the key religious conflicts since then. From its very beginnings, the emergence of Saudi Arabia stemmed from a marriage of religious zealotry with raw political power. On the religious side was Wahhabism, which grew out of the teachings of an eighteenth-century religious reformer named Muhammad ibn Abd al-Wahhab. Wahhab advocated a return to a simple life of intense and pure worship, emphasizing strict monotheism while opposing "luxuries" such as smoking and music. Wahhab would not have gotten far with the scattered and fiercely independent Arabian tribes but for his partnership with Muhammad ibn Saud, a tribal leader with a keen sense of power politics. Saud and his ferocious warriors provided the muscle to coax recalcitrant tribes to accept the puritanical message of Wahhabism. Wahhab, on the other hand, provided the religious ideals that united the disparate groups. The result of their collaboration was the emergence of the first Saudi state in 1744, a country founded on the recognition that the ruling elite could not govern through coercion alone, but would also need some overarching message to appeal to the people. Although the Saudi state founded by Saud and Wahhab eventually collapsed, the combination of political power legitimized — and threatened — by deeply felt religious beliefs would once again serve as the basis of the modern Saudi state that emerged in the twentieth century.[48]

The creation of modern Saudi Arabia began when Ibn Saud, a descendant of the founder of the first Saudi realm, set off on a crusade in 1902 to unite the fractious tribes in the Arabian desert who had come under the influence of a rival clan, the Al-Rashid. Like his forebear, Ibn Saud turned to religiously driven Wahhabi tribesmen to accomplish his task. These supporters, called the Ikhwan (brothers of the faith) zealously responded to Ibn Saud's leadership, conquering tribe after tribe in the name of Islam. The Ikhwan, however, proved to be a most troublesome ally. They opposed modern developments such as taxes and the telegraph that Ibn Saud needed to consolidate his rule. The Ikhwan attacked indiscriminately, including tribes in neighboring Iraq (then under British control), threatening to bring the might of the British Empire against Ibn Saud's primitive forces.[49] Ibn Saud tried to rein them in, but the Ikhwan ignored him, claiming he was not sufficiently Islamic. Finally, in 1929, the Ikhwan turned on Ibn Saud himself, launching a major rebellion. By that time, however, Ibn Saud had amassed sufficient support among non-Ikhwan tribes to suppress the revolt. Ibn Saud emerged triumphant, establishing the modern state of Saudi Arabia in 1932, though recognizing how close he came to losing all. From that time through the present, Saudi leaders have had to live with the knowledge that the religious groups necessary to consolidate power also constitute the primary threat to the regime.[50]

The victory over the Ikhwan meant that a less strict version of Wahhabism would dominate Saudi Arabia, enabling the emergence of a modern state. But it also meant that the zealous supporters of Wahhabism, the descendants of the Ikhwan, would forever be at odds with some of the practices of that state. A clear illustration of this conflict occurred with the 1979 uprising that seized the Grand Mosque in Mecca. The leader of Saudi Arabia at the time, King Faysal, had good relations with the religious authorities in Saudi Arabia and had established several administrative bodies of Islamic scholars to ensure that his rulings were consistent with Islamic teachings. His efforts to appease the religious forces, however, proved inadequate. On November 20, 1979, a date that corresponded to the first day of a new Islamic century, several hundred insurgents seized the Grand Mosque. They were led by Juhayman bin Muhammad al-'Utaybi, a grandson of one of the Ikhwan killed in the revolt against Ibn Saud. The rebels, who ominously appeared to have support within the National Guard, quickly gained control of the Grand Mosque. From their platform at the holiest site of Islam, they called for the abolition of the Saudi monarchy, establishment of an Islamic republic, breaking off relations with the West, cleansing of the kingdom of all foreigners and Western innovations, and an end to all exports of Saudi oil. It took Saudi troops with foreign help (including forces from France) an embarrassingly long two weeks to reclaim the Mosque. More than 200 people were killed in the bloody operation. 'Utaybi was taken prisoner and beheaded.[51]

The seizure of the Grand Mosque shook the very foundations of the Saudi regime. Although the Saudi government blamed foreign agents, there was no denying the revolt's indigenous roots and leadership. Equally alarming to the royal family was the reaction of the Islamic establishment in Saudi Arabia. When asked to issue a *fatwa* (religious decree) condemning the attack, the clerics did so only after a considerable delay and pointedly omitted any condemnation of the insurgents' call for the toppling of the regime, reserving their criticism for the seizure of the Grand Mosque itself.[52] The revolt also appeared to have substantial public sympathy, with only the revulsion at the violation of the Mosque limiting more widespread support. After the attack, the Saudi regime wasted no time seeking to appease its religious opposition. The royal family ceded control over education, the courts, and cultural affairs to the imams. Many of the rigid features of Saudi life, such as not allowing women to appear on television, no public mixing of the sexes, or music in any media, and smothering doses of religious indoctrination in schools came about in the early 1980s as a response to the Mosque takeover.[53] As with most efforts to appease, however, the Saudi government's actions left open the question as to whether they would satisfy the demands of the religious extremists or simply whet their appetite for further actions against the regime.

Another major challenge to the legitimacy of the regime, also stemming from religious conflict, took place following the 1991 Persian Gulf War. A decade of falling oil prices and the ascendance of a new generation of Saudi religious leaders educated in Islamic universities made Saudi Arabia ripe for turmoil. The introduction of a half million American troops, almost none of whom were Muslim and a substantial number of whom were women, shocked the Saudis. It did not matter that the troops were sent to Saudi Arabia to protect the kingdom following Saddam Hussein's invasion of Kuwait and to serve as a base from which Kuwait would be freed from Iraqi occupation. Nor did it much matter that the Saudi leadership obtained a *fatwa* from the senior Islamic cleric, Chief Mufti bin Baz, allowing the American troops to enter Saudi Arabia. The *fatwa* itself lacked enthusiasm and did little to assuage the feeling many Saudis had that the American presence was an insult to Islam. Led by two young Saudi clerics, Shaykh Salman bin Fahd al-Awda and Shaykh Safar bin 'Abd-al-Rahman al-Hawali (known as "the Awakening Shaykhs"), followers blanketed the kingdom with cassettes condemning in the most virulent terms not only the American troops but also the Saudi regime that allowed them in the country.[54] Pointing to the dying statement of the Prophet Muhammad, who was said to have declared, "Let there be no two religions in Arabia," the radical clerics railed against the presence of Christian American troops as blasphemy of the worst kind. Some Saudis believed so strongly that only Muslims belonged in Saudi Arabia that jihad, or holy war, was not only justified but *required* to rid the Arabian peninsula of the infidels. Later, in 1998, Osama bin Laden would issue a *fatwa* declaring the American deployment of forces in Saudi Arabia as the principal reason for his attacking the West.[55]

Not only was the Saudi regime illegitimate by inviting the hated Americans into the country, the government forfeited its right to rule by demonstrating that it could not defend the kingdom on its own. Tens of billions of dollars had been spent over the past decade to protect Saudi Arabia from threats from other countries such as Iraq. Countless resources were poured into the Saudi military to purchase the most technologically sophisticated aircraft, tanks, and ships. Saudi officers trained at the best schools in the United States and Britain, all to ensure the security of the state and the holy cities. Nevertheless, as soon as an external threat materialized, the Saudis had to run to the Americans, to the "infidels," to protect the kingdom. The very raison d'etre of the Saudi government is to serve as the guardian of the holy cities of Mecca and Medina. If, despite untold oil wealth, it is unable to do so, it is understandable that its right to rule would be subject to question.[56]

In the wake of the American troop presence in Saudi Arabia, radical fundamentalists took several actions directly challenging the royal family. In May 1991, a group of clerics issued a "letter of demands," the first organized effort of religious figures to increase their role in governance. The letter called for a council independent of government influence, the repeal of all laws not conforming to the Sharia, an end to corruption by the royal family, and greater attention paid to Islam in foreign policy. As Joshua Teitelbaum relates, the letter attempted to return Saudi Arabia to the time of the Ikhwan, when religious figures had more influence and policymakers acted strictly in accordance with the Koran.[57] As many as 400 religious officials, both radicals and moderates, are believed to have signed the letter.

Despite this level of support (or perhaps because of it) the royal family reacted harshly, harassing the signatories and even imprisoning some. The clerics, however, would not be silenced. They escalated the war of words by charging the royal family with *takfir*, or pronouncing one's disbelief in true Islam. This is the most serious charge that could be made against a Muslim, much less a government whose legitimacy derived from Islam. The charge of *takfir* had been made against the Saudi regime on two previous occasions, during the Ikhwan rebellion and the seizure of the Grand Mosque, at which times the religious establishment came to the government's defense. But this time, notably, the senior clerics said nothing.[58] The divide between the royal family and the religious establishment clearly had grown, again calling into question the very legitimacy of the Saudi regime.

The 1990s saw renewed strife between religious and governmental authorities. To respond to growing discontent, King Fahd created a Consultative Council in March 1992, in which clerics could voice their concerns, but it never had any real power and did little to mollify the religious critics of the regime. In May 1993, six radical clerics announced the establishment of the Committee for the Defense of Legitimate Rights (CDLR). Despite its reassuring name and seeming emphasis on human rights in Saudi Arabia, the group sought mostly to increase the influence of extremist Islam and bring Saudi laws more into conformity with the Sharia. Although the CDLR would eventually collapse due to Saudi repression and internal discord, it nevertheless made its mark as one of the first institutionalized forms of religious opposition to the Saudi regime. In its wake, other groups, such as the Movement for Islamic Reform in Arabia (MIRA), have emerged. They too have been repressed, but live on to challenge the Saudi regime.[59]

With the legitimacy of the Saudi regime increasingly being called into question by religious authorities, the 1990s saw an outbreak of serious violent acts against the government and its American patrons. In 1995, four Saudis bombed the headquarters of the Saudi National Guard, killing five Americans and two Indians. The Saudis, three of whom had fought the Soviets in Afghanistan, claimed the American troop presence of 1990 drove them to act as they did. It is believed they were influenced by Osama bin Laden. In June 1996, 19 American servicemen were killed and 373 injured when the Khobar barracks, located near the Saudi air base at Dhahran, was destroyed by a massive truck bomb. The Saudis blocked the ensuing American investigation of the bombing, perhaps to prevent worsening relations with Iran, which may have had a hand in the attack through its support of Saudi Shiites.[60] In these and other actions, extremist groups called into question whether the Saudi regime was truly behaving as an Islamic authority should. In so doing, they laid the basis for even greater challenges that would surface in the opening years of the twenty-first century.

OSAMA BIN LADEN AND THE SAUDI JIHADISTS

The greatest threat faced by the Saudi regime, and the one most likely to lead to civil war, comes from the jihadists, a loose network of groups who believe that the Saudi monarchy is not legitimate because it is not authentically Islamic and thus cannot command their loyalty. Unlike reformers, the jihadists believe the royal family is too corrupt and Westernized to change. They seek the overthrow of the Saudi regime and its replacement by a government that is guided by "true" Islamic principles. The jihadists adhere to an Islamic movement known as the *Salafiyya*, which seeks to purify Islam by returning to the time of the Prophet Muhammad. The jihadists follow the works of Sayyid Qutb, an Egyptian scholar whose works in support of *Salafiyya* resonate among Islamic extremists in Saudi Arabia and elsewhere in the Muslim world. Writing as an Egyptian prisoner in the 1950s and 1960s (he was executed by the Egyptian government in 1966), Qutb argued that most states, including Islamic ones, are in *Jahiliyyah*, that is, ignorance of Islam. The only way to remove oneself from *Jahiliyyah* is through jihad against those who keep their people in this condition. This means not only fighting against countries like the United States (the "far enemy") but also overthrowing Islamic regimes such as Saudi Arabia (the "near enemy") who have strayed from the Islamic path.[61]

In the place of the Saudi government, jihadists seek to establish a Taliban-like regime that harkens back to the days of the Ikhwan and rejects the efforts, however modest, of the royal family to embrace modernity. There would be no room for Westerners in this new-old society and few modern inventions. Instead of struggling to enter the twenty-first century, Saudi Arabia would return to where it belongs, the idyllic times of the seventh century, when the Prophet Muhammad spread his message across the Arabian peninsula.

A key figure in the Saudi jihadist movement is Osama bin Laden. Bin Laden, a scion of one of the most prominent and wealthy families in Saudi Arabia became radicalized when fighting the Soviets in Afghanistan during the 1980s. Although best known as the architect of the 9/11 terror attacks and the founder of Al Qaeda (in 1988), bin Laden is first and foremost committed to the destruction of the Saudi regime. The main purpose of Osama bin Laden's terror attacks against the United States was not to defeat America—he knew that was impossible.

Rather, many believe bin Laden struck the United States to provoke an American reaction against Muslims that would inflame anti-American sentiment in the Arab world. This in turn would undermine the legitimacy of Arab regimes allied with the United States, notably Saudi Arabia, promoting their downfall. Attacking the United States, therefore, is simply a means to a greater end, that being the over-throw of the royal family and restoration of Saudi Arabia to its rightful place as the land where true Islam would be practiced.[62]

Bin Laden's background leaves little doubt of his intentions to topple the Saudi regime. As a student in Saudi Arabia's King Abdul-Aziz University, he came under the influence of Mohammad Qutb, the brother of Sayyid, and the radical Muslim Brotherhood. Just after graduating in 1979 with a degree in civil engineer-ing, he joined Muslim rebels fighting the Soviet Union in Afghanistan, where he reportedly became even more radicalized. Following the Soviet defeat, bin Laden returned to Saudi Arabia, where his military exploits and pious living had made him a well-known and admired figure. Bin Laden, however, quickly lost favor with the Saudi royal family through his persistent criticisms. He attacked the regime for its corruption and its failure to enact the Sharia. He bitterly denounced the regime for arresting the "awakening shaykhs," announced his support for groups critical of Saudi Arabia, such as the CDLR, and established the Advice and Reform Committee, a group harshly critical of the royal family. Fearing for his safety, he left Saudi Arabia for Sudan in 1991, where he established a base of operations, which, among other aims, promoted the downfall of the royal family. The Saudi government revoked his citizenship in 1994.[63]

While bin Laden disliked the Saudi regime for many of its actions, it was King Fahd's 1990 decision to allow American troops into the kingdom that convinced him the royal family had lost its right to rule. Bin Laden's anger at this decision, which he saw as a violation of core Islamic principles, is clearly expressed in his 1996 "Declaration of War against Americans." In this *Bayan* (statement) bin Laden calls upon Muslims to kill Americans in order to bring about a U.S. with-drawal from Saudi Arabia. Less remarked upon, bin Laden's statement is also a "Declaration of War" against Saudi Arabia. Throughout the text, bin Laden vi-ciously lashes out at Saudi Arabia — not even using the name of the country (be-cause it includes the royal family's name, Saud), instead referring to it as the "land of the two Holy Places." Bin Laden is highly specific in his claims against the Saudi regime. He castigates the government for spending billions of dollars on a military that cannot defend the state, having a government-controlled press, and widespread corruption in the royal family. He then gets to the heart of his com-plaints about Saudi Arabia when he condemns it for "ignoring the divine Shari'ah law; depriving people of their legitimate rights; allowing the Americans to occupy the land of the two Holy Places; imprisonment, unjustly of the sincere scholars [the awakening shaykhs]."[64]

Bin Laden goes on to attack bin Baz's *fatwa* supporting the introduction of American troops into Saudi Arabia and in so doing challenges the very legitimacy of the Saudi state. As bin Laden wrote, "These apostate rulers [the Saudi royal family] who are fighting against God and His Messenger have no legitimacy or authority over Muslims, and they are not acting in the interests of our *umma* [Islamic community]. Both through these juridical decrees of yours you are giving legitimacy to these secular regimes and acknowledging their authority over Muslims, in contradiction of the fact that you have previously pronounced them to be infidels."[65]

Bin Laden reinforced this theme in his February 1998 statement, "Declaration of the World Islamic Front for Jihad against the Jews and the Crusaders." He attacked American policy for its sanctions against Iraq and support of Israel, but what most enraged him was the U.S. troops in Saudi Arabia. As he wrote, "For more than seven years the United States is occupying the lands of Islam in the holiest of its territories, Arabia, plundering its riches, overwhelming its rulers, humiliating its people, threatening its neighbors, and using its bases in the peninsula as a spearhead to fight against the neighboring Islamic peoples . . . We call on the Muslim ulema [religious authorities] and leaders and youth and soldiers to launch attacks against the armies of the American devils and against those who are allied with them from among the helpers of Satan."[66] It is clear that when bin Laden refers to "those who are allied with them," he is talking about Saudi Arabia. These two documents are nothing less than a call to jihad, not only against the Americans but the royal family as well.

Since 9/11, bin Laden's words and perhaps even active leadership produced an unprecedented wave of violence against the Saudi regime. Under the name of Al Qaeda of the Arabian Peninsula (QAP), bin Laden's followers launched a series of deadly attacks that at times appeared to be a prelude to civil war. The carnage began in May 2003, when three cars packed with bombs exploded in a residential compound in the Saudi capital of Riyadh, killing 34 people (including 10 Americans) and wounding 200. In November 2003, QAP members dressed in police uniforms again attacked a residential complex in Riyadh, killing 17 and wounding 120. The following month the United States ordered nonessential foreign service officers to leave Saudi Arabia because of the deteriorating security situation. On April 21, 2004, suicide bombers attacked government buildings in Riyadh, killing 5 people and wounding over 150. Less than two weeks later, on May 1, gunmen struck at the heart of Saudi power — its oil wealth — by killing six people in a Western oil company office in the city of Yanbu, on the Red Sea. On May 29, one of the most horrific assaults occurred when 4 gunmen killed 22 oil workers in Khobar, in eastern Saudi Arabia. The militants specifically sought out non-Muslims for slaughter, dragging one bound man behind them in their car to his death.[67] QAP launched two additional attacks in December 2004, one against the U.S. Consulate General office in the western city of Jeddah and the other a car bomb targeting the Saudi Ministry of Interior in a (failed) effort to kill the interior minister.[68] Al Qaeda also took credit for another direct assault on Saudi oil, the 2006 attack on the Abqaiq oil facility. The Saudi regime fought back, killing many of the terrorist leaders and eliminating many of the extremist cells, but the jihadists had demonstrated that they could act with impunity throughout the kingdom.

These attacks presented a serious threat to the royal family for several reasons. Most, if not all, of the assaults were believed to be the work of Al Qaeda. As such, the terrorist cells operating in Saudi Arabia are part of a much larger organization, led by bin Laden and dedicated to the overthrow of the royal family. The ease in which the attacks had been launched and the escape of several of the perpetrators led some to conclude that the Saudi security services have been penetrated.[69] Moreover, there is a seemingly large group of religiously motivated insurgents that a jihadi movement can draw from. It is estimated that between 15,000 and 25,000 Saudis have trained in Islamist camps in foreign countries over the past several years. Many had fought in Afghanistan against the Soviets. These "Afghan Saudis" combine military knowledge with a strong desire to remove the Saudi regime.[70] The American occupation of Iraq has created a new crop of battle-hardened Saudi fighters numbering in the hundreds or even thousands who, when they return to their country, can be expected to join the Afghan veterans in fighting against the Saudi government and its U.S. backers. Add to them the many Saudis who are unemployed after years of indoctrination in extreme Islam, and the potential for serious violence becomes great indeed.[71]

Religion in the form of extreme Islam has served as a source of legitimacy for a succession of Saudi leaders, providing a sense of stability and cohesion in a forbidding environment. Unfortunately for the Saudi regime, however, what religion gives it can take away. It is not easy running a country under the unforgiving eyes of the Wahhabi establishment, which will always find something to suggest that the Saudi leadership is insufficiently Islamic. Giving in to the Wahhabis, as the Saudis have done since the 1979 Grand Mosque revolt, provides some respite, but it is not a viable long-term strategy. Just as Saudi legitimacy depends on religious approval, so too does it rely upon the government meeting the needs of an exploding population. Since the Wahhabis oppose virtually everything that did not exist at the time of Muhammad in the seventh century, including computers, televisions, and telephones, and since Saudi security depends on American support, there are limits to how far the royal family can go to appease the faithful. As a result, what little legitimacy the Saudi regime enjoys will erode over time, strengthening Al Qaeda and other jihadist groups who seek to topple the government.

PROSPECTS FOR SUCCESS

Groups are not likely to engage in violence unless they believe they will gain by doing so. Standing in the way of potential Saudi insurgents are the internal security forces who protect the kingdom and the oil fields from domestic unrest. It appears at first that the Saudi forces are more than adequate to meet the challenges posed by rebel groups, thus making the resort to violence highly improbable. The Saudi leadership knows full well that its major threats come from within the country. Throughout its history, despite some minor incursions, Saudi Arabia has never been invaded by a foreign foe. On the other hand, beginning with the 1929 Ikhwan rebellion, followed by the 1979 seizure of the Grand Mosque, the Shia riots of the early 1980s, and the terror attacks post-9/11, Saudi Arabia has suffered through a series of devastating internal assaults. In response, Saudi Arabia has developed what looks like a formidable array of forces designed to squelch domestic disturbances before they can pose a threat to the state.

The National Guard plays an especially critical role in defending Saudi Arabia from domestic threats. Established in 1956, and now with around 100,000 men, the National Guard's primary mission is to ensure internal security, including the defense of Islamic holy places and the oil fields. The National Guard draws heavily from tribal areas, especially from the Najd and Hasa regions, which are seen as loyal to the regime.[72] The Guard has played an important role in suppressing major threats to Saudi security, including the attempted seizure of the Grand Mosque and the Shiite uprisings. Supplementing the Guard are a range of security forces under the Ministry of Interior Affairs, which watches over the Islamic clergy and groups, seeking signs of anti-Saudi activism. Added to these efforts are some 25,000 paramilitary police, specially trained antiterror units and a Royal Guard whose purpose is to protect the royal family. The oil fields have special units assigned to their protection made up of National Guard and other forces. From 25,000 to 30,000 troops guard the oil installations on any given day, with terminals and platforms also protected by some 5,000 Saudi Aramco security forces. A pervasive intelligence presence, complete with countless informers, blankets the country, seemingly alert to any developing threat. Should the internal security forces be overwhelmed, Saudi Arabia could turn to its regular forces in the army, air force, and navy to assist in any counterrevolutionary effort. These forces are among the best-equipped militaries in the world.[73]

Although the Saudi security apparatus looks daunting on paper, it is far less powerful than it appears and would not likely be able to deter or defeat a determined domestic assault. The Saudi forces reflect Saudi society, with all its weaknesses and divisions. They are made up of poorly educated, pampered recruits, who are subject to the tribal and religious passions of their fellow citizens. Precisely because the Saudi regime fears internal threats emanating from the military, it has prevented its armed forces from behaving in a coordinated manner, drastically limiting its effectiveness. Saudi Arabia's first line of defense, its intelligence apparatus, is woefully ill prepared to meet the threats against the kingdom. When the director of the Saudi Ministry of the Interior, Prince Nayef, argues that the Israelis were behind the 9/11 attacks,[74] it gives some indication as to how the pathologies of the kingdom infect the very highest levels of Saudi intelligence, calling into question its ability to respond to threats in the real world.

The high number of Saudis involved in terrorist activities, both within the kingdom and in Iraq, Afghanistan, and Europe attests to the inability of Saudi intelligence to control its own population. When put to the test, Saudi security forces have often failed to meet the challenges arrayed against them. In 1979, Saudi forces required outside help and several weeks to remove the occupiers of the Grand Mosque. In 1990, the billions of dollars poured into the Saudi military left them unable to defend themselves against the gathering threat posed by Saddam Hussein. In 2003 and 2004, the Saudi security establishment proved initially unable to anticipate or to adequately respond to the series of Al Qaeda attacks in the heart of the kingdom. Although the Saudi security forces have since done better in countering terrorist attacks, there is great uncertainty about how it will perform when once again confronted by extremist forces.

Arrayed against Saudi Arabia's dysfunctional security establishment are highly motivated fighters driven by fanatical beliefs that they are called upon by God to defeat the apostates who have taken over the holiest lands of Islam. It is true that they may lack the strength to overcome the Saudi forces, hapless though they might be. Nevertheless, victory to these insurgents need not mean toppling the Saudi regime immediately. Rather, they may simply seek to strike out at the Saudi government, undermining its hold on the country bit by bit, as they await a more propitious time for a decisive strike. Because "winning" for these insurgents simply means attacking the hated Saudi royal family and all that it stands for, they are unlikely to be defeated and cannot be deterred.

HOW MIGHT CIVIL CONFLICT EMERGE?

In this morass of conflict and threat, the catalyst for civil conflict might emerge from several sources. First, a split in the royal family could bring about civil war as princes come into conflict over some issue. A division in the royal family would be critical, because different members of the royal family control different portions of the military, heightening the prospects for civil war. A likely source of dispute is the proper role of Islam in Saudi society. While all the Saudi princes claim to follow the precepts of Wahhabism, there are major differences in how strictly they would apply their beliefs to governing the kingdom. The role of Wahhabism in everyday life is central to the Saudi conception of the state and one that resonates with the Saudi population. Open disagreements over religion among the princes could well produce violent conflict in its wake.

A battle over succession could also rupture the royal family. The principal Saudi leaders are all in their seventies and eighties, including King Abdullah. When they pass from the scene, power will need to be transferred to a new generation of princes. With no institutionalized procedures for determining who will be the next king, a dispute among the younger princes could degenerate into violence, with civil war lurking in its wake.

Civil war might also arise through a challenge from outside the royal family. Such a threat is most likely to stem from religiously driven extremists inspired by or directed from Al Qaeda or one of its allied groups. As the terrorist violence that erupted in 2003 so visibly demonstrated, these groups are capable of launching murderous attacks against the Saudi state. Anti-Saudi militants have already received some support from the Saudi population and, even more ominously, possibly from the Saudi military and internal security forces themselves. Just as the contemporary jihadist movement emerged out of the anti-Soviet Afghan war of the 1980s, fallout from Saudi fighters returning from the anti-American civil war in Iraq could jump start a revolt in the kingdom. American efforts to democratize Saudi Arabia could also lead to a violent challenge from groups opposed to the existing regime. Pushing for free elections can have unintended effects, such as occurred with the 2006 elections of Hamas in the Palestinian territories. The Saudi population is even more conservative and religiously driven than its government. Free and fair elections may select a leadership at odds with the royal family, setting the stage for a violent confrontation.

Finally, the catalyst for civil conflict may come from a drop in oil prices, sending the economy into a downward spiral. The Saudi regime has been able to maintain itself in power essentially by buying support from a wary and spoiled citizenry. When oil sells for around $100 a barrel there are ample funds to go around, ensuring the support of key constituencies. Oil prices, however, are extraordinarily volatile, placing the Saudis in a most precarious position. Since Saudi Arabia depends on oil to sustain the standard of living for its citizens, should the price of oil again plummet, all those who have come to depend on Saudi largesse will find themselves suddenly out of cash. Disgruntled groups, including the urban unemployed, students, tribal minorities, and the military, might react violently to being deprived of the benefits they expect. The Saudi regime will be placed in an impossible situation when forced to respond to mounting demands without the financial cushion that has bailed it out in the past. The result could well be protracted domestic conflict leading to a full-blown civil war.

These paths to civil war are mutually reinforcing. Divisions in the royal family could push princes to seek alliances with religious extremists outside the government. A succession crisis will embolden antigovernmental groups to strike out at the regime. Success by militant forces is likely to exacerbate splits in the royal family. A drop in the price of oil will foment popular unrest, which in turn will increase the power of the jihadists. The troubles of Saudi society and the royal family will be reflected in the military, enhancing the prospects for widespread unrest.

Civil war in Saudi Arabia is likely to be bloody. Given the division of the armed forces, and especially the rival commands of the Saudi National Guard and the regular army, a leadership crisis might quickly degenerate into protracted conflict. Since control of the oil fields would likely determine who leads Saudi Arabia, they would be a probable target in any violent civil conflict. The losing side might well choose to torch the fields or otherwise render them inoperable, as Saddam Hussein did in his 1991 retreat from Kuwait. The fields may be destroyed inadvertently, in the course of fighting, or key choke points may be rendered inoperable by determined jihadists. The victor in the civil war may choose to drive up the price of oil, as Osama bin Laden promised, or not sell oil at all, as the leaders of the 1979 Grand Mosque revolt pledged. Whatever happens, the effects of civil conflict in Saudi Arabia would spill over its borders, inflicting catastrophic damage on the United States and the wider world community.

CHAPTER THREE

Pakistan

Loose Nukes

The greatest threat to the security of the United States is a nuclear attack on American soil. As bad as 9/11 was, it does not take much imagination to contemplate how much worse it would have been if a nuclear bomb, instead of civilian aircraft, proved to be the weapon of choice. If the nightmare of a nuclear strike against the United States occurs, it almost certainly would not come about as a result of a deliberate decision by a government. Even hostile leaders recognize that any attack on the United States would bring about their own destruction. These leaders may be driven by fanaticism, they may hate the United States, they may wish to harm America, but they also want to live. Rather, if the United States is to become the victim of a nuclear attack, it most likely would occur because of events beyond the control of governments. Unauthorized strikes, especially by terrorist groups who seize or otherwise acquire nuclear weapons present the most pressing threat of nuclear attack against the United States. American concerns, therefore, need to center on those countries where nuclear weapons coexist with violent extremist groups, which brings us to Pakistan.

Pakistan poses a uniquely horrific threat to American interests because it brings together a witches' brew of capability and instability. Pakistan has from 50 to 90 nuclear bombs and enough nuclear material to make many more.[1] It is home to fanatical groups, including Al Qaeda and the Taliban, whose possession of nuclear weapons would place millions of American lives at risk. Pakistan verges on collapse, a collapse that would facilitate the transfer or seizure of nuclear weapons to terrorists. Much of Pakistan's population is desperately poor, separatist movements exist in three out of four of its provinces, prodemocracy groups launch violent protests against dictatorial rule, Islamists rail against leaders deemed insufficiently religious, and large sections of the country are beyond government control. Close ties with the United States and the government's inability to deliver services to its people dog the Pakistani regime. Although Pakistani military and security forces are well trained, they are forever spread thin dealing with multiple insurgencies and outbreaks of terrorist violence. Worries persist about the penetration of extremist religious influences in the Pakistani armed forces and intelligence community, raising questions about how they would react if confronted with an Islamist revolt. Should a regional insurgency get out of hand or should war once again break out with India, it is easy to see Pakistan unraveling. Pakistan is the only nuclear-armed state ever to have experienced a successful coup. If it becomes the only nuclear-armed state to collapse into civil war, America could face its worst security nightmare since the Cuban Missile Crisis.

Understanding the nature of Pakistan's threat requires an examination of how Pakistan came to develop nuclear weapons. The lack of control Pakistan maintains over its nuclear arms and the threats this poses to the United States are then considered. The likelihood of civil war in Pakistan and how such a conflict would undermine Pakistan's already shaky control of its nuclear forces completes the picture of what may be the most dangerous threat to the safety of Americans in the post–Cold War world.

PAKISTAN DEVELOPS NUCLEAR WEAPONS

Pakistan sought a nuclear capability to deal with pressing threats to its security. It borders India, a country which has roughly seven times the population and more than twice the armed forces. India is also a nuclear power, having tested a nuclear "device" in 1974 and detonated several atomic bombs in 1998. In the less than 60 years of its existence, Pakistan has gone to full-scale war with India three times (1947, 1965, 1971) and fought with India or been on the brink of war on many other occasions, including major crises in 1990, 1999, 2000, and 2001. The issues dividing India and Pakistan, especially the province of Kashmir, whose population is mostly Muslim but is largely under Indian control, remain mostly unresolved. Meanwhile, India's economy, population, and military potential continue to grow. Since it confronts an adversary that has more powerful conventional forces and has nuclear weapons to boot, it is hardly surprising that Pakistan has sought to acquire nuclear arms of its own.

Pakistan's efforts to develop nuclear weapons are long-standing. Following the test of the Indian nuclear device in 1974, its then–prime minister Zulfikar Ali

Bhutto famously declared that "even if Pakistanis have to eat grass, we will make the bomb."[2] Under Bhutto's leadership, Pakistan began its nuclear program even before the Indian test, in the spring of 1972. With help from China (which sought to counter India), Pakistan initially focused on reprocessing uranium as its path toward developing nuclear weapons. Reprocessing involves removing spent fuel rods from nuclear reactors, then separating out the plutonium that forms on the rods in a special plant before finally fabricating the plutonium into bombs. Pakistan was well on its way to making nuclear weapons in this manner when its plans hit a snag. France, which had promised to build a separation plant in Pakistan, withdrew its offer in 1977 under American pressure. Although Chinese help continued, without the separation plant Pakistan was not able to make a plutonium-based nuclear weapon at that time.[3]

With the plutonium option blocked, Pakistan placed its hopes on a second path toward making a nuclear bomb, through the enrichment of uranium. The enrichment process takes natural uranium and increases the level of uranium-235 from the 0.7% that exists in uranium ore to the 90% that is necessary to produce a fission (or nuclear) explosion. Enriching uranium does not require a separation plant or nuclear reactor, as is the case with a plutonium-based bomb, but the enrichment process is very difficult to achieve. Enrichment typically requires the ability to transform uranium into a gas and then to spin the gas in thousands of centrifuges until enough amounts of the lighter U-235 isotopes can be separated and collected.

Soon after the 1974 Indian nuclear explosion, while Pakistan was still pursuing the plutonium route, it embarked on a parallel enrichment program. Key to the program was a German-trained, Pakistani metallurgical engineer, Abdul Qadeer Khan. A. Q. Khan, as he came to be known, stole critical blueprints for centrifuges while working at an enrichment plant in the Netherlands, returning with them to Pakistan in 1976. Khan also proved to be a skilled organizer, establishing dummy firms to purchase the technology and hardware needed to produce a nuclear bomb from Western Europe. The determination to acquire a nuclear bomb did not waver when General Mohammad Zia-ul-Haq ousted Bhutto in 1977, though Zia did transfer control of the nuclear program from the civilian sector to the military. As Khan continued to amass the necessary ingredients for a nuclear weapon throughout the 1980s, the United States turned a blind eye to his efforts. Washington concluded that it was better to enlist Pakistani support to expel the Soviets from Afghanistan (following the USSR's 1979 invasion) than to stop Pakistan from becoming a nuclear power. By the late 1980s Pakistan was believed to have amassed enough enriched uranium for a bomb. In late May 1998, all doubts evaporated when Pakistan followed a series of Indian nuclear tests with six nuclear explosions of its own, thus publicly joining the nuclear club.[4]

With enrichment programs in place later supplemented with an indigenous plutonium production capability, Pakistan has become a full-fledged nuclear power.[5] In addition to its existing arsenal of nuclear weapons, Pakistan can probably produce from five to ten additional bombs each year. Pakistan has scores of ballistic missiles and nuclear-capable aircraft that can deliver its nuclear weapons to targets within a range of 2,000 kilometers.[6] If smuggling of nuclear arms is considered, there is not a target on earth, including the United States, that is beyond the reach of a Pakistani nuclear weapon.

THE THREAT TO THE UNITED STATES

The development of Pakistani nuclear weapons is so frightening because nuclear arms have the potential to inflict greater damage than any other weapon. A single device the size of a suitcase can incinerate an entire city in an instant. Because nuclear bombs produce sudden destruction, there is usually no defense against its effects.[7] That the United States has the largest and most powerful military forces in the world means nothing in the face of a nuclear attack. A small group or even a single individual can wreak catastrophic destruction on the mightiest of countries, including the United States. The ability of the very weak to do so much damage against the very powerful is unprecedented in world history. Previously, to hurt the very strong one had to be very strong as well. A country needed large armies, a developed industrial base, and advanced technology to threaten another state.

With nuclear weapons, none of this is necessary. No other "weapon of mass destruction" equals what nuclear weapons can accomplish. Chemical weapons do not cause any more damage than conventional arms, though they pack a significant psychological wallop. Biological weapons are potentially devastating, but they take time to do their mischief, time in which defenses can be mounted against them. Radiological weapons, the so-called dirty bombs, contaminate large areas, but kill few people, and their effects can be lessened through intensive cleanup campaigns. In a world of frightening weapons, nuclear weapons stand alone. Nothing else places millions of innocent lives at risk in the blink of an eye.

How might a nuclear attack happen? The source of a nuclear strike has been a subject of morbid fascination from the very dawn of the nuclear age in 1945. Countless articles and books have been written exploring how nuclear weapons may be used. Overwhelmingly, their focus has been on nuclear war between countries, particularly between the United States and the Soviet Union. During the

Cold War, scholars and policymakers agonized over how best to protect American nuclear weapons from a Soviet strike that would disarm its retaliatory capability, over whether limited nuclear war could be kept limited, and how to communicate to the USSR the futility of nuclear conflict. Nuclear crises, especially the Cuban Missile Crisis, reinforced the belief that the world stood at the brink of nuclear war. The development of a Chinese nuclear force under Mao Tse-tung in the mid-1960s increased American anxieties that nuclear war was a realistic threat.[8]

In retrospect, however, fears of superpower nuclear war or nuclear attacks on the United States from other countries were exaggerated. Even at the height of the Cold War, leaders of the United States, the Soviet Union, China, and other major powers recognized that launching a nuclear attack against another nuclear-armed adversary would provoke retaliation in kind. Since no interest was worth being annihilated, deterrence worked and nuclear war was averted.

The same attributes of nuclear weapons that kept the nuclear peace during the Cold War remain now that the Cold War is over. Leaders know now as they did then that nuclear war would be suicidal, making it highly unlikely that any would initiate a nuclear attack. To be sure, nuclear powers must still take actions to make certain their nuclear forces cannot be disarmed in a first strike or that their leaders would survive to order a retaliatory attack. But this is less of a problem than is commonly understood. It is exceedingly difficult to have supreme confidence of completely destroying a hidden and protected nuclear force in another country or killing all of a country's political and military leaders. Especially so, since the consequences of a nuclear first strike that failed to disarm even a handful of nuclear weapons or to kill a single individual with the means to order a counterstrike would likely be devastating retaliation. Seen in this light, the political theorist Kenneth Waltz is correct to argue, nuclear proliferation will make war less likely and, as far as the spread of nuclear weapons to other countries goes, "more may be better."[9]

The pacifying effect of nuclear weapons applies to India and Pakistan. Despite their intense hatred of one another, the two countries have been governed by a succession of rational leaders who appreciate the suicidal nature of nuclear conflict. Even when religiously driven heads of state were in office, they showed no signs of ignoring the costs of nuclear war. So long as both countries possess nuclear weapons, of course, the possibility of nuclear war exists, but its likelihood remains low. There is even evidence that their possession of nuclear weapons prevented India and Pakistan from going to full-scale *conventional* war, as they had done so often in the past when both countries lacked nuclear arms. In crisis after crisis, the mutual fear of nuclear war may have prevented a major escalation of hostilities between Pakistan and India. Just as nuclear weapons kept the peace between the United States and the Soviet Union during the Cold War, so have they helped deter a major war between Pakistan and India in the post–Cold War era.[10]

If nuclear war among countries is not likely, what about leaders giving or selling nuclear arms to terror groups? After all, the prospect of Saddam Hussein transferring nuclear weapons to organizations such as Al Qaeda became one of the main rationales for the United States invading Iraq in the spring of 2003. The possibility of leaders providing terror groups with nuclear weapons is, however, very remote. Nuclear arms contain isotopic identifiers, making it possible in some cases to identify the country that is the source of the weapon in a process known as "nuclear attribution." The Pentagon has put together a team of nuclear experts who use sensitive instruments and robots to study the radioactive fallout from a bomb and compare the results with data collected from various bomb programs around the world. Since leaders of countries know they might be identified as the origin of a terrorist attack, they are less likely to back such attacks out of fear that they would become the target of retaliation.[11] Moreover, terrorists are unstable and unreliable. It is hard to imagine any leadership that would give nuclear arms to organizations they cannot control and who may even turn against their supplier. In the post–Cold War era, as during the Cold War, deterrence will probably remain in effect, meaning that leaders are not likely to order nuclear attacks on other countries with nuclear weapons nor give nuclear weapons to nonstate groups.

Pakistan very much fits this reassuring model. It is certainly true that Pakistan abounds with groups whose possession of nuclear weapons would be a nightmare for the United States. But there has never been a Pakistani leadership, including those sympathetic to Islamic extremism, that ever gave any sign they would risk the security of their country by handing over weapons of mass destruction to others. Neither is it likely that the Pakistani military, an essentially moderate and conservative force, would stand for such a transfer. The fear that the weapons would be traced back to Pakistan or that the terrorist groups would use them in a manner harmful to Pakistani interests would be enough to stop any decision to hand over nuclear weapons to fanatics dead in its tracks.

INADVERTENT USE

While the chances of a deliberate decision by a country's leadership to use or transfer its nuclear weapons are remote, the same cannot be said for the inadvertent use of these arms. If nuclear weapons are to be used in the coming years against the United States or others, it is far more likely to happen because a government loses control over its nuclear arsenal than a conscious choice by a head

of state to initiate nuclear war. One way a nuclear weapon could be used without governmental intent is an accidental detonation. How badly this would affect
American interests depends on the specific conditions of the nuclear blast. If it
is localized, in an area of sparse civilian population, its effects would be limited.
Even the nuclear taboo in effect since 1945 might not be eroded, if there is little
damage and it was clear there was no warlike intent.[12] If an accidental detonation
destroyed a Pakistani city, it would have much more of an impact, obviously, on
Pakistan itself, but it would affect the United States as well. The humanitarian
dimension alone would be devastating and there might also be global environmental effects. Moreover, a nuclear bomb going off accidentally could be just the
catalyst to push the already fragile Pakistani society into collapse, with untold regional implications.

An even worse development would be the deliberate use of nuclear weapons
without government authorization. One way this could come about is if a lower-
ranking officer decided to launch a nuclear weapon in defiance of the Pakistani
government, most likely against India. The motivations to commit such an act
range from individual madness to an overwhelming sense of anger at some Indian
policy. Whatever the cause, the comforting logic of nuclear deterrence cannot be
relied upon to constrain the actions of individuals. Leaders of countries are likely
to be rational in the sense that they are sensitive to costs. After all, to achieve power
and hold on to power requires the ability to make sound calculations about the
(often hostile) world that leaders face. Such individuals are not likely to commit
suicide by initiating a nuclear exchange.[13] No such confidence can be applied to
random individuals who are capable of engaging in all kinds of bizarre behavior.
It is hard to imagine a more deadly combination than irrationality and nuclear
weapons, but that is precisely what could happen if nuclear arms fall into the
hands of fanatics. Should nuclear war with India arise through an unauthorized
Pakistani strike, the United States would be endangered, even if Washington remained aloof from the actual conflict. The environmental fallout, the surge of refugees, the devastation of two key allies, and coping with a postnuclear world would
likely haunt the United States — and the rest of the world — for decades to come.

Most frightening is the prospect of terrorist groups gaining control of nuclear
weapons either by seizing the arms by force or having someone give the nuclear weapons to them. The possibility of a group like Al Qaeda (or Al Qaeda itself) acquiring nuclear weapons is so alarming because traditional means of deterrence will have no effect. Deterring terrorist groups by threatening to punish
them stands little chance of success. The aims of many of these groups are so extreme that hurting the United States becomes an end in itself, making the threat

of retaliation pointless. Many embrace death, calling into question what threat of punishment would be enough to cause them to choose not to harm the United States when they are fully capable of doing so. The locations of these groups are often unknown — they have no "return address" — making it virtually impossible to hit them even if such an attack might do some good.

If nuclear weapons fall into terrorist hands, there is little the United States could do to prevent an attack on its cities. Once in the arms of extremist groups, nuclear weapons could easily be smuggled into the United States. More than 50,000 cargo containers enter the United States each day delivered by some 30,000 trucks, over 6,000 railroad cars, and 140 ships. Less than 5% of these containers are ever inspected. The United States has a 4,000-mile border with Canada and a 2,000-mile border with Mexico, both of which are lightly guarded. Thousands of noncommercial ships and boats sail into American harbors, with fewer than 10% ever inspected by U.S. Customs. Even when inspections occur, detection of nuclear material is very difficult, especially if it is shielded with lead or tungsten to inhibit radioactive emissions. Efforts to prevent smuggling are handicapped, since they also inhibit the free flow of goods and people, essential to the American economy. After acquiring nuclear arms, sneaking them into the United States would be as easy as smuggling drugs or illegal aliens — an everyday occurrence.[14] It is hard to avoid the conclusion that if terrorists such as Al Qaeda get control over nuclear weapons, they will use them against the United States. Not surprisingly, during the 2004 Bush-Kerry presidential debates, both candidates, who agreed on little else, named the threat of a terrorist attack with nuclear weapons as the single most serious threat to the United States.

PAKISTANI CONTROL OF NUCLEAR WEAPONS

Since the principal danger presented by Pakistani nuclear weapons is accidental or unauthorized use, the key question is determining how well the regime controls its arsenal. The Pakistanis claim they have no problem in overseeing their nuclear arms. Prior to the 9/11 attacks, Pakistani president Pervez Musharraf told an American journalist that the manner in which Pakistan deployed its nuclear weapons made terrorist seizure or theft virtually impossible. As Musharraf described it, control of nuclear weapons was exercised through "a geographic separation between the warhead and the missile . . . In order to arm the missile, the warhead would have to be moved by truck over a certain distance. I don't see any chance of this restraint being broken." Following the 9/11 attacks, President Musharraf again tried to allay American concerns about the security of the Pakistani arsenal, saying in a CNN interview, "We have an excellent command and control system which we have evolved and there is no question of their falling into the hands of the fundamentalists." Showing that this was not just empty rhetoric, Musharraf established a National Command Authority in December 2003, which gave him ultimate control over both Pakistani nuclear weapons and fissile material that could be used to make those weapons. The image conveyed was of a country whose nuclear weapons were under tight security whose use would only follow a direct presidential order.[15]

Despite Musharraf's assurances, there is ample reason to believe that Pakistani nuclear weapons could be used against the wishes of its leadership, especially in the context of major civil unrest. Because Pakistani weapons are so unsophisticated, as befits a new nuclear power, they are much more likely to be detonated accidentally than the weapons of the United States or Russia.

Modern American nuclear weapons have what is called the "one point safety rule," whereby there is less than one chance in a million that a weapon will go off due to explosion, fire, or some other extraneous stimulus.[16] There is little chance that Pakistani bombs have been made to this exacting standard. Pakistan developed its bomb in secret, which often means less attention is paid to safety issues. It has had scant experience in conducting exercises or in handling nuclear weapons.[17] The design of many primitive bombs are such that if they are shot, hit with artillery, or even jostled badly, there is no guarantee they would not go off.[18]

Even more worrisome is Pakistan's vulnerability to having extremist groups seize its nuclear weapons. Pakistan is filled with groups who hold a deeply felt hatred of the United States and would like nothing better than to launch an attack against an American city. One of the most extreme, Al Qaeda, is well entrenched in Pakistan. Believed to have founded Al Qaeda in the Pakistani city of Peshawar in 1988, its leader, Osama bin Laden, is thought to be hiding in Pakistan. Al Qaeda commanders, such as Khalid Sheikh Mohammad, Ramzi Ahmed Yousef, and Mir Aimal Kasi, hail from Pakistan, where they have received a good deal of support from Pakistani tribes. Al Qaeda has thousands of fighters on the Pakistani-Afghan border and has maintained close ties with elements of the Pakistani military and some 25,000 other radical jihadis.[19] A 2007 U.S. National Intelligence Estimate concluded that Al Qaeda had regained its pre-9/11 strength in large measure by establishing itself in safe havens in the Pakistani tribal areas.[20] At least two and as many as eight Pakistani nuclear scientists had met with Osama bin Laden in the summer before 9/11, where the subject of a nuclear bomb for Al Qaeda was apparently discussed.[21] No greater nightmare exists for Americans than Al Qaeda getting control of a nuclear bomb, and no place provides a better opportunity for it to do so than Pakistan.

The possible absence of effective locks on Pakistani nuclear weapons makes them an especially attractive target for those seeking to use nuclear arms without approval of the government. American nuclear weapons have "PALs" — permissive action links — which are electronic locks that require a special code for activating the weapon. Just as stealing an ATM card without a PIN will do a thief no good, stealing or transferring a nuclear weapon with a PAL and not the correct code will also be of little use to the recipient. This is especially true with the more sophisticated PALs that deactivate a nuclear weapon if a wrong code is tried.[22] Pakistani weapons are believed to have some version of PALs, but they are not the highly effective ones of American design. Instead, Pakistan has reportedly placed its own locking devices on its nuclear weapons, but they are unlikely to work as well as American PALs. The United States has reportedly discussed providing PALs to Pakistan but is inhibited by legal obligations that prevent nuclear assistance to countries not parties to the Non-Proliferation Treaty. More important, Pakistan has resisted American efforts to place PALs on their weapons for fear that America would be able to disable the nuclear arms without the approval of the Pakistani leadership.[23] Without effective PALs, Pakistani nuclear weapons might be useable by any group that seizes control over them.

NEVER/ALWAYS

The likelihood that the Pakistani government will lose control over its nuclear weapons is increased by the way Pakistan deploys its nuclear forces. Like all nuclear powers, Pakistan confronts what political scientist Peter Feaver has described as the "never/always" dilemma in deciding how to exercise control over its nuclear forces.[24] Leaders need to be certain that nuclear weapons will *never* be used against their wishes, but that they will *always* be used if they order them to do so. If all the Pakistani leadership was concerned about were accidents and unauthorized use of its nuclear weapons, it could take effective steps to prevent either from occurring. Pakistan would simply keep its weapons unassembled with their components separated, under tight governmental control, just as President Musharraf said it does. In this way, accidental detonations of nuclear weapons will not occur, because with its parts scattered there is no bomb to go off. Keeping the weapons unassembled also means there are no bombs for terrorist groups to seize or be given. Securing all the possible components of a nuclear bomb and putting them together in a manner that would result in a working weapon would be far more difficult than just grabbing a bomb off the shelf. Moreover, a safe nuclear system would have a very limited number of individuals who had the authority to order the launch of nuclear weapons. If only the president, and perhaps a small number of his subordinates, were able to initiate a nuclear strike with a special code that only they knew, the possibility of unauthorized use or transfer to terrorist groups would be substantially diminished. So, in theory, Pakistani nuclear weapons can be deployed in a manner making them impervious to unintentional use.

The problem, however, is that leaders of nuclear-armed countries, especially new proliferators, also want to be sure that their nuclear force will "always" be ready to respond to an order to launch. It is not accidents and unauthorized use that is their main cause for worry, but disarming and decapitating strikes from an outside adversary, that keep leaders up at night. In a disarming strike, the leadership survives, but its nuclear forces are destroyed on the ground before they can be launched. Without a surviving nuclear force, there can be no retaliation, making a first strike that much more attractive for the enemy. In a decapitating attack, the leadership is killed (or otherwise neutralized) before they can give the order to launch a counterstrike. If the authority to launch a nuclear attack is held by only a small number of people and they are incapacitated in a decapitating strike, retaliation against the aggressor might not take place, undermining deterrence.

A leadership that worries about a disarming strike will attempt to convince a would-be aggressor that it will be unable to prevent nuclear retaliation by destroying its nuclear forces before they can be launched. Especially for countries like Pakistan that face an enemy only minutes away, it would be necessary to launch one's weapons quickly, before they can be eliminated on the ground. Nuclear weapons must be kept fully assembled, on hair-trigger alert and armed for immediate detonation. It would also be best that nuclear forces be kept constantly moving to complicate efforts to locate and destroy them. Coping with a decapitating attack requires convincing a potential aggressor that they cannot forestall a nuclear counterattack by killing a handful of officials, because the authority to launch a counterstrike would be delegated to a large number of subordinates. The message to the would-be attacker is clear: even if you succeed in eliminating the top leaders of the country, others who have the authority to launch nuclear weapons will survive to order a devastating retaliation. These choices create a horrible dilemma. Steps taken to deal with a threat from an outside adversary make accidents and inadvertent use more likely, while actions taken to protect the country from accidents and inadvertent use make it more vulnerable to external attack.

The choice leaders make as to which of the "never/always" dangers to emphasize is never easy. It depends on whether the leadership believes it confronts a greater threat from internal forces or from outside countries. Pakistan, which faces both internal and external threats, has an especially tough choice. From the American perspective, though, Pakistan's decision is not difficult. The Indian threat to Pakistan, though real, is manageable through deterrence. Internal threats, however, abound and need to be taken much more seriously. Most important, the United States has much more to fear from "loose nukes" falling into the hands of terrorist groups than from an Indo-Pakistani nuclear war. Clearly, American policymakers would prefer a Pakistan that worried more about the "never" side of the always/never divide.

The leadership of Pakistan, however, believes otherwise. President Musharraf's claims notwithstanding, Pakistan does not always deploy its nuclear weapons in ways that would prevent their inadvertent use. It may be true that when relations with India are peaceful, the Pakistani leadership pays more attention to preventing accidents or unauthorized use, and nuclear weapons are kept unassembled in secure storage. But relations with India often are not peaceful. On at least three occasions when Pakistan's leaders believed it faced the possibility of an Indian attack, Pakistani nuclear forces were placed on alert. This happened in 1999, when Indian and Pakistani forces clashed in Kargil; following the 9/11 attacks on the United States; and in December 2001 after a terrorist assault on the Indian parliament in New Delhi by a group with links to Pakistan. For the latter two episodes, Pakistan removed its nuclear weapons from storage sites and dispersed them throughout the country.[25] During the Kargil episode, Musharraf even considered transferring Pakistani nuclear weapons to western Afghanistan to guard against a preemptive strike from India.[26] Following the "always" logic of protecting themselves from an Indian nuclear strike, the Pakistanis almost certainly assembled their nuclear weapons and gave authority to use them to lower-ranking officers during these crises. Having fully armed nuclear weapons on the move with field commanders empowered to use them is the mother of all nightmares, but this is apparently what Pakistan does whenever a crisis erupts with India.

CIVIL WAR HEIGHTENS THE DANGER

The already frightening prospects that Pakistan would lose control of its nuclear weapons get much worse should civil war break out. If a government is toppled or threatened by civil strife its ability to protect nuclear weapons — likely targets for insurgents — will be severely compromised. While there have been no cases of nuclear weapons actually being used or transferred during civil strife, there have been close calls. In one instance, several French generals seeking to overthrow President

Charles de Gaulle came close to getting control of a nuclear weapon being prepared for testing in Algeria in 1960. Only a quick detonation of the bomb by loyalist forces — in a test that fizzled — prevented it from falling into the hands of the insurgents.[27] During the Cultural Revolution in China, a senior military officer launched a missile with an armed nuclear warhead 500 kilometers across Chinese territory without governmental approval and (in a different action) a party boss threatened to take over China's Lop Nor nuclear assembly plant and testing site in the remote Xinjiang province. Both threats stemmed from concerns over attacks by Red Guards on the Chinese military. In each case, the government backed down, reining in the rampaging Red Guards.[28] Although nuclear weapons were not used by insurgent forces in either France or China, these are clear illustrations of how states undergoing civil strife can lose control over their nuclear arsenals.

A Pakistani civil war would dramatically increase the chances of the government losing control of its nuclear arms to those who would use them against its wishes. The onset of civil war would almost certainly cause Pakistan to place its nuclear forces on alert either in response to the domestic strife or to an Indian alert, an alert that would surely be called as the Indian leadership reacted to the implications of Pakistan engulfed in violence. In the midst of violence and confusion, therefore, the Pakistani leadership can be expected to order the assembly of its nuclear bombs, move them from place to place, and give the authority to launch a nuclear attack to lower-ranking subordinates. The risk of Pakistani military or governmental officials ordering the use of nuclear arms without governmental authorization would be greatly increased. Officials newly empowered with the ability to launch nuclear weapons may choose to do so without governmental approval as the passions unleashed by civil war convince them now is the time to settle scores with domestic or regional foes. Even if the Pakistani government refused to predelegate authority for nuclear weapons use, it could not ensure that the nuclear arms would remain under its control. Since Pakistani nuclear arms probably lack effective locking mechanisms, the mere physical possession of the weapons would be enough to allow for their use, increasing the likelihood that someone would decide independently to initiate a nuclear attack.[29]

The greatest danger to American interests — the seizure of nuclear weapons by terrorist groups — would be greatly enhanced by a Pakistani civil war. The alerting of nuclear forces that would come about in response to civil conflict in Pakistan will make nuclear weapons much more vulnerable to falling into the hands of terrorists. Not only will fully assembled nuclear weapons be moving around from place to place, there is a very good chance radical groups will know where these weapons are. Extremists launched two nearly successful assassination attempts against Musharraf in 2003, demonstrating that they penetrated the president's inner circle to the extent of knowing his exact travel plans.[30] It is not much of a leap from knowing the president's secret itinerary to knowing the location of nuclear weapons in time of crisis. Given the Islamist penetration of the military, it can be assumed that some of these nuclear weapons will be guarded by soldiers with sympathy for radical causes.

The prospect of civil war exacerbates this already perilous situation. The intense emotions that surround civil conflict may be enough to push closet radicals in the military to turn over the weapons to fellow Islamists. Guards may assist radical groups launching assaults on nuclear compounds, increasing their chances of success. Even without inside help, a civil war is likely to spur attacks by religious extremists on nuclear sites that may result in the accidental detonation of the primitive weapons or, even worse, their seizure. A Pakistani military busy fighting on many fronts, especially if it is divided within itself, will not be able to offer the kind of defense of the nuclear weapons that may be needed. The result is that terror groups such as Al Qaeda or one of the many Pakistani groups affiliated with Al Qaeda would gain control of Pakistani nuclear arms, placing the lives of millions of Americans in jeopardy.

Civil war also increases the chances of Pakistan accidentally plunging into nuclear war with India. With both India and Pakistan placing their nuclear forces on alert, the already tense standoff between the two countries becomes much more dangerous. The leaders of Pakistan and India have roughly five minutes — the time it would take nuclear-armed missiles to reach their targets — to determine if a suspected attack was real. To wait longer means risking having their retaliatory forces destroyed on the ground or their leaders killed. As discussed, achieving a successful disarming or decapitating strike is staggeringly difficult, but for a leadership that believes it is under attack the first impulse would be to ensure that retaliation against the aggressor would be carried out. This can be accomplished by placing one's nuclear forces on "launch on warning," that is, forces are launched as soon as it appears an attack is underway, not waiting for the missiles and bombs to actually fall. This posture increases the chances that a false radar reading or other mistake would precipitate a decision to launch a nuclear strike, plunging both countries into nuclear war. In the wake of civil war in Pakistan, with tensions reaching a fever pitch and with many fingers on many nuclear triggers, the chances of these kinds of miscalculations rise astronomically. A nuclear war that neither Pakistan nor India sought could well be the outcome.

Equally frightening, civil conflict in Pakistan raises the likelihood of a deliberate nuclear war with India. Notwithstanding an official posture of committing itself not to use nuclear weapons first, a January 2003 official statement issued by the Indian government left the door open for first strikes under certain circumstances.[31] An earlier semiofficial statement that was posted on the Indian government's website warned potential aggressors that "any threat of nuclear weapons against India shall invoke measures to counter the threat," presumably including India's launching a preemptive attack against Pakistan.[32] A Pakistani civil war might pose just the "threat of nuclear weapons against India" that would precipitate a nuclear war. Since civil war in Pakistan raises the prospect of nuclear weapons falling into the hands of groups who would use them against India, the Indian leadership may decide that despite the huge risks, it must attempt to disarm Pakistan before it launches an attack. A civil war in Pakistan also might provoke an Indian first strike if the Indians conclude that Pakistani nuclear capabilities have been so degraded that India could disarm the remaining nuclear forces. Conversely, Pakistan may be tempted to launch a first strike against India if its leadership believes that India would take advantage of Pakistani civil strife to launch an attack. Whatever the scenario, it is hard to escape the conclusion that civil war in Pakistan makes the nightmare of an Indo-Pakistani nuclear war much more likely.

PROSPECTS FOR A PAKISTANI CIVIL WAR

There is no doubt that any use of nuclear weapons by Pakistan would threaten American interests. There is also no doubt that the outbreak of civil war or widespread domestic violence would dramatically increase the chances that these arms would be used. The critical issue, then, is the likelihood of civil strife breaking out in Pakistan. Unfortunately, the prospects that civil violence in Pakistan will soon tear the country apart are distressingly high and — if present trends continue — will only get worse.

Pakistan has undergone or been on the brink of civil conflict ever since its creation in 1947. It has been under formal military rule for roughly half its existence and informal military rule for the other half. No elected government has ever succeeded another in office. Pakistan has fought three wars with India, all of which it has lost. Demonstrators pressing for democratic rule regularly challenge the authority of Pakistan's autocratic leaders in major cities. Separatist movements are active across the country, leaving many areas free of governmental control. Terrorist groups such as Al Qaeda flourish along the Pakistani-Afghan border and in the cities. They are supported by a growing indigenous Islamic movement that openly seeks to topple the state. Against these forces is the army, the one institution that holds the country together. But its willingness and ability to suppress antigovernment forces, especially Islamic groups, is increasingly in doubt.[33] If Pakistan continues on its current path — and there is little to argue that it won't — it is difficult to avoid the conclusion that it could well collapse in a frenzy of violence.

The likelihood for civil war in Pakistan is so high, because the conditions that typically generate internal conflict are all present. Pakistanis are intensely angry at their government and fellow citizens, setting the stage for more violent confrontations. The regime's legitimacy, shaky at best, erodes with each passing day, providing would-be insurgents with the sense that they have a *right* to violently challenge Pakistani rule. As extremist influences infiltrate a police force and military already weakened by having to cope with multiple threats, opponents of the regime are becoming more confident that they can defeat the security forces arrayed against them. The coming together of intense grievances, lack of governmental legitimacy, and belief that violence will successfully advance your cause has been at the root of civil wars throughout history and there is little to believe that Pakistan will be an exception.

GRIEVANCES

The anger felt by the Pakistani people against their government comes in two forms. First are complaints stemming from overall dissatisfaction with their lot in life, particularly with the way the government acts to cope with problems they face. Second are more specific complaints from groups who believe they have been maltreated because of their ethnicity or adherence to Islam. The Pakistani government does a terrible job in dealing with both sets of grievances.

General grievances abound in Pakistan because life is so miserable. The *Human Development Report,* which ranks quality of life in such areas as education and longevity, places Pakistan 135th in the world, in the same category as such countries as Ghana, Sudan, and Botswana. Pakistanis have a life expectancy of only 63 years, with an adult literacy rate of less than 50%.[34] More than one-third of its people live in poverty and its educational system is ranked among the 15 worst in the world. Nor does the future hold much promise. Pakistan's population is growing at a rate of 2.9% per year — one of the highest in the world. Its population has increased from 32 million at the time of its independence to about 165 million in 2006 and will be over 255 million by 2025, making it the fifth most populous state in the world. Exacerbating population pressures is a rising rate of urbanization. Approximately 18% of the Pakistani people lived in cities at the time of partition, growing to 33% in 2004 as the young now flock to urban areas. Many will not find work, because aside from a troubled textile industry, Pakistan produces little of export quality. While the Pakistani economy at times has grown at a healthy 6% per year, its high level of foreign debt has made it hostage to outside investment and foreign aid. If Pakistan does come apart, or if its strategic role is diminished, it will no longer be able to depend on critical Western assistance to meet the basic needs of its people. Add to this a crumbling infrastructure, weak political institutions, poor public health, and rampant crime, and it is easy to understand why the Pakistani people are so angry with their government.[35]

The fury of the Pakistani people is fueled by the thoughtless manner in which its leaders have dealt with their problems. The military has run Pakistan, either directly or indirectly, from the time of its founding. If the military proved to be a good manager, its governance might have been acceptable, but its members have proven to be extraordinarily inept rulers. Democratically elected civilian leaders have turned out to be even worse. Whether civilian or military, governments collect taxes from less than 1% of the people, making them incapable of meeting the escalating demands of their citizens.[36] Instead, a large informal economy flourishes, making the regime increasingly irrelevant. How is the government going to build schools and bridges, pay policemen, and stimulate the economy if it cannot even collect money from individuals and businesses? Neither has the Pakistani government kept its people safe. With the possible exception of the 1947 clash, none of Pakistan's conflicts with India were wars of self-defense. Instead, Pakistan blundered into needless wars and crises with a much stronger adversary, exposing its people to death and destruction.

The Pakistani government has not done much better in providing for domestic security. Large areas of the country are no-go zones, where lawlessness prevails and governmental authority simply does not exist. Urban centers have become battle zones as ideological and religious conflicts are settled violently in the streets with the police unable or unwilling to intervene. Few have faith in a government that is ranked among the most corrupt in the world.[37] With the military unwilling to allow civilian governments to act on their own and incapable of governing effectively by itself, democracy — or just competent governance — appears to be a distant dream. The lives of most Pakistanis are miserable and they understandably blame their government for not making them better.

SEPARATIST MOVEMENTS

Pakistan is a multiethnic state where loyalty to one's ethnic group often takes precedence over loyalty to the country. You may be a citizen of Pakistan, but you are a Baluchi or Punjabi first, and only then a Pakistani. Pakistan's lack of a national consciousness mirrors the experience of other states in the Third World. Pakistan too is an artificial and mostly arbitrary creation of a colonial power. Ripped from India by Great Britain, its disparate peoples were never a single nation. Pakistan's six decades of independence have not given it time or the means to create the sense of common identity that took centuries to develop in the West.

There is no national glue holding Pakistan together. While most Pakistanis are Muslim, they adhere to different sects, creating violent divisions. Pakistan has the misfortune of being broken into four provinces, each of which is the primary home of a distinct ethnic group. The Pashtuns live mostly in the North-West Frontier Province (NWFP), the Punjabis in Punjab, the Sindhis in Sindh, and the Baluchis in Baluchistan. As demonstrated by the Bengalis, whose 1971 secession from Pakistan created the new state of Bangladesh, concentrations of ethnic groups in particular regions facilitate separatist movements and civil war. While each ethnic group has its own list of grievances, all chafe under the domination of the Punjabis, who run the government and the economy. The weakness of the Pakistani state exacerbates these problems. Vast areas of Pakistan are untouched by central authorities. Basic goods and services are delivered not by the government, but by traditional tribal leaders. If a well needs to be dug, a school built, or food provided to feed one's family, the government is not there to help. In such a situation who will the Pakistanis trust to look after their interests? A government that is largely invisible and can change overnight? Or their ethnic brethren with whom they have shared an identity for millennia and who are actually on the ground to give them what they need? Not surprisingly, nationalism flourishes, but it is ethnic-provincial nationalism, not Pakistani nationalism.[38]

The group most likely to challenge the Pakistani government are the Pashtuns. There are about 28 million Pashtuns living in Pakistan, mostly in the NWFP and the largely lawless tribal areas, with another 13 million Pashtuns living across the border in Afghanistan. Efforts to unite the Pashtuns into a single country arose even before the creation of Pakistan and continue to bedevil Pakistani governments today. These activities have often been aided by Afghan governments seeking to bring together the Pashtuns on both sides of the border. The coming to power of the Taliban, itself a movement that originated in Pakistan and was made up of Pashtuns, delighted the Pakistani government because it ended Afghan support for absorbing the Pashtuns into Afghanistan. In the wake of 9/11, however, the problem of Pashtun separatism reawakened with a vengeance. Following 9/11, the United States, with President Musharraf's approval, sent covert American forces to northwestern Pakistan to support operations against Al Qaeda in Afghanistan and to search for Osama bin Laden.[39]

The Pashtuns, who support Al Qaeda far more than they do the United States, deeply resented their government's decision to cooperate with Washington. One consequence of that resentment was the 2002 election of a coalition of Islamist parties to run the NWFP. For the first time, a province of Pakistan fell under the control of religious parties, raising the possibility of a religious-ethnic alliance committed to a separatist movement. Across the border, the post-Taliban Afghan government also revived Pashtun separatism. Unhappy that the NWFP was supporting many of the remnants from the old Taliban regime and that the Pakistani government was doing very little to hinder its efforts, the Afghan government threatened Pakistan with renewed support for an independent Pakhtoonistan (a state for the Pashtuns) if these policies continued. Either an indigenous Pakistani separatist movement or one supported by Afghanistan could seriously challenge the Pakistani regime's already tenuous control over this key province.[40]

Making matters worse, the tribal areas abutting the NWFP have increasingly come under the control of the Taliban and Al Qaeda. Following an ineffectual truce in 2006 with local tribal leaders, the Pakistani Interior Ministry acknowledged in the summer of 2007 that Islamic extremists were rapidly overwhelming Pakistani security forces in a growing revolt that threatened to spread throughout the rest of the country. If the tribal areas continue to serve as a haven for Al Qaeda and the Taliban, and if the Pakistani military is unable to regain some semblance of control, the entire northwest region might break away, setting into motion a process that could rip apart the state.[41]

Only slightly less dangerous is the separatist movement in Baluchistan. The Baluchis make up the largest province in Pakistan, with almost half the country's total area, but only 5% of its population. The Baluchis speak their own language and see themselves as ethnically distinct from Pakistanis. Baluchistan had been independent for nearly a year before being forced to become part of Pakistan and since then has resisted efforts at integration into the Pakistani state. Many Baluchis want to regain their short-lived independence by seceding from Pakistan. Toward that end, they have engaged in several armed conflicts with Pakistani forces, with the most serious being a civil war fought in the early 1970s. The immediate spark of the conflict was the firing and imprisonment of Baluchi leaders by Prime Minister Bhutto, who accused them of fostering separatism. Local fighting soon grew out of control as 80,000 Pakistani troops eventually stormed into Baluchistan to counter some 55,000 poorly armed insurgents. Some 3,300 Pakistani troops and over 6,000 Baluchi rebels died in the war.[42] The large-scale fighting, coming so soon after the successful secession of East Pakistan, posed a serious threat to the existence of the Pakistani government. The civil war ended only when Bhutto was replaced in a military coup by General Zia, who quickly reached agreement with the rebels and withdrew the Pakistani troops. Successive Pakistani governments largely left the province alone, except to play some 17 major tribal leaders off against one another.[43]

The politics of divide and rule did not work. A low-level insurgency that had been simmering for years escalated markedly in 2005, when Baluchi rebels, members of the Baluchistan Liberation Army (one of several guerrilla groups that have emerged since the 1970s), attacked Pakistan's biggest gas field, threatening a major source of income for the regime. The assault revealed the growing resentments of the Baluchis against the increasing Pakistani military presence in Baluchistan (estimated at some 23,000 Pakistani troops) combined with anger at not being given what they believe is their fair share of revenue from the province's natural resources. President Musharraf's determination to exploit Baluchistan's gas and oil wealth — unmatched elsewhere in Pakistan — along with his intention to build a pipeline across the province sparked widespread unrest that the Pakistani army was unable to quell. The rebels deploy as many as several thousand fighters and have launched operations throughout the province. It is unlikely that they will be able to secede on their own, but if the Pakistani government is weakened by other challenges, the Baluchis may seize the opportunity to set up their own state, thus hastening the dissolution of Pakistan itself.[44]

The Sindhis also pose a separatist threat, though not as severe as the Pashtuns and the Baluchis. Sindh is the source of much of Pakistan's food and its principal outlet to the sea. Sindh borders India, which has backed Sindhi separatists in the past. A Sindhi independence movement emerged in the 1970s but has been largely dormant because the central government has placated the Sindhis by providing jobs and ensuring that the Sindhi language is given official protection. Nevertheless, tensions persist, as illustrated by a four-month revolt in 1983 in which over 400 people died. While the approximately 40 million Sindhis have many grievances, their biggest concern is being swallowed up in a Punjabi-dominated India, with their language and customs disappearing. The influx of large numbers of Punjabis and Mohajirs — Muslim immigrants from India — have exacerbated Sindhi fears that their culture may not survive another generation. The mostly moderate Sindhis also resent the growing power of Islamic extremists and the violence which pervades the country. It is unlikely these concerns will lead to secession, in part because the central government would act quickly to forestall such a move. It cannot be comforting, however, that such a vital province harbors such anti-Pakistani sentiments.[45]

Separatist movements are likely to become full-fledged civil wars if either of two conditions are met. First, separatist movements will need the support of an outside country to pose a credible threat to Pakistani rule. The secession of East Pakistan would not have been possible if the Bengalis had not received massive military assistance from India. Since the Pashtuns have ties to Afghanistan, the Baluchis to Afghanistan and Iran, and the Sindhis to India, this condition could well be realized.[46] The second condition for separatist strife to morph into civil war is the emergence of other major threats to Pakistani rule, especially from Islamist forces, that would divert the resources of the Pakistani security forces. Unfortunately for Pakistan and the United States, there is a very good chance these threats will indeed emerge, exacerbating the dangers posed by separatist movements while presenting a formidable danger to Pakistani stability in their own right.

ISLAMIST GRIEVANCES

If civil war comes to Pakistan, religious grievances are likely to be at their core. Since Pakistan was created as a Muslim state, successfully challenging the regime's adherence to Islamic principles strikes at the heart of Pakistani rule. There is little question that the power of Islamist groups is growing in Pakistan. If the various Islamist groups are able to resolve their differences and act together, they may amass enough power to topple governments they view as not sufficiently Islamic. Pakistani regimes have traditionally opted not to confront the Islamists, but cooperate with them. President Musharraf in particular has used Islamist parties to advance his agenda in the belief that he can control them. Thus far, Musharraf has been successful, but it is not difficult to see how riding this tiger can backfire, with widespread violence as the outcome.

The central grievance of the Islamists is their belief that Pakistan has betrayed its birthright by choosing a secular path. Their resentments increased during the first 30 years of Pakistan's existence, when Islam was indeed given short shrift by a succession of military and civilian regimes. Pakistani governments were not able (or in some cases willing) to eliminate religious influence but did manage to keep Islam on the margins. This changed with the 1977 coup that placed General Mohammad Zia-ul-Haq in power. Zia was the first (and so far only) Pakistani leader committed to transforming Pakistan into an Islamic state. Zia believed that only Islam kept Pakistan together and by weakening Islam, you risked destroying the state.[47] He instituted Islamic law (the Sharia), hired tens of thousands of Islamic activists to man the government and the courts, overhauled the educational system to reflect Islamic teachings and, most ominously, increased the influence of Islam in the military. Although Zia died in a suspicious plane crash in 1988, his policies of Islamic rule lived on. It is this Islamic legacy that is at the center of much of what bedevils Pakistan today. Once having tasted power, the Islamists have been reluctant to relinquish it. The perennial question of the role of Islam in Pakistan has resurfaced with a vengeance, the resolution of which cannot fail to alienate large numbers of the population.

Who are the Islamists? They are a broad range of groups who believe that political affairs, particularly those of Pakistan, need to be guided by the precepts of Islam. Most are Sunni, reflecting the 75% to 20% Sunni-Shia split in Pakistan itself. Some are followers of mainstream political parties, such as the Jama'at-i-Islami, who pursue relatively moderate policies and maintain close links with figures with the government and military. Others are extreme fringe groups who openly seek the violent overthrow of the Pakistani government and keep close ties with terrorist organizations such as Al Qaeda. Some of these groups openly call for jihad against the United States and India, while others focus on Pakistan, seeking to return it to the pristine form of Islam that existed at the time of the Prophet Muhammad. All the Islamic groups oppose India's domination of Kashmir and Israel's policies toward the Palestinians. All are anti-American, reflecting displeasure with Washington's support of Pakistani governments as well as America's backing of Israel and India. They oppose America's war on terror and are enraged by Pakistan's cooperation with the United States in this effort.[48]

To be sure, the overwhelming majority of Pakistanis are not radical Muslims. They may be religiously devout, but have little patience for transforming Pakistani society or radicalism in general. Up until 2002, the religious parties had never won an election, usually receiving less than 5% of the national vote. When Islamist groups have done well, it has been because the government and the military have supported their efforts, mostly to counterbalance the influence of secular parties whose popularity makes them an even greater threat against the regime. The military keeps a watchful eye on Islamic activity and has expressed confidence that it can control the more violent elements if need be. While Pakistani military governments may raise the threat of Islamic violence to secure American support, the ability of the Muslim groups to take over the government or plunge the country into civil war is seen by some as not very great.[49]

Nevertheless, there is growing cause for concern as Islamic extremists gain in strength. In October 2002, a coalition of six religious parties, the Muttahida Majlis-e-Amal (MMA) emerged as a major political force in Pakistan. It won 11% of the national vote, thereby securing over 50 (out of 342) seats in the National Assembly and making it the leading opposition party. The MMA did especially well in those parts of Pakistan where separatist tendencies are greatest, gaining control of the government in the NWFP and becoming part of the ruling coalition in Baluchistan. Previously, no province had been ruled by an Islamist party and no religious party had ever gotten as many as ten seats in the National Assembly.[50] With this victory, the Islamist and separatist movements became one and the same, posing a major challenge to governmental rule.

Despite the threat posed by these groups, a major reason for the success of the MMA was the support of President Musharraf. Unlike Zia, Musharraf, a former army chief of staff who seized power in a 1999 military coup, never was a pious Muslim. Because he feared the appeal of secular political parties led by former prime ministers Benazir Bhutto and Nawaz Sharif, he crippled their electoral efforts, leaving the MMA as the only real alternative to his rule.[51] The other reason for the success of the MMA was its hatred of the United States. The parties making up the MMA coalition disagree on much, but they all deeply resent the United States and oppose any Pakistani efforts to cooperate with Washington. This common anger at America proved to be enough to hold together an otherwise discordant coalition.[52]

The power of the religious parties became apparent when Musharraf sought to renege on earlier promises by extending his rule at least until 2007. The secular parties resisted this power grab, but the Islamists stood by the Pakistani leader, enabling him to get the extension he sought. Musharraf's alliance with the Islamic parties, however, came at a steep price. The MMA made no secret of its agenda to Islamize Pakistan, with some members of the coalition even arguing for Taliban-like policies to do so. In order to achieve these ends, it reinforced ties with radical jihadi groups, many of whom already supported the aims of the MMA. Musharraf had won his victory, but only at the cost of moving the Islamic parties, once at the fringe of Pakistani politics, to its very center.[53] Although the religious parties suffered a major setback in the 2008 elections, their organizational strength and continuing appeal to the disaffected suggest that they will be a major force in Pakistani politics for decades to come.

Along with their support for Islamic parties, Pakistani governments have also backed Islamic terrorist groups against India. Especially since the late 1980s, Pakistan has supported the efforts of extremists in Kashmir to evict the Indian presence from the disputed province. Even if it fails to bring Kashmir under its control, by supporting terrorist attacks against Indian forces Pakistan is able to tie down some 400,000 Indian troops in Kashmir, at little cost to itself.[54] Pakistani governments also gain public approval through their Kashmiri operations, especially from the Islamists. By supporting radical Islamic groups, however, especially those engaged in terror, Pakistani regimes buy short-term peace at the price of long-term instability. Large numbers of Pakistani terrorists in Kashmir have returned home, where they make up a dozen or so private Islamic armies.[55] In December 2001, a pro-Pakistani terrorist group attacked the Indian parliament, almost plunging the countries into war (and causing Pakistan to place its nuclear forces on alert). This was followed in May by another terrorist attack on the family quarters of an Indian army base, killing 34 people, mostly women and children, and again nearly causing an Indo-Pakistani war. The Pakistani regime believes it can control the terror groups, just as it does the Islamic parties. Nevertheless, if the government is weakened or if opposition to its policies mount, these same Islamic armies could well turn on the regime or push it into war in order to punish it for not doing enough to "liberate" Kashmir.

Pakistan's support of Islamic extremist groups has also gotten it into trouble with its most important ally, the United States. Following the 9/11 attacks, Washington presented Musharraf with an ultimatum: you are either with the United States in its campaign against Islamic jihadists or you are against it. With little choice, Musharraf opted to support the United States, albeit with some reluctance and foot-dragging.[56] As a result, Pakistan has received over $10 billion in American assistance (mostly to the military) since 9/11.[57] Musharraf's decision, however, was exceedingly perilous. On the one hand, the United States expressed its disappointment and anger at Musharraf for what Washington believed was a lack of effort in suppressing Islamic terrorists. As American officials pointed out, Musharraf would make a big show of arresting jihadi leaders and disbanding their groups, but then quietly let them out of jail and turn a blind eye when the groups resurfaced with different names.[58] Musharraf has also been accused of not attacking Al Qaeda sanctuaries along the Afghan-Pakistani border with sufficient vigor and allowing Al Qaeda to reestablish itself in strength, particularly in the tribal areas.[59] So long as Musharraf does not appear to be doing what the United States asks of him in the war on terror, he (or a successor) runs a significant risk of losing vital American support.

Musharraf, however, also encountered problems when he took actions to suppress Islamic militants, actions which were very unpopular with the Pakistani people. In the spring of 2004, the Pew Research Center found that only 16% of Pakistanis supported the campaign against terrorism, only 7% had a favorable view of Bush, while 65% had a favorable view of Osama bin Laden.[60] Not surprisingly, efforts Musharraf has undertaken against terror groups have produced significant backlashes at home. In 2006, attacks on alleged Al Qaeda terrorists by unmanned American Predator aircraft in Pakistan killed many innocent civilians, further increasing the hatred of the United States and Musharraf. Suicide bombings and attacks on foreign interests in the cities of Pakistan have become increasingly common, a sign that Al Qaeda's influence is growing. Most ominous have been at least four assassination attempts against Musharraf, two of which in December 2003 came very close to killing the Pakistani leader. There is little question that Islamic groups, perhaps with ties to Al Qaeda, backed these efforts.

The Pakistani government has been placed in an untenable situation. Cooperating with the United States increases armed resistance to the regime and the prospect of assassination, but refusing to cooperate with America means losing the support of a key patron. Whatever the fate of Musharraf may be, future Pakistani leaders will face a similar choice, with the prospect of civil war looming regardless of which direction is taken.

This threat of Islamic extremism, and the dilemmas it creates for the Pakistani government, will almost certainly grow in the coming years because of the rise of the madrassas. The madrassas are Islamic religious schools that have come to dominate the educational landscape of Pakistan. The number of madrassas has exploded in Pakistan, with only 137 at the time of partition and over 10,000 in 2005.[61] The growth of the madrassas reflects the failure of the Pakistani state to educate its young. Public education is deplorable or absent throughout much of Pakistan and private schooling is beyond the reach of all but a tiny fraction of Pakistanis. Madrassas not only offer free education, they also provide room, board, and clothing to their needy students. With many madrassas financed by Saudi Arabia and Iran, they also provide a radical anti-American, anti–Pakistani government curriculum.

Among the alumni of the madrassas are the Taliban, who applied what they learned in neighboring Afghanistan. With little state supervision of the madrassas and growing enrollments, the number of students sympathetic to Taliban (and Al Qaeda) ideas are skyrocketing in Pakistan. Their growth has corresponded with a rise in religious violence throughout the country. The extreme Sunni teachings of the madrassas have already contributed to the deaths of some 4,000 Pakistanis over the past two decades, killed in Sunni-Shiite clashes. Of particular concern is the spread of madrassas to the capital of Islamabad, where enrollments in schools emphasizing the most radical forms of Islam have exploded. The bloody siege of the Lal Masjid ("Red Mosque") mosque complex in July 2007 in which Islamic extremists seeking to impose Sharia had to be violently suppressed in the heart of Islamabad (leaving over 100 dead) dramatically illustrated the threat posed by groups schooled in madrassas to governmental rule. This violence is likely to worsen as a generation of poor Pakistanis with few job prospects are taught that their lives will improve only by following the path of radical Islam.[62] How to deal with angry extremist groups rising out of the teachings of the madrassas, whether to confront or appease them, could well determine the survival of Pakistani governments for decades to come.

RIGHT TO FIGHT

As attested to by its many coups, insurgencies, and assassination attempts, Pakistan is filled with groups who believe they have the right to engage in violence against the government. Much of this belief in the illegitimacy of the regime stems from Pakistan's confusion over its identity. From its very beginnings, it was unclear just what Pakistan was meant to be. For some, including its founder, Mohammad Ali Jinnah, Pakistan was to be a refuge for Muslims who wanted to practice their religion free from the Hindu persecution they found in India. As Israel is for the Jews, Pakistan would be for Muslims, that is, an Islamic homeland where Muslims of different sects and orthodoxy would live together in mutual tolerance and safety. For others, Pakistan was not so much a country where Muslims lived, but an Islamic state. The government derived its authority from adherence to Islamic principles, from the Islamic code of Sharia and adherence to the Koran. So, is Pakistan to be a state for Muslims or a Muslim state? And if it is to be a Muslim state, what branch of Islam would rule? The failure to answer these questions, or even address them adequately, is at the root of Pakistan's problems with legitimacy.[63]

Pakistan's inability to sustain democratic rule also cripples its efforts at achieving legitimacy. Although Pakistani officials like to describe their country as a democracy, the reality is much different. Most of Pakistan's history has been marked not by democracy, but military leadership that pays only lip service to democratic principles. Under President Musharraf two democratically elected prime ministers were forced into exile because they opposed the Pakistani leader and the chief justice of the supreme court was removed from office for investigating the disappearances of governmental critics. Attorneys and other professionals engaged in widespread protests in 2007 over Musharraf's actions, illustrating that problems with legitimacy come not only from religious extremists, but also from secular democrats. These protests and Musharraf's belief that the supreme court was about to declare his reelection (in 2007) illegal, led the Pakistani leader to declare emergency rule in November 2007, thus ending what little sense of democracy remained in the country. The assassination of opposition leader Benazir Bhutto in December 2007 and the crushing defeat of Musharraf's party in the February 2008 elections further weakened the Pakistani leader's tenuous hold on legitimacy. Musharraf (or his successors) will attempt to remain in power by relying on the army and the United States to prop up their rule, but such a course is unlikely to prove successful. Without widespread agreement that the government in power has a right to rule, it is difficult to see how any Pakistani government can maintain itself in office over the long haul.

A government that cannot derive legitimacy because of the ideals it stands for needs to try to attain legitimacy by convincing its citizens that they are fortunate because of what their government does for them. If the government can provide for its people's welfare, make their lives better, give them hope for the future, then a lack of legitimacy is not such a crippling factor and, in time, people will come to believe in the right of the government to act in their interests. As seen, however, in the miserable lives so many Pakistanis live, the government is spectacularly unable to deliver the goods and services that its people need. With the government lacking any compelling rationale for rule and unable to provide for the good life, it is not surprising that the only point of agreement among Pakistan's disparate groups is the view that all who oppose it are justified in seeking its overthrow, by violence if necessary. If civil strife is to be avoided in Pakistan it will not be because forces in Pakistani society believe they lack the right to act against the government.

PROSPECTS FOR SUCCESS

The major question regarding Pakistan is not whether civil war will break out, but why has it not done so already. As it is one of the most mismanaged countries in the world, where ethnic, regional, and religious hatreds abound, the answer cannot be that the Pakistani people are happy with their lot in life. Few believe in the government's right to rule over them, as evidenced by widespread and mounting attacks on the regime. The reason, then, for relative peace in Pakistan is that those who would seek to topple the government do not attempt to do so because they do not believe they will succeed. The basis for this lack of confidence, in turn, lies in the belief of regime opponents that the Pakistani military has the will and capability to suppress any challenge they might mount.

There are good reasons to assume that the Pakistani armed forces are up to the challenge of keeping Pakistan peaceful and whole. The Pakistani military is the strongest and most respected institution in Pakistan. The Pakistani armed forces see themselves as the principal defender of the state. While this mission has caused it to launch periodic coups against civilian governments it judged not up to the job, it has also imbued the military with a sense of responsibility to protect Pakistan against all enemies, domestic and foreign. Through the wars with India and many crises that placed Pakistan on the brink of war, through countless campaigns against separatist movements, and through an unpopular war on extremist Islamic groups, the Pakistani military has hung together. It is indeed a formidable fighting force which, if it can maintain its historic unity, is powerful enough to defeat any domestic challenger.

There is reason to believe, however, that the cohesiveness of the military is being undermined, calling into question its motivation and capacity to deal with future threats. Foremost among the factors that could weaken the military is the danger of Islamic influences dividing the military along religious lines. For the first decades of its existence, under the influence of British and then American advisers, religion was largely kept out of military affairs. General Zia's seizure of power changed all that. Zia allowed religious groups to openly operate in the military, encouraged officers to adopt Islamic principles to guide military strategy, and advanced the careers of devout Muslims. Many of the officers who began their tenure under Zia have begun to assume positions of authority in the military. The military's support of Islamic groups in Afghanistan and Kashmir has also contributed to the rise of Islamic influence. During the 1980s, the Pakistani military, and especially its intelligence bureau, the Inter-Services Intelligence Directorate (ISI) essentially ran the Afghan resistance and created the Taliban. The close ties the Pakistani military maintains with the Taliban and (some would say) Al Qaeda stem from this time. In the 1990s, the backing of Kashmiri terror groups by the Pakistani military and ISI in part led to the ill-fated 1999 Kargil campaign that brought about armed clashes with India. The Pakistani military not only influences radical Islamic groups, but is influenced by them. These groups may support the agenda of the Pakistani military, but at some point they might turn on their patrons and bring many of their supporters in the armed forces with them.[64]

The military is becoming more Islamic because it more closely reflects Pakistani society. Increasing numbers of officers come from the countryside, where radical Islam is propagated in the madrassas.[65] Larger numbers of Pakistanis from the lower classes have made the armed forces their career, while the wealthy choose other paths. These poorer Pakistanis are more likely to be religious Muslims and to have narrow, unsophisticated outlooks. When Musharraf was asked what bothered him most about the armed forces, he replied that 75% of his officers have never been out of Pakistan, making them more open to Islamic incitement.[66] The officer corps that has emerged is much more Islamic and more supportive of radical Islamic groups than it was in the past and where some military officers are nothing but radical Islamists in uniform.[67] Evidence of pernicious Islamic influence on the Pakistani military is not hard to find. In 1995, an Islamist Pakistani general developed a plan to kill the leadership of the armed forces during a corps commander meeting. He planned to then impose Sharia on Pakistan and launch a jihad against India. The plot failed, but it is telling that someone of these beliefs could reach the rank of general in the Pakistani army and come so close to decapitating its leadership.[68] More recently, senior Pakistani officers continued to support the Taliban's anti-Afghan rebellion from bases in Pakistan despite direct orders from Musharraf for them to desist.

The efforts of A. Q. Khan to spread nuclear technology throughout the world, especially to Islamic states such as Iran and Libya is also a cause for concern.[69] Given that the military controls Pakistan's nuclear weapons and that many of Khan's deliveries were made with military aircraft, the Pakistani military, or at least some elements in it, had to back his efforts. Whether this was done with or without government approval is still unclear. If the Pakistani government supported Khan's efforts, then it was complicit in spreading nuclear weapons to some of the world's most notorious leaders. If Musharraf's denial of responsibility is true, then it demonstrates a frightening lack of control over Pakistan's nuclear activities. In either case, the A. Q. Khan affair raises disturbing questions about the extent to which military factions may be pursuing their own agendas.

The growing anti-Americanism of the Pakistani military along with U.S. efforts to enlist Pakistan in the war on terror can also split the armed forces. As with Pakistani society, the Pakistani military has become more hostile to the United States since 9/11. In part, this reflects anger at American policies felt throughout the Muslim world, such as American support for Israel and its occupation of Iraq. Closer to home, many Pakistani officers resent the American intervention in Afghanistan that toppled a friendly Taliban government and replaced it with a regime less favorable to Pakistan's interests. Many also see an American tilt toward India, with some even believing that there is a Zionist-American alliance against Pakistan.[70] Protests by Pakistanis angry at the erosion of democracy that led to Musharraf's declaration of emergency rule in 2007 has unsettled the Pakistani military, worried about keeping together a country that appeared to be spinning out of control.

Most upsetting to the military is Musharraf's agreement to actively support the United States against "terrorist" groups, many of whom are Pakistani. Many in the Pakistani military opposed American efforts in northwest Pakistan to hunt bin Laden, seeing this as an affront to Pakistani sovereignty. Nor was the military happy about the hundreds of casualties it incurred in operations to remove foreign militants (many of whom the Pakistani military supports) from areas near the Pakistani border.[71] That efforts such as these have forced the military to confront thousands of demonstrators in the streets of Pakistani cities makes them even less enthusiastic for doing America's bidding. Musharraf may have had little choice in supporting American efforts in the war on terror, but in doing so he (or a successor) runs the risk of weakening the Pakistani military's support for the government, which could be critical if the regime is challenged.

The key question facing potential insurgents is how the Pakistani military would react if confronted with a violent rebellion. For most of its existence, the answer was clear: the armed forces would suppress any effort to topple the government (unless of course, the military was behind the attempt itself). Now, however, it is much less certain what the Pakistani military would do if confronted with an Islamic revolt, urban riots, or a separatist movement that spread throughout the country. Insurgents do not require the active support of the army to win. They simply need the military, or large portions of it, to step aside and let events take their course. If the military leadership is divided, perhaps because of sympathy with Islamic radicals or prodemocracy protestors, or anger at the government's support of the United States, or if the rank and file will not obey orders to fire on fellow Pakistani Muslims, then the seeds of civil war are planted. It is a divided, ambivalent military that poses a far more likely threat of civil war than one that is united behind rebel forces, and that is exactly the kind of military that is emerging in Pakistan today.[72]

HOW A CIVIL WAR MIGHT BEGIN

The fundamental causes for civil conflict are all uncomfortably in place in Pakistan. The majority of the people resent the circumstances in which they live, whether it be the overall decay of the nation, the desire of ethnic minorities for more autonomy, the demands of many for true democracy, or the growing Islamist movement that does not want to follow the dictates of what they see as secular regimes. Pakistan's governments lack legitimacy, so few will be inhibited from contesting their rule out of concern that they have no right to do so. Standing in the way of civil war is the one institution that works in Pakistan, the military. But increased Islamic influence, ties with radical groups, lack of confidence in an increasingly unpopular political leadership, resentment against the American war on terror, and the seeping decay from a failing state all call into question its willingness and ability to contain the rising tide of insurgent forces.

Pakistan, then, is ripe for civil war. What is missing is some catalyst to ignite its long-festering problems to produce civil conflict. Pakistan has been fortunate that such a catalyst has not yet emerged. Pakistan's luck, however, is not likely to hold out forever. There are too many events that may plausibly occur that could push Pakistan into civil war to have confidence that its period of relative domestic peace can last for long.

Civil war is most likely if the Pakistani military disintegrates. This could come about in the wake of another defeat against India. If the Pakistani military performed poorly, as in 1971, its cohesiveness may shatter, with the army splitting along ethnic, religious, or ideological lines. The monumental decision of whether to use nuclear weapons could also divide the military. If faced with defeat in a war with India, passions would be high both for those who wished to use nuclear weapons to stave off surrender and those who would argue that any use of nuclear weapons would be suicidal. Leaders of the different factions might call upon troops under their command to support their view. An attempted coup, especially if launched by Islamists, might also provoke civil war. Pakistan has already had many coup attempts, several of which have been successful. If an Islamist coup toppled the regime, those seeking to preserve the integrity of the military are likely to launch a countercoup, which could easily morph into civil war. If the coup failed, Islamists in the armed forces may try to topple the government through an armed insurrection, provoking a response by the regime's defenders that could also escalate to all-out civil war. Rising violence in the streets could tear apart the military. If massive demonstrations appear in Pakistan, elements of the military may be reluctant to suppress them. Armies traditionally do not like being used as police forces. If some in the military sympathize with the demands of the protestors, as might be the case if demonstrators are objecting to Pakistani government support of the American campaign against militant groups, they might refuse to fire on the crowds. The unwillingness of the armed forces to confront protestors led to Ayatollah Khomeini's ascension to power in Iran in 1979, raising the possibility that something similar could happen in Pakistan.[73]

Civil war is also likely through separatist violence. A group, most probably the Pashtuns or Baluchis, might seek to take advantage of a weakening of the military to launch a determined effort to secede. If they had the backing of an outside state, such as an Afghan-Pashtun alliance, or an Iranian-Baluchi connection, civil war is likely to erupt. Even a revolt that began without the help of an outside power might nevertheless provoke external intervention, similar to what occurred with Indian support for East Pakistan. If India joins a budding rebellion, what began as a local insurgency could soon escalate into a nationwide civil — and international — war.

Finally, civil war is likely if Pakistan collapses. It is easy to imagine a situation where population growth, economic failure, incompetent leadership, and the lessening of outside assistance combine to produce a situation in which the state ceases to function. Already in many areas of Pakistan, particularly in the tribal areas along the Afghan border, the government is nowhere to be seen, with Al Qaeda and the Taliban rapidly filling the vacuum. Given that Pakistan, with the exception of the military, has no strong institutions, centrifugal forces are likely to continue to be stronger than the power of the central government to keep the country together. The many no-go areas in Pakistan will get bigger, perhaps eventually leading to the collapse of the central government itself. Domestic anarchy in Pakistan could produce a situation similar to that in the Balkans in the 1990s, where in the absence of a strong central government, people relied on their religious and ethnic brethren to ensure their security. In such a Hobbesian world, groups arm themselves and launch preemptive attacks on other groups, all to ensure their safety in a hostile and violent climate.[74] A war of all against all could easily emerge in Pakistan, with its regional, ethnic, and religious divisions. Some argue that because it possesses nuclear weapons, the world's major powers will not allow Pakistan to fail. It is just as possible, however, that if Pakistan is torn by domestic conflict, no one would wish to intervene for fear of becoming the target of a nuclear attack, allowing the horrific events to take their course.

More than the Soviet Union ever did during the Cold War, Pakistan presents a threat to American security. The threat originates in Pakistan's possession of nuclear weapons and the material to build additional nuclear bombs. It is compounded by a deployment posture that makes the weapons vulnerable to seizure or unauthorized use, especially in the case of civil war. What makes this so worrisome is that civil war is such a likely possibility for the dysfunctional Pakistani state. Should civil war happen, there is an alarming risk that nuclear war would ensue with India, with horrific regional and international consequences. Nuclear weapons may also fall into the hands of terrorist groups who seek to use them against American cities. If such a group gained control of a nuclear weapon, there is little the United States could do to deter or defend against a catastrophic nuclear attack. Although a nominal ally, Pakistan has become one of the greatest threats to American security in the post–Cold War world.

CHAPTER FOUR

Mexico

A Flood of Refugees

At first glance, it seems puzzling to talk of instability in Mexico. After all, in the first years of the twenty-first century, Mexico appeared to be doing very well. An increasingly privatized economy grew at a healthy rate of more than 4% per year in 2005 and 2006. The 1994 North American Free Trade Agreement (NAFTA) generated huge increases in bilateral trade, spreading prosperity throughout Mexico. Regional insurgencies, such as the 1994 Chiapas uprising, have been largely absent. Most important, Mexican democracy came of age in 2000, when the 70-year reign of the authoritarian Institutional Revolutionary Party (PRI) ended with the election of Vicente Fox, head of the rival National Action Party (PAN) in a free and fair contest. It would be easy to conclude that Mexico had moved into the ranks of the developed world, where threats of economic collapse and violent instability have all but vanished.

Such a conclusion would be wrong. Mexico faces deep-seated problems that have penetrated into the fabric of its politics and society and may yet plunge the country into prolonged and widespread disorder. Far from being robust, Mexico's economy depends on shaky pillars, which could crumble suddenly, driving the country into recession or worse. The 2006 elections for Fox's successor demonstrated the fragility of Mexican democracy, as the razor-thin victory of the conservative PAN over the leftist PRD (Democratic Revolutionary Party) produced violent protest in the capital, a crisis of legitimacy, and an exacerbation of the north-south divide that threatens to tear Mexico apart. No matter who rules Mexico, the structure of the government ensures continued paralysis, as three lame-duck parties square off against each other and a lame-duck president. The cancer of drug trafficking and rampant crime continue to eat away at the rule of law, making a mockery out of any hope for justice and accountability. More than a dozen armed groups, quiet but far from dead, wait for a national emergency to set their violent agenda in motion. Unlike Pakistan and Saudi Arabia, Mexico does not face imminent collapse. Nevertheless, the trends are worrisome and could lead to a prolonged period of instability that flies in the face of recent optimism.

All this matters to the United States because Mexico matters to the United States. A wide range of American vital interests depend on Mexico, most of which stem from the 2,000-mile border shared by the two countries. America's national security and economic health are inexorably linked to what goes on in Mexico. Concerns for Americans living and traveling abroad, the demands of the growing Hispanic bloc in the United States, and fears of spreading disorder and environmental degradation all have roots in what happens in Mexico. If Mexico's seeming move to stability is illusory, it behooves Washington to pay close attention.

The wide range of vital American interests in Mexico makes it difficult to think of *any* country whose fate is more important to the United States. Why conditions in Mexico have created intense grievances, the belief in the right to engage in violence, and the sense that violence will succeed are then examined. As will be seen, the difficulties Mexico faces are overwhelming and chronic, with the prospect of major disorder a realistic possibility. Whether Mexico is up to the challenges it confronts is unclear, but whatever Mexico may do, Washington ignores the gathering dangers south of its border at its peril.

AMERICA'S VITAL INTERESTS IN MEXICO

There is little question that the United States maintains a wide range of vital interests in Mexico. Most of these interests stem from the United States being the only First World country to share a long border with a Third World state, a situation that is the source of much that is beneficial to both countries but which also threatens key American concerns. Foremost among these concerns is safeguarding American security, especially in the wake of the 9/11 attacks. In 2005 alone, the U.S. Border Patrol arrested over 1 million illegal aliens attempting to enter the United States from Mexico.[1] The great majority of this traffic is Mexicans seeking better-paying jobs, but the same paths used by illegal immigrants can be exploited by terrorists with weapons of mass destruction. In 2005, some 650 people from "special interest countries," that is, states terrorists are known to inhabit, attempted illegally to cross the Mexican border into the United States. Included in this number were members of Hezbollah, an Islamic organization declared to be terrorist by the U.S. government. Since it is estimated that only between 10% and 30% of illegal aliens are arrested, the number of those crossing into the United States who pose at least a potential risk of terrorism could well be in the thousands.[2]

The shared border also accounts for America's problems with illegal immigration. Some 6 million Mexicans already live in the United States illegally, making up more than half the total of all illegal immigrants.[3] Mexicans are 325 times as numerous as the next largest group of illegal immigrants (from El Salvador). As Samuel Huntington has remarked, illegal immigration is largely a Mexican phenomenon. Given the tremendous disparity in wealth between the two countries (Mexicans who make $5 a day at home can make $50 a day in the United States), geographical contiguity, regional concentrations of Mexicans in the southwest, and the inability of the Mexican economy to produce enough jobs for its citizens, it is to be expected that Mexicans will continue to try to enter the United States legally or not.[4] Just how big a problem this is, is the subject of fierce debate. Some argue Mexicans take jobs that no one else wants and pay a substantial amount in taxes, while others assert that Mexicans take jobs away from American citizens while overwhelming social services. Although both views have merit, this dispute misses a bigger issue. A vital interest for any country is the control of its borders. Whether because of security concerns or economic worries, a government has to be able to determine who can and cannot enter its territory, something the United States has thus far been unable to do.

Stopping disorder in Mexico from spilling over the U.S. border is another critical American concern. The United States has intervened militarily in Mexico on four occasions, each time citing the need to protect itself and its citizens from violent instability. The most serious episode occurred in 1916 following a raid on the New Mexico town of Columbus by the rebel forces of Pancho Villa. In response to the raid and growing fear of an American-Mexican war, the United States sent some 10,000 troops into Mexico to capture Villa and deployed nearly the entire American army along the Mexican border.[5]

Another Pancho Villa may not be on the horizon, but fears of Mexican disorder are very much alive in the twenty-first century. Over 9 million people live along the U.S.-Mexico border and for those on the American side, there are rising fears that the ill effects from crime-ridden Mexican cities will spread to them. These fears are well founded. Skyrocketing numbers of murders and kidnappings in the border region led the American ambassador to Mexico to issue a record number of diplomatic protests to the Mexican government and threat advisories to Americans contemplating travel to Mexico in 2005.[6] In the Mexican city of

Nuevo Laredo, just across the Rio Grande from the Texas city of Laredo, the mayor was forced to suspend the entire police force of over 700 officers in 2005 because they were suspected of serving as hit men and lookouts for the criminals they were supposed to arrest. Anarchy reigned in the city, where the police chief and a city councilman were assassinated, at least 43 were kidnapped in 12 months, and the American ambassador had to close the consulate for a week to evaluate the security situation. The Mexican government sent in federal agents to restore order, but the potential for renewed outbreaks of violence remained. At around the same time, the governors of New Mexico and Arizona declared their border areas with Mexico a disaster area that were (in the words of then-governor Bill Richardson of New Mexico) "devastated by the ravages and terror of human smuggling, drug smuggling, kidnapping, murder, destruction of property and death of livestock."[7] Intriguingly, one of the areas hardest hit by the disorder was the same town of Columbus, pillaged by Pancho Villa some 90 years earlier. Despite efforts by Mexican presidents Fox and Calderon, the level of violence on the border, much of it drug related, has been escalating year by year, threatening the security of Americans as well as Mexicans.

Every government, including the American government, has a vital interest in protecting its citizens who live and travel abroad. Mexico is of special concern because more Americans live there than in any other foreign country. The lure of inexpensive housing, favorable climate, and a low cost of living is especially attractive to retirees who have established numerous American "colonies" in Mexico. Just how many Americans live in Mexico is the subject of some dispute, as estimates range from 124,000 to 1 million, with perhaps the State Department figure of around 500,000 being most widely accepted.[8] Even more numerous are American visitors to Mexico, who average about 10 million a year. If Mexico falls victim to violent instability, particularly if the instability occurs in cities and in border areas, there is a good chance that American lives and property will be at risk. The United States may be forced to act on its own to protect its citizens if the Mexican government proves unwilling or unable to do so.

American interests are engaged in Mexico because there are so many Mexican Americans who care about what happens in their ancestral homeland. About 25 million people of Mexican descent live in the United States, with Mexican immigrants constituting 32% of its total foreign population (the next largest group is Chinese Americans, with less than 5%).[9] Mexicans make up the largest percentage of Hispanic Americans, who have become America's biggest minority, and are especially prevalent in the southwest. The number of Mexican migrants in the United States has shot up in the past 35 years, growing from 760,000 in 1970 to over 11 million in 2004. In the past decade, the Mexican population living in the United States has been growing by about 500,000 per year, with 80–85% of that increase consisting of illegal immigrants.[10] Mexican Americans keep especially close ties to Mexico because of the encouragement of the Mexican government (which welcomes remittances from Mexicans living in the United States), the ease of traveling back and forth to Mexico, and the large numbers of Mexican Americans for whom Spanish is still their first language. Six out of twelve of the major cities on the American side of the border had populations that were over 90% Hispanic in 2000.[11] Virtually all of these Mexican Americans have family and close friends across the border in Mexico. Mexico matters to the United States because the lives of so many Americans are inextricably tied up with what happens there.

Mexico is also important to the United States because illegal drugs have become such a pressing American problem. Nearly 35 million Americans used an illegal drug in 2004, and almost 4 million Americans are dependent on or abusers of illegal drugs. Arrests and incarceration of drug dealers have increased from fewer than 42,000 in 1980 to more than 480,000 in 2002.[12] The financial and human costs of the illegal drug trade are staggering. The American federal government spends over $11 billion each year for drug education, incarceration, and treatment, and billions more are spent by the states.[13] Illegal drug use kills 20,000 Americans each year, is a major contributor to crime, and costs the American economy at least $67 billion in lost productivity.[14] These figures do not include the personal toll of emotional turmoil and lives ruined. No wonder that President Reagan declared in 1986 that drug use had been transformed from a crime problem into an issue of national security.

No country plays a larger role in illegal drug trafficking than Mexico. Most of the illegal drugs that come into the United States come from Mexico. This includes over 90% of the cocaine, most of the marijuana (that is not grown in the United States), most of the methamphetamines, and much of the heroin.[15] Once in America, according to the U.S. government, "Mexican criminal groups exert more influence over drug trafficking in the United States than any other group."[16] Stopping the drug traffic from Mexico is virtually impossible. Every day, about a million people and 300,000 trucks and cars cross into the United States from Mexico. It only takes a minuscule percentage of those coming to smuggle drugs to feed America's problem. Despite major efforts to contain drug traffic, the price of most illegal drugs in the United States has dropped and the purity has risen over the past decade, lending support to the belief that America is losing the drug war.[17] Although America's drug problem is not caused by Mexico, because it is the source of so many drugs entering the United States, Mexico plays a central role in its severity. Getting the Mexicans to do more to stem the illegal flow of drugs has dominated U.S.-Mexican relations over the past decades and all signs indicate that it will continue to do so.

The American economy, in large part, is dependent on a prosperous and stable Mexico. Mexico is the third largest trading partner of the United States (after Canada and China). Trade has more than tripled after the establishment of NAFTA, growing from $81.5 billion in 1993 to $290.5 billion in 2005.[18] The United States exports over $120 billion of goods to Mexico each year, accounting for hundreds of thousands of American jobs. In northern Mexico, a healthy American economy has fueled the growth of maquiladoras, the for-export-only factories that bring jobs to Mexicans and low-cost products to Americans. Mexico is a leading exporter of apparel, automobiles, and sophisticated electronic equipment to the United States. Mexico is also one of its top three suppliers of oil (along with Canada and Saudi Arabia). Insofar as the health of the American economy is a vital interest, so too is maintaining the robust economic relationship between the two countries.[19]

Finally, Mexico matters to the United States because of the environment. Mexican environmental standards are far more lax than what exists in the United States. Because pollution does not stop at a country's borders, the United States pays the price for Mexican policies. Aquifers have become polluted, air is contaminated, and land is poisoned along the entire border. Making matters worse, the exploding economic relationship between Mexico and the United States has attracted large population growth, precisely at the time that the resources to sustain that growth are becoming tainted. Lack of clean water has become an alarming problem since there are no new sources of water to meet the needs of the border residents. Some 300,000 Americans living near the Mexican border do not have safe drinking water or adequate solid waste disposal facilities. The maquiladoras that have done so much to stimulate the Mexican economy lack the anti-pollution equipment required in America. The resulting air and water pollution seeps into the United States. The prolific use of pesticides and herbicides in Mexico to enhance agricultural production causes particular difficulties on the northern border. Sewage from Mexican rivers flows into the United States, affecting major urban areas such as San Diego, while industrial pollution is especially acute in southern Arizona. NAFTA was supposed to deal with many of these problems as one of the first major treaties to link trade and the environment, but it has not lived up to expectations.[20]

There is no question that if violent instability engulfs Mexico, American vital interests would be threatened. Widespread civil conflict is likely to produce a flood of illegal immigrants, dwarfing the already huge numbers, as masses of Mexicans flee escalating violence. Civil unrest could erode Mexican border controls, allowing for the transport of even greater amounts of drugs and the entry of terrorists into the United States. The disruption of trade would cost America hundreds of thousands of jobs and undermine America's overall economic prosperity. Violent turbulence on the Mexican side of the border would almost certainly spread to the United States, especially among the border towns with large Hispanic populations. A Mexican civil conflict with well-defined sides might drag in Mexican Americans in support of one faction or another, perhaps replicating the conflict in parts of the United States. While a Pancho Villa–style American intervention may be remote, the deployment of American troops on the Mexican border backed up by Reserve and National Guard forces to evacuate the hundreds of thousands of American tourists and residents living in Mexico threatened by violence is a distinct possibility. Civil conflict is likely to produce environmental degradation in its wake, further polluting American air, water, and land. By almost any measure, prolonged severe instability in Mexico would be a nightmare for the United States.

The type of instability that would threaten vital American interests would be one of prolonged disorder that shakes the foundations of the country. This might include causing extralegal regime change, or violence that takes place over several months (or years) throughout the country in a manner that calls into question the ability of the central government to contain the disorder. The likelihood of this kind of instability occurring will be determined by the extent to which Mexican groups have intense grievances against the government (and each other), their belief in the right to engage in violence against authorities to redress those grievances, and their view that violence will be successful in advancing their cause. What is so frightening for the United States — and Mexico — is that conditions in Mexico provide critical support for each of these factors, making the likelihood of widespread violent internal conflict impossible to dismiss.

GRIEVANCES

There are an overwhelming number of reasons for Mexicans to be angry with the government and their fellow citizens. They can be roughly divided into those grievances that currently exist (most of which are getting worse) and those grievances which are not yet manifest but have the potential to undermine Mexican society should they emerge. In the former category is anger over income inequality, the failed potential of NAFTA, crime, and the judicial system. In the latter category are the possibilities of economic collapse, violent attacks against the government by drug traffickers, and the resurgence of rural revolts such as the 1994 Chiapas uprising. As dire as any of these possibilities emerging is, the chance that several may erupt at once is what is most likely to produce the horror of widespread Mexican instability.

A major reason why many Mexicans are angry is that after decades of economic liberalization, income inequality has increased markedly in Mexico.[21] Mexico's Gini coefficient — a measure of inequality where 0 equals perfect equality and 1 equals perfect inequality — was 0.48 (in 2002), placing it among the very worst of the countries in Latin America.[22] It is estimated that more than half of the Mexican people live in poverty, defined as those whose incomes are not sufficient to provide adequate clothing, shoes, housing, and public transportation. These poor earn less than $3 a day in rural areas, and only $4.50 in urban centers.[23] All the while, Mexico during the 1990s earned the dubious distinction of producing its first homegrown billionaires. Across the country, the unequal distribution of wealth has created an unhealthy situation, with the top 1% of the population earning more than three times as much as the poorest 40%. This maldistribution is most pronounced between rural and city inhabitants, with rural poverty seven to ten times higher than urban poverty.[24] While poverty in itself will not cause violence and instability, when the poor live in the shadow of the very rich it is to be expected that anger and resentment will spew forth. All the more so because in Mexico there is a widespread belief that the wealthy did not earn their money but achieved their position through corrupt means.

NAFTA has not lived up to expectations for the Mexican people. After a decade's experience with NAFTA, Mexican wages (adjusted for inflation) have dropped, levels of poverty have risen, and economic inequality has grown. Many of the manufacturing jobs that Mexico had hoped would be created by NAFTA have failed to materialize as the United States has turned to other countries, such as China, where labor costs are lower, for its manufacturing needs. Part of the problem has been the inefficiency of the Mexican government, which has not devoted needed resources to job training, infrastructure, and education necessary to create a workforce able to compete in a globalized world. NAFTA itself is also to blame for Mexican shortcomings, as it has led to a drop in tariff revenues that ideally could have been allocated to improve Mexican competitiveness. Wherever the responsibility lies, NAFTA has been at best a mixed blessing for Mexico.[25]

Another major grievance in Mexico is crime. The first requirement of governments is to protect its citizens. Mexico is fortunate in not having any outside enemies, but the state has proven woefully inadequate in protecting its people from each other. Public opinion polls consistently rank crime as the number one concern of most Mexicans.[26] A particular worry is kidnapping, which has reached epidemic proportions. It is estimated that some 3,000 kidnappings occur in Mexico each year, as compared to around 350 in the United States, a country with three times Mexico's population.[27] A person is more likely to be kidnapped in Mexico than in just about any other country. The situation is most grave in the capital of Mexico City, where in 2004 hundreds of thousands of Mexicans marched through the capital to protest the epidemic of abductions.

Other crimes, such as homicide, are also on the rise. Approximately 350 Mexican women have been murdered in the border area alone from 1995 to 2005, where state police have done little to solve the crimes, aside from torturing and imprisoning innocent people.[28] Drug-related murders in Mexico have more than doubled from around 1,000 in 2001 to over 2,100 in 2006.[29] Robbery and rape have also seen dramatic increases. Exactly how far the numbers of crimes have risen is difficult to determine because it is estimated that only 20% of crimes are reported and of that number, the great majority are not solved.[30]

One reason why so few crimes are reported is that most Mexicans do not expect the police to do much about combating unlawful behavior. It is not so much that the police are unable to defeat the criminals, it is that in many situations the police *are* the criminals. In the mid-1990s, most of Mexico's 900 criminal rings were made up of former or current police officers and the situation has not improved since then.[31] An especially brutal crime wave in 2007 forced President Calderon to call out the army, since turning to the corrupt local police forces was not an option.[32] It is bad enough to have a government that cannot provide security for its people, especially in the capital. It is far worse to have a government whose police actively contribute to the sense of unlawfulness and insecurity that most Mexicans must endure. As crime continues to dominate people's lives in Mexico, it is only to be expected that the anger of the Mexican people against their government will continue to grow.

There is also widespread — and justifiable — anger in Mexico about the judicial system. Many Mexicans, perhaps most, do not believe the system is fair. Wealth and connections guarantee acquittals, while the poor are imprisoned whether they are guilty or not. Mexico's legal system has its origins in the Napoleonic tradition, in which prosecutors make the key decisions as to the accused's guilt or innocence, with judges serving mostly to support their choices. Faced with an aggressive prosecutor, a defendant can do little to exonerate himself. Nor are the grievances about the judicial system confined to Mexicans. A major reason why foreign investment in Mexico has been curtailed is because investors worry about

being hauled into court to face corrupt judges making arbitrary rulings. Senior ex-
ecutives have been routinely jailed for seemingly no reason, creating a sense of
unease throughout the financial community.[33] Some reforms have been made on
the local level, but because virtually any case can be appealed to the federal courts
(in a process called *amparo*), so long as the federal system remains unchanged
these reforms will carry little weight. Mexicans simply do not trust their judicial
system and have little hope that substantive change will occur in the future.

A COLLAPSE OF THE MEXICAN ECONOMY?

As bad as things are in Mexico, they can get a lot worse. Embedded in Mexican
politics and society are potential problems, "ticking time bombs," which if they
explode will wreak havoc across Mexico. Foremost among these potential disasters is the prospect of the collapse of the Mexican economy. To many, the Mexican economy is a success story, not something to fret about. Beginning in the early
1980s, Mexico has liberalized its economy, ending state control of most corpora-
tions. Mexican exports have increased over 300% from 1995 to 2005, especially important because 20% of Mexicans are employed in export-oriented jobs. Agricultural production, the mainstay of rural Mexico, rose over 50% between 1993 and
2001. After decades of reckless borrowing and spending, the Mexican administrations of Carlos Salinas and Vicente Fox have pursued prudent fiscal and monetary policies. The Central Bank, long an institution devoted to opaque dealings,
is operating much more transparently. The dramatic rise in oil prices beginning in
2005 has provided the government with a massive influx of new revenues. It would
appear that the economy provides a strong basis for optimism for the future.[34]

There is, however, another side to Mexico's success story. As detailed by Luis
Rubio and Jeffrey Davidow, Mexico's economic picture is darker than many ob-
servers have acknowledged. The economy has grown but not quickly enough to
employ those seeking work or deal with rising problems of poverty and social security. President Fox had promised economic growth of 7%, but the Mexican
economy only averaged 3%. Instead of 1 million new jobs, only about 100,000
were created each year. The effects of globalization have been especially severe
for the already poverty-stricken peasants and workers in the south.[35] Half the labor
force works in the informal sector, as power-hungry unions prevent meaningful
reform of labor laws. While American productivity has increased by more than a
third since 1990, Mexican productivity has actually declined. In large measure
this is due to low levels of education in Mexico. Only slightly more than 5 million
Mexicans have completed any postsecondary education.[36] In an increasingly

globalized world where the advanced nations' advantage lies in the quality of their workforce, Mexico is at a distinct disadvantage.

The Mexican social security system is also in deep trouble. Mexico has an unusually generous system of benefits. For those employed by the government, workers can retire with a pension providing them with 100% of their last year's salary. Especially with overtime, workers can inflate their last year's wages, leaving them with a very comfortable retirement. Finding money for those retirees will become more and more difficult. In 1983, 20 workers supported each retiree, but by 2020 it is estimated that there will be only 2 workers providing such support. A quarter of Mexicans are expected to be 65 or over by 2050; providing for this group will become prohibitively expensive. Mexico's taxation rate of 11% of GDP is lowest among the OECD (Organisation for Economic Co-operation and Development) countries (which average 27%), making raising money to pay for an aging population (or anything else) exceedingly problematic.[37]

Optimistic views of the Mexican economy have been made before, only to be crushed due to some unforeseen cataclysm. Economic crises have erupted with disturbing regularity in Mexico, including in 1954, 1976, 1982, 1987, and most tellingly in 1994.[38] If a lesson was needed as to how a Mexican economic crisis could come seemingly out of nowhere with catastrophic effects for America, one need look no further than the collapse of December 1994. Prior to the crisis, Mexico had been touted as having become a "world class economy" ripe for increased American investment. Instead, Mexico had an economy that was rotting from within. Despite the oversight of international foreign institutions, Mexican foreign reserves were criminally inadequate to meet its responsibilities. In a shocking move, Mexico devalued its currency, which quickly led to the near collapse of the economy. Over the next year, more than a million Mexicans were laid off, producing an unofficial unemployment rate of 13%, a 20% decline in wages for those who managed to keep their jobs, and an over $70 billion loss in the stock market value of Mexican corporations. Interest rates reached 100% per year while Mexico's GDP declined by a staggering 7%. Alarm quickly spread to the United States, where American investors lost over $30 billion in a matter of weeks and fears grew for the hundreds of thousands of workers dependent on the Mexican economy. American economists and government officials worried that a Mexican collapse would reverberate through the world economy. In response, President Clinton put together a $50 billion international bailout package, including $20 billion in American loan guarantees. The plan eventually got Mexico back on its feet, but the 1994 financial collapse remains a potent warning to those who are complacent about Mexico's economic future.[39]

AMERICAN TIES

As bad as the 1994 crisis was, much worse could happen to the Mexican economy in the future. Mexico's prosperity rests on three foundations: ties to the United States, oil exports, and drug trafficking. Each of these factors is critical to keeping the Mexican economy on a solid footing. Each, however, is subject to changes that could plunge Mexico into a depression far more severe than what began in the waning days of 1994. Most disturbing, there is little Mexico or anyone else can do to ensure that such disastrous changes do not occur.

The well-being of the Mexican economy depends on the United States. Sixty-nine percent of Mexico's bilateral trade is with the United States, including 90% of Mexico's exports. If the United States lessens the amount of Mexican goods it buys, the heart of the Mexican economy will be destroyed. The over $24 billion in annual remittances from Mexicans in the United States (including Mexican Americans) sent to Mexico also plays a central role in the health of the Mexican economy. Any sharp cut in these remittances would spell disaster for Mexico.[40] Mexican emigration to the United States — both legal and illegal — is a critical safety valve for unemployed Mexicans. The Mexican economy has never produced enough jobs to meet the demands of its growing population. The United States provides gainful employment to millions of Mexicans who cannot find work and who would otherwise be idle — and angry — at home.

It is dangerous for both Mexico and the United States to have the Mexican economy so dependent on the United States. If conditions in the United States change, this could have horrific consequences in Mexico, which, in turn, would harm the American economy as well. If the American economy experiences a downturn, the United States will buy fewer exports from Mexico, eventually harming both economies. Rising American interest rates can cause investors to leave Mexico for more attractive opportunities in the United States, a development that did much to precipitate the December 1994 crisis.[41] An American decision to adopt protectionist policies to safeguard the wages of U.S. workers would likely produce massive Mexican unemployment. Most serious would be a determined American effort to stop Mexicans from crossing the border into the United States, a process that had already begun in earnest as the American presidential campaign of 2008 got underway. Especially if the United States becomes the victim of another terrorist attack from perpetrators who sneaked in from Mexico, the pressure to tighten controls on the border would become overwhelming. Whatever the rationale, with Mexicans prevented from coming into the United States, remittances would fall and the number of Mexicans without jobs would skyrocket.

The relationship between the United States and Mexico, as with all countries, is subject to change. If the extensive ties between Mexico and the United States falter, either for economic or security reasons, both countries will suffer. Those areas where some progress has been made could be wiped out in an instant, leaving resentment and anger among those who were just beginning to enjoy the fruits of economic progress. Should the Mexican economy collapse because of events in the United States, the fact that it was not Mexico's fault will do little to allay the burning sense of grievance many Mexicans would have toward their government.

OIL

The second wobbly pillar holding up the Mexican economy is oil. Mexico is a major oil power, producing (in 2007) over 3 million barrels per day, of which around half are exported. The United States purchases almost all of the Mexican oil that is not consumed domestically. The health of the Mexican economy depends on these oil exports. Fully one-third of the federal government's budget comes from oil. More than half of Mexico's revenue increases are due to higher oil income, a proportion certain to rise along with the price of oil.[42]

The critical dependence of the Mexican economy on petroleum exports is frightening because there are signs that Mexico is running out of oil. Many analysts argue that Mexico will be able to produce appreciable amounts only until 2015, after which it will have to import its oil. Mexico's biggest source of oil, the Cantarell field in the Gulf of Mexico provides over 60% of Mexico's output, but it is being rapidly depleted. Beginning in 2006, production is declining by about 20% per year. Without Cantarell, Mexico is finished as an oil exporter. Increased domestic consumption of oil also hastens the day when Mexico will need to start importing oil. If in the next decade Mexico must begin buying oil, the most important source of funding for the Mexican economy will disappear. Mexico has done little to diversify itself from its dependence on oil, raising the prospects for a catastrophic fall if and when the oil supply vanishes.[43]

Some hold out hope that Mexico will discover vast untapped reserves in the Gulf of Mexico that will preserve its position as a major oil exporter, but this is far from certain. It is not clear that these reserves exist and even if they do, Mexico might not be able to exploit them. The problem lies with PEMEX, the government-owned company that has been given a monopoly over Mexican oil development. As with most government-owned enterprises in Mexico, PEMEX is notoriously inefficient. It produces only 24 barrels of oil per employee per day, which is about half the level of production of other oil companies in Latin America.[44] PEMEX is also chronically in debt. Since 60% of its revenues go to the government, it is frequently short of cash, crippling efforts to discover new sources of oil. Complicating matters further, the Mexican Congress establishes PEMEX's budget. This makes it difficult for the company to establish its own plans and set priorities for the exploitation of oil. Without technical expertise, financial resources, or coherent planning, PEMEX is ill suited to find, much less develop, any new sources of oil that may exist.[45]

If PEMEX cannot be counted upon to keep Mexico as an oil exporter, the obvious solution would be for Mexico to turn to foreign firms to do the job, but this may prove to be impossible. Mexico nationalized its oil industry in 1938, making it the only major Latin American country that does not allow outsiders to have meaningful participation in the oil industry. The notion that Mexican oil belongs to the Mexican people alone is one of the core principles of the Mexican Constitution. In order to bring about foreign investment in the oil sector, there would have to be a sea change in attitudes by the Mexican people and a constitutional amendment approved by at least two-thirds of the Mexican Congress, but neither development is probable. While in office, President Fox tried to modify the foreign prohibition, only to retreat rapidly in the face of virulent opposition.[46]

That opposition has only grown in the wake of the 2006 elections, in which the leftist PRD emerged as the second largest party in the legislature. The PRD fervently supports the continuation of the PEMEX monopoly and is adamantly opposed to any foreign participation in Mexican oil development. Its increased clout makes it highly unlikely that any government would be able to modify the constitution so as to change Mexican policy. In less than a decade's time, instead of oil keeping the Mexican economy afloat, the cost of buying oil may well sink any hopes of future Mexican prosperity.

Mexico's reliance on oil also causes problems because it breeds complacency, inhibiting Mexican efforts to undertake needed economic reforms, such as improving tax collections or regulating unions. Every once in a while, falling oil prices cause an economic panic, as happened in 1998, but the price of oil has always rebounded, allowing Mexico to continue doing business as usual. The crunch will come if oil prices do not rebound or, more likely, there is no more oil to sell. It is the height of folly for the Mexican economy to depend on oil reserves that may soon be gone, on a state-owned company that is unable to find or exploit new reserves, and on a price of a commodity that is subject to wild fluctuations.

DRUGS

The third pillar of the Mexican economy that calls into question Mexico's long-term economic health is illegal drugs. The Mexican economy is addicted to the funds it gets through drug trafficking, without which the economy might simply collapse. Estimates of just how much money Mexico earns from drug trafficking range enormously. On the high end, some suggest Mexican drug dealers earn $30–40 billion per year, with more modest estimates placing the revenue from drug traffic at between $5 and $10 billion each year.[47] Whatever the amount, these revenues are central to Mexico's economy. As an illustration, in 1994 the Mexican attorney general's office estimated Mexican drug profits to be $30 billion, which was four times Mexico's oil revenues, five times its international reserves, and over 7% of Mexico's GNP.[48] These profits — and their role in the Mexican economy — have only increased in the past decade, making drug trafficking one of the most, if not *the* most, important economic activity in Mexico.

The money earned from illegal drug sales does not simply sit in home vaults. Instead it is recycled and invested in legitimate business, such as tourism and banking. If the drug money is removed, these industries and the jobs that depend on them would be undermined, with dire effects for the Mexican economy. The economic importance of drug trafficking to overall prosperity has put Mexico in a precarious position. If the government gets serious about eradicating the drug trade that is central to the Mexican economy, it risks undermining the economic health of large numbers of Mexicans. If the government continues to engage in an elaborate charade in which it tolerates large-scale drug trade, it risks alienating its most important trading partner, the United States, which will not be always forgiving of halfhearted Mexican drug efforts. Mexico finds itself in an untenable situation where its economy depends on an illegal activity that cannot be forever sustained.

Despite its robust appearance, the Mexican economy is in deep trouble because its viability depends on conditions that are largely beyond its control and that can disappear virtually overnight. A downturn in the American economy, a shift in American trade and investment to other countries, or a serious effort to police the American-Mexican border could all be catastrophic for Mexico. Mexico may soon find itself without any oil to export, thus losing the money to build infrastructure, pay government workers, and finance pensions without any alternative source of funding to put in its place. If Mexico truly attempts to stop the drug trade, there is no telling the impact that would have on a Mexican economy flush with the proceeds of illicit drug money. If events such as these do indeed occur, they will seriously destabilize the Mexican economy, which in turn would have horrific consequences for the American economy. Worse, the unraveling of the Mexican economy will enrage millions of Mexicans, raising the prospect of political instability and widespread domestic violence, thus creating enormous problems for Mexico — and its northern neighbor.

ANGRY DRUG DEALERS

Aside from their impact on the economy, drug traffickers themselves are the source of critical grievances that could undermine Mexican stability. The continued tolerance of illegal drug activity and the lawlessness it engenders angers many Mexicans who feel powerless to change the course of events. No society can maintain itself indefinitely while tolerating pervasive criminal activity in its midst. Cracking down on the traffickers, however, might not be an option. The drug traffickers have become so powerful that if any Mexican government challenges their position, *they* will become enraged and could well seek to topple the regime. When President Felipe Calderon declared war on drug dealers in 2007, lawmakers of two major political parties became so alarmed that they proposed that the military be called up to defend the capital from the wrath of the cartels.[49] As has occurred in Colombia, the fury of the drug traffickers might turn into civil war, throwing Mexico into violent chaos.

The Mexican drug industry has always been a creature of American demand. Mexico's long border with the United States — most of which has never been adequately patrolled — combined with lax law enforcement, made Mexico a natural transit point for drugs headed for America. Prior to the Mexican Revolution (1910–1920), drug trafficking was not a major factor in Mexico. Domestic consumption was light, and American demand modest. Following the Mexican Revolution, however, and the onset of Prohibition in the United States, drug traffickers began to emerge as a significant force. As American demand grew, so too did the Mexican drug organizations, but their size and influence was modest, especially compared with their counterparts in Colombia. The Mexican organizations essentially were family-based local organizations dealing with locally grown products. The situation changed markedly in the 1980s, when Colombian drug traffickers sought new routes for smuggling cocaine into the United States following an American crackdown on their traditional pathways in the Caribbean and Florida. The Colombians saw Mexico as their best alternative and began flying Boeing 727s filled with drugs onto makeshift airstrips in Mexico. The drugs would then be offloaded into trucks and planes for transshipment to the United States. By the 1990s, Colombian drug lords working in partnership with their Mexican counterparts transformed Mexico into the principal source of illegal drugs into the United States.[50]

The huge amounts of illegal drugs pouring into the United States from Mexico generated tremendous profits not only for the Colombians, but for the Mexicans as well, leading to development of Mexican cartels as powerful as their Colombian counterparts. Five major drug organizations emerged in Mexico as large and deadly as any that can be found throughout the world. These cartels operate with impunity in Mexico, beyond the control of government and law enforcement. They have their own security forces or act in tandem with government forces. The cartels deliver social services, build roads, and enforce the law.[51] They have succeeded in creating what former Mexican Federal Deputy Attorney General Eduardo Valle Espinosa called "a state within a state," that is, a protected area where even the government will not intrude.[52] The cartels have sophisticated arms, intelligence capabilities, and communications equipment that at times can overpower even American law enforcement bodies. No wonder that the U.S. Border Patrol is sometimes counseled to shy away from direct confrontations with drug armies.[53] Mexican security forces too tend to avoid confrontations with drug lords out of fear of being outgunned or concerns that their troops are on the take. Mexican political leaders are little better, worrying, among other things, that strong efforts to suppress the drug trade could lead to their assassination.[54]

The nightmare Mexico faces is Colombia. An ongoing civil war in Colombia had brought the country to near collapse. Revenues from the drug trade are central to this civil war, as they support both sides of the brutal conflict. Using drug money, insurgents have established vast ministates where the Colombian government has little or no presence. Cooperation between drug cartels and the rebels has become so close that in many instances it is impossible to tell the difference between the two groups. On the governmental side, paramilitary forces supportive of the regime regularly use drug profits to finance their attacks on the rebels. The result is an ongoing civil war and massive criminal violence that has claimed the lives of 30,000 in the past ten years and threatens to turn Colombia into a failed state.[55]

Mexico has not yet reached the point of Colombia. Mexico has a stronger civil society than Colombia and its rebel groups are nowhere as strong. Drug traffickers in Mexico have thus far coexisted (and at times cooperated) with the government and so have little incentive to try to bring it down. Nevertheless, if the Mexican government cracks down on the cartels, angering their leaders, peace between the traffickers and the regime could easily fall apart. Drug traffickers might directly strike out at the government either through assassination or military assault, or they may seek to subvert it from within. If insurgent groups gain strength in the countryside, they may make common cause with the drug cartels in a manner reminiscent of Colombia. Mexico is not Colombia, but neither can it be certain of avoiding its fate.

RURAL DISQUIET

Another source of grievances arousing the Mexican masses lies among the poor in the rural areas, where an estimated 25% of the Mexican population live. Most Third World revolutions begin in rural areas, and while Mexico is far from being on the brink of revolution, if anger in the countryside continues to mount, widespread civil conflict could erupt. The Mexican National Defense Ministry has identified 15 armed insurgent groups, the best known of which are the Zapatistas and the Popular Revolutionary Army (EPR).[56] The activities of the insurgents are widespread, with rebel groups maintaining a presence in 20 of Mexico's 31 states and in the Federal District.[57]

Their support stems from the extreme poverty in the rural areas, which is especially acute among the indigenous people of Mexico. There are approximately 10 million indigenous people in Mexico, most of whom live in the central and southern regions. Fully 81% of the indigenous population lives in poverty, and very few have broken into the Mexican political and economic elite.[58] The indigenous peoples share a history of exploitation, discrimination, and grinding poverty, making them ripe for rebellion. The rebel organizations they create persist because the Mexican government and military is too weak to destroy them. These problems are unlikely to be addressed, at least in the short to medium term, by Mexico's halting steps toward democracy. The elimination of the PRI monopoly has made the state less capable of confronting insurgent groups and thus far has done little to eliminate the intense grievances (such as gross income inequality) that give rise to the rebels in the first place.[59]

The most visible manifestation of rural unrest in Mexico, and a possible portent for future insurgencies is the 1994 uprising in the southern Mexican state of Chiapas. What happened in Chiapas is important because the causes of the rebellion have largely not been addressed, suggesting that violence can reoccur there at any time. Moreover, the conditions that gave rise to the Chiapas insurgency are found throughout much of rural Mexico, especially in the southern states, making the understanding of this event all the more important in assessing the prospects for widespread instability in Mexico.

The details of the Chiapas uprising are not in serious dispute. On New Year's Day 1994, armed insurgents, mostly Mexican Indians, mobilized about 5,000 armed fighters and attacked several villages and towns in the southern Mexican state of Chiapas. The insurgents claimed they were an "Indian" army and called themselves the Zapatista National Liberation Army (EZLN in its Spanish acronym). They promised to end over five centuries of repression against the Indians by the Spanish invaders and a succession of Mexican governments. The Zapatistas seized several towns and villages, meeting only token opposition by Mexican authorities, who were taken completely by surprise. Flushed with victory, the Zapatistas announced their intention to march on Mexico City to overthrow the government and replace it with a regime that would treat the Indians fairly. Within a week of the uprising, the armed struggle had gone beyond Chiapas with the destruction of electric towers in the states of Michoacan and Puebla and the explosion of a car bomb in Mexico City. Fears that the uprising would spread throughout the country gripped Mexico.[60]

The fighting between the Zapatistas and the government went on for some ten days until halted by a cease-fire. The costs of the uprising were high. At least 145 dead, hundreds wounded, and some 25,000 residents of Chiapas became refugees.[61] Although the violence ended, its roots were not addressed. The insurgent forces remained intact, confronting an increased military presence policed by an uneasy truce. Not surprisingly, incidents continued to occur, threatening to unravel the fragile peace. In December 1994 (nearly a year after the initial rebellion) the rebels announced they had occupied 38 towns in a renewed offensive. By the time the report was discredited — no towns had been taken — foreign investors panicked, contributing to the 1994 economic crisis.[62] In 1997, a formal peace agreement was finally signed, but its provisions granting the Chiapas residents autonomy were never carried out. Instead, in December 1997, armed supporters of the PRI killed 45 sympathizers of the Zapatistas, mostly women and children, after the EZLN had taken over a small village. The coming to power of Vicente Fox held out some hopes of ending the insurgency, especially as aid began to pour into the embattled province, but many of his efforts to change conditions in Chiapas died in Congress. Reacting to the continued unrest, in 2003 the EZLN established de facto autonomous zones in Chiapas, where government forces hesitated to travel.[63] By 2005, hundreds of people had been killed and 20,000 people forcibly removed from their villages.[64] The Zapatistas and backers of the PRI continued to engage in a limited war of sorts, largely unseen and unremarked upon. While this conflict lacked the drama of the 1994 rebellion, the inhabitants of Chiapas are hardly satisfied and the potential for renewed widespread conflict remains.

The causes of the Chiapas uprising are not difficult to discern. The people of Chiapas are dirt poor, with a poverty rate 40 times higher than in the Federal District (home of Mexico City). According to government figures, over half the population in Chiapas suffers from malnutrition, one of the highest incidences in the country. Chiapas has an illiteracy rate of 30%, three times Mexico's average, almost half its people do not have access to clean drinking water (compared with 20% with Mexico as a whole), and more than a third have homes without electricity (compared with 12.5% in Mexico).[65] It is not only, then, that the people of Chiapas are so poor, they are substantially worse off than the rest of Mexico. Problems of scarcity also explain the Chiapas revolt. A common cause of civil unrest is rapid population growth in poverty-stricken areas, a characteristic that fits Chiapas all too well. From 1970 to 1990, the population of Chiapas doubled from a little more than 1.5 million to 3.2 million.[66] This reflected a population growth rate of 5.4% per year, more than twice the rate of 2.1% for the rest of Mexico.[67] Arguments that Mexico's overall low rate of population increase will bring stability fail to recognize that in some places, such as Chiapas, population growth has reached alarming proportions.

Complicating the skyrocketing population growth is lack of land. In 1992, President Salinas amended Article 27 of the Mexican Constitution in an effort to attract private investment in agriculture and increase food production. One of the effects of the changes was to make it easier for large landowners to evict peasants.[68] Given that the peasants had already suffered due to inequitable distribution of land, the constitutional change came as a bitter shock. The economic liberalization that began in the 1980s but gained momentum in the 1990s, meant major cuts in state subsidies and increased global competition. While many Mexicans elsewhere did indeed benefit from lack of governmental controls on the economy, the Indians of Chiapas were badly hurt, since they depended on those subsidies to live and lacked the skills to compete in the global marketplace.[69]

With the ample grievances of the Chiapas peasants at a boiling point, all that was needed was skilled organizers to transform those grievances into a political movement. Some of that organization came from "Subcommander Marcos," a Marxist professor with no trace of Indian ancestry whose real name was Rafael Sebastian Guillen.[70] Marcos's flair for publicity and skill with modern forms of communication, such as the Internet, did much to draw attention to the Chiapas revolt throughout Mexico and the world. Of equal importance was the role of the Catholic Church, which for centuries had been identified with wealthy landowners. So long as Catholicism was the only organized religion, this caused the Church no great harm. Increasingly, however, in Chiapas and other poor regions,

Protestant missionaries had taken up the cause of the peasants, attracting many to their fold. To counter the appeal of the Protestant missionaries and to show they could take up the mantle of the disenfranchised, the Catholic clergy organized protest movements for the Indians. The Zapatistas grew out of these movements.[71]

The combination of extreme poverty, weak government presence, a rapidly growing Indian population, erosion of property rights, economic changes that made it harder for peasants to earn a living, and the organizational efforts of the Church gave root to the Zapatista rebellion. Similar conditions exist throughout Mexico, especially in the poorer states of Mexico's south, including Guerrero, Michoacan, Oaxaca, Hidalgo, and Puebla. In some of these states, dangerous guerrilla movements already exist. In Guerrero, for example, the EPR has committed more attacks than the Zapatistas (but lack Marcos's attention-getting skills). The EPR also made a comeback in Oaxaca in 2006, when thousands of teachers and other workers engaged in massive demonstrations, paralyzing the state. Politically motivated violence continues to bedevil other southern states such as Chiapas and Guerrero, while elsewhere the threat is mostly latent. None of these movements will be able to topple the Mexican regime, but each has the potential to spread havoc and cause economic uncertainty. Moreover, if an alliance forms with drug traffickers, such as occurred in Colombia, a serious threat to the stability of the Mexican government will have emerged.

Growing discontent in the south, as manifested by the Chiapas rebellion and violent protests in other southern states, raises the threat that Mexico will be split along regional lines. While NAFTA has contributed to the Mexican economy growing at a consistent rate of over 4% per year, the southern states of Mexico, such as Chiapas, Oaxaca, and Guerrero, are lucky to reach growth rates of 1%. Increasingly, Mexico is being divided, with an industrialized north benefiting from close trade ties with the United States separated from a largely agricultural and poverty-stricken south. The political implications of this regional split surfaced during the 2006 elections, when Felipe Calderon's victorious PAN drew overwhelmingly from the north, while Andres Manuel Lopez Obrador's PRD garnered his support from the "losers" of Mexico in the south. As income inequality continues to grow, Mexico is rapidly becoming two countries, a wealthy north and a sullen, angry south generating insurgency and perhaps one day, civil war.[72]

RIGHT TO ATTACK

There is no doubt that there are many groups in Mexico who are angry and desperate for change. The question remains, however, whether they believe they have the *right* to use violence, especially against the government, to achieve their ends. To be sure, for some groups this is not a primary concern. As criminal organizations, drug traffickers by their very nature are not going to anguish over whether they are justified in acting violently to advance their agenda. For others, the question of the right to engage in violent means is indeed central. Whether that right exists depends on whether the Mexican government is seen as legitimate. If Mexico's citizens believe the government has the right to rule over them, then the government will not be the target of violent action, at least not to any great extent. If the Mexican government is not legitimate, however, there is little to stop the intense grievances from turning into bloodshed against the ruling authorities.

How legitimate is the Mexican government, including related institutions that underlie Mexican society? At first glance, the Mexican government appears highly legitimate. The 2000 elections of Vicente Fox, ending the PRI's 70-year monopoly, were widely seen as free and fair. The peaceful transition from one party to another is the hallmark of democracy and Mexico carried it off with nary a hitch. One would expect that changeover to confer a healthy level of legitimacy to the victors, protecting them from the wrath of violent protest. In fact, however, the legitimacy of the Mexican government is weak, and is likely to decline over time. The principal threats to Mexico's legitimacy are governmental paralysis in the face of mounting problems and pervasive corruption that has infected and at times dominated all levels of government and law enforcement. Because Mexico is a new democracy with fragile institutions, these threats pose a realistic danger of undermining Mexican legitimacy and with it, the stability of the state.

PARALYSIS

Throughout much of its history, Mexico has enjoyed many years of stable and effective rule thanks to the dominance of the PRI. Established in 1929, the PRI was created to bring order to Mexico after the chaos and carnage of the Mexican Revolution. Much more than a political party, the PRI quickly became the governing body, ruling as a patronage machine with ties to groups throughout Mexican society, especially labor. The PRI's appeal rested with a grand bargain it offered the Mexican people. In exchange for their unquestioning loyalty, they would be rewarded with jobs, access to government officials, and cash. Going against the PRI, on the other hand, would bring about punishment and impoverishment. In order to prevent political power struggles from once again bloodying the nation, the presidency was limited to one six-year term, with the outgoing president typically anointing his successor. It was far from ideal democracy, but it worked. Mexico enjoyed both stability and economic growth for decades.[73]

The PRI, however, began to lose its iron grip over the country beginning in the late 1960s. In 1968, student riots rooted in anger over university and governmental policies, resulted in at least 30 being killed. A series of economic crises beginning in the mid-1970s shook people's confidence in the PRI, especially its ability to provide for its followers. In the 1980s, economic liberalization resulted in the government giving up ownership over large firms while allowing a much bigger role for the market. The reforms spurred economic growth, but only at the cost of limiting the patronage of the PRI, thus weakening its ties to key groups. At the same time, new legal structures emerged, making free and fair elections possible for the first time. Taking advantage of all this, PAN and its charismatic leader Vicente Fox mounted a vigorous electoral challenge of the PRI. The PRD also joined in the election fray with attractive candidates of its own. Their efforts bore fruit in 1997, when for the first time both houses of the Mexican Congress lost their PRI majority. Instead of the PRI running the show on its own, a genuine three-party system had emerged with no single party exercising dominance. The era of one party dictating the course of Mexican politics had come to an abrupt end.

While Fox's victory in the 2000 presidential elections finally ended PRI rule, his triumph did not substitute one ruling party for another. Rather, it ushered in a new era of Mexican politics that produced governmental paralysis rather than effective rule. The inability of the government in the post-PRI era to get anything done emerged first because the office of the president is so weak. The Mexican president, for example, cannot issue temporary decrees or veto legislation like most of his Latin American counterparts. Throughout most of Mexico's history, the constitutional limits on the presidency did not present insurmountable problems. Since the president also led the PRI, he commanded this immensely powerful organization that could intimidate or coopt virtually all of Mexico's important players. Once the connection between the PRI and the presidency was broken, however, much changed. The PRI no longer could provide access to the highest levels of government that so many demanded, and the president no longer could command the PRI's pervasive machine to reward his friends and punish his enemies.[74] The president was reduced to seeking to persuade unruly elements to adopt his agenda, an effort that all too often ended in failure.

Exacerbating the effect of a weakened presidency has been the emergence of a divided Congress. The Mexican president used to be effective because he worked with a Congress that also belonged to the PRI. The emergence of PAN and PRD as serious electoral contenders, however, ended the era of one-party dominance not only for the presidency but for Congress as well. Although Fox won the presidency in 2000 with over 42% of the vote, his PAN controlled just 30% of the seats in the lower house of Congress and 38% in the Senate, with the rest taken up by PRI and PRD (and some smaller parties).[75] In the 2006 elections that propelled Felipe Calderon into office, the PRI again lost major ground to both PAN and the PRD, and while PAN won a plurality in both houses, it continued to face a legislature divided among the three parties. So long as this pattern of multiparty congresses continues and as long as the parties refuse to cooperate with one another, no president will be able to work with the legislature to bring about the major changes needed to address Mexico's chronic problems.

Contributing to this stalemate are the constitutional rules governing Congress. As with the presidency, members of Congress cannot run for consecutive terms. The intent of this law was to prevent the entrenchment of power, which contributed mightily to the horror of Mexico's civil war. In the modern era, however, the law produces a Congress that has little incentive to be responsive to the needs of its constituents. Moreover, the inability to run for reelection means that congressional expertise is limited, preventing sustained, informed attention to critical issues. It also impedes the president's abilities to negotiate with Congress, given that both recognize they will soon be out of office with little or no hope of returning. The result is a Congress that is unable to cooperate with the president or do much of anything on its own.[76]

The inability of the president and Congress to rule cannot help but affect people's perception of their *right* to rule. Mexico faces a staggering array of problems, including crushing poverty, rampant crime, an overdependence on oil, rural insurrection, a growing north-south divide, and drug traffickers running amok. Thus far, democratization and the liberalization of the economy have done little to address these issues, while increasing the demands Mexicans have placed on their government. The key will be how the Mexican government responds to these escalating demands. If progress is made toward meeting them, then patience and accommodation from the Mexican people will be the rule. However, all signs point to a political system in which no single party or coalition can govern effectively, leading to gridlock.[77] Under conditions of prolonged paralysis, what legitimacy the Mexican government enjoys will quickly dissipate, heightening the chances of major violence both among Mexican groups and directed at the failed leadership itself.

No clearer example of the weakness of Mexico's legitimacy exists than the reaction to the summer 2006 elections, in which Calderon of PAN triumphed over the PRD's Lopez Obrador by a half of a percentage point. Lopez Obrador and his followers flagrantly refused to accept the electoral verdict, even after the Federal Election Tribunal (one of Mexico's most effective and least corrupt institutions) validated Calderon's victory. Instead, Lopez Obrador declared himself winner of the election, promised to create a "parallel government," mobilized hundreds of thousands of his supporters to occupy the main plaza of Mexico City, and called for demonstrations throughout the country to reverse the "fraud" at the polls. In an especially embarrassing move, congressmen loyal to Lopez Obrador prevented outgoing president Fox from delivering his final State of the Union message. As the candidate who won most of the southern states, Lopez Obrador's actions called into question the government's right to rule for a major portion of Mexico's population. A hallmark of a healthy democracy is accepting defeat, even when the margin is tantalizingly close. Lopez Obrador's failure to abide by the results of Mexico's elections combined with the fervent support bestowed upon him by Mexico's dispossessed, suggests that legitimacy for Mexico's government remains an elusive goal.[78]

CORRUPTION

Aside from political weakness, corruption also eats away at Mexico's legitimacy. From its very origins in the aftermath of the Mexican Revolution, through the hopeful period of the transition to democracy, corruption has infected all levels of Mexican government. Corruption ranges from the routine bribing of police officers to make traffic offenses go away to active cooperation with drug dealers at the very highest levels of government. Corruption produces a populace that is understandably skeptical of the willingness of officials to better their lives. It undermines the sense of the rule of law in Mexican society, making extralegal solutions the rule rather than the exception. Because of corruption, Mexicans have lost confidence in their police and are rapidly losing confidence in their army and political leaders. For Mexicans to believe their government has a right to rule over them, they have to believe the government is acting in their interests, but increasingly this is not the case. The danger is that one day corrupt forces will not simply influence the government, but take it over, provoking widespread violence in its wake.

The most likely way that corrupt forces would take control over the Mexican government is through the actions of drug traffickers. From the drug trade's very beginnings in the 1920s, drug dealers worked hand in hand with the Mexican government. As Luis Astorga explains, it is misleading to think of drug dealers and government officials as two opposing sides. Instead, drug dealers and government

officials worked closely together to the point where it became difficult to distin-
guish between the two. Drug dealing was institutionalized so that drug traffickers
would pay a "tax" to government officials to enable them to do business.[79] The
government could control the drug dealers, because for the most part they were
local organizations with limited influence and not powerful cartels on the Colombian model.[80]

The balance of power between the drug dealers and government began to
change in the 1980s when Mexican drug traffickers began to replace the Colombians. Flush with cash, the Mexican cartels then proceeded to get the Mexican
political establishment to do its bidding. The long rule of the PRI made it an easy
target for corruption. With one party in charge of political power, jobs, and funding, it provided "one stop shopping" for the drug lords to increase their influence
and ensure noninterference.[81] Mexican institutions such as the PRI, the presidency, the courts, and even the Church proved no match for the allure of some
$500 million in bribes per year.[82] The Arellano brothers alone, leaders of Tijua-
na's cartel, spent as much as $75 million each year on payoffs to local, state, and
federal officials.[83]

The corrupting influence of the drug lords on Mexican politics became
painfully apparent as the administration of Carlos Salinas (1988–1994) came to an
end. During the Salinas period drug traffickers acquired unprecedented power
that reached into the president's office itself. President Salinas's brother and chief
assistant, Raul, was credibly linked to a major drug trafficker, Juan Garcia Abrego,
and was believed to have played a central role in the murder of Jose Francisco
Ruiz Massieu, a prominent leader of the PRI. In February 1995, Raul was arrested
for the Ruiz Massieu assassination as well as for all the money he received from
drug traffickers. The investigation that followed his arrest showed how the Salinas
administration was riddled with the influence of drug lords. As if to underscore
the penetration of the illicit drug dealers, Deputy Attorney General Mario Ruiz
Massieu, the brother of the murdered Jose Francisco Ruiz Massieu, and the man
in charge of investigating the crime, was himself arrested for covering up Raul's
involvement. It was later learned that Mario Ruiz Massieu may have been involved with drug traffickers. These and other developments raised questions
about whether Carlos Salinas himself (who left Mexico for Ireland after his presidential term ended) was involved in the drug trade.[84]

The inroads achieved by drug traffickers during the Salinas years were so deep
that subsequent administrations have been unable to uproot their influence. President Ernesto Zedillo, who succeeded Salinas, was personally honest, but he accomplished little against the drug dealers. The election of Fox raised hopes that

with a non-PRI president, the power of the drug lords would finally be confronted, but those hopes quickly evaporated. Drug arrests under Fox dropped from previous periods, while violence connected to drug trafficking increased, especially in the northern states.[85] While Fox himself was not suspected of being corrupt, those around him were less honest. Incident after incident demonstrated the reach and power of the drug lords. In January 2001, drug kingpin Joaquin Guzman Loera escaped from a federal prison in Mexico. The warden of the prison and some 70 others were placed under house arrest in the belief that they freed Guzman in exchange for $2.5 million.[86] The head of Fox's travel staff was arrested on suspicion that he was feeding information to drug lords regarding Fox's itinerary. Not only did this raise concerns that the president's staff had been penetrated, it also made the president vulnerable to possible assassination attempts by drug interests. Fox's failure to deal with the drug trade and the corruption it has spawned turned out to be one of the biggest complaints the Mexican people made against his administration.[87]

One reason Fox did not accomplish more is that his election may have facilitated efforts by drug dealers to extend their control. The end of PRI dominance opened up Mexican politics to an unprecedented degree. As welcome as this was, it left in its wake a government that was weaker than its predecessors because it lacked the PRI's ties and patronage. The fragility of the new regime meant that major antidrug efforts were more difficult to undertake. In addition, the advent of competitive elections created increased needs for campaign contributions. Even under the old PRI regime, the Cali cartel is suspected of contributing tens of millions of dollars to PRI candidates. With contested elections, the quest for campaign cash intensified, playing into the hands of drug dealers.[88] The point is not that democracy is bad for Mexico or that drug trafficking was not a problem under the PRI. Rather, the transition to democracy places the state in a position where it is especially vulnerable to being corrupted by powerful nonstate actors, lessening any legitimizing benefits that democracy was supposed to bring.

Along with the corruption of high-level political officials, the tentacles of the drug traffickers have reached into all levels of Mexico's security forces. Local police have long been implicated in the drug trade, with officers often serving as bodyguards and enforcers for drug lords. The termination of the entire police force of the border town Nuevo Laredo in 2005 because of its work for the drug trade illustrates the enormity of the problem honest officials face when trying to get a handle on illicit drug dealing. As bad as the local police are, the state police are not much better. In 1997, for example, President Zedillo got rid of the Baja California state police because of their ties to the drug trade. The border city of

Ciudad Juarez, with a population of some 1.3 million people, is Mexico's most violent city in part because the state police, including its former head, were in league with drug traffickers.[89] The federal police are not much better, as they too are riddled with officers serving the drug cartels. The director of the American Drug Enforcement Agency reflected the prevailing wisdom when he said (in 1997), "There is not one single law-enforcement institution in Mexico with which the DEA has an entirely trusting relationship."[90]

President Fox's efforts to create a new, corruption-free federal force to target the drug dealers failed miserably. The Federal Investigation Agency (AFI by its Spanish acronym) established by Fox at the beginning of his term was mired in scandals, with over 1,400 of its officers investigated for wrongdoing (457 had been indicted by December 2005), including engaging in kidnapping and torture while under the employ of drug cartels.[91] What respect can one have for law enforcement officials when, instead of upholding the law, they are actively working on the side of criminals?

In despair, President Calderon enlisted the military as the centerpiece of his anticartel efforts, sending some 24,000 soldiers and police to the state of Michoacan in December 2006 to do battle with drug cartels, but little success was achieved. Historically, Mexican attempts to do an end run around its thoroughly corrupt police forces by enlisting the army to deal with drug trafficking have backfired badly. At first, hopes were high that the army, one of the most reliable institutions in Mexico, could wage a war against the drug lords without being corrupted. These hopes never were realistic, as the Mexican military has a long and undistinguished record of working with drug dealers.[92]

Any beliefs to the contrary were dashed with the arrest of General Jesus Gutierrez Rebollo in early 1997. The appointment of Gutierrez in December 1996 as the leader of the antidrug effort was welcomed in the United States, where U.S. drug czar Barry McCaffrey called Gutierrez "a guy of absolute, unquestioned integrity."[93] Some nine weeks after taking office, Gutierrez was found to be working for Amado Carrillo Fuentes, one of Mexico's premier drug lords. Instead of fighting drugs, Gutierrez placed his 38,000 soldiers, weapons, and airfields at the service of Fuentes. What looked like antidrug actions were really Gutierrez murdering and torturing members of drug gangs that threatened Fuentes's control.[94] Since his arrest, several other generals have been jailed for involvement with drug traffickers and in 1999, the entire elite 96th Infantry Battalion was suspected of selling the cocaine it had confiscated.[95] The secretary of defense under Zedillo, General Enrique Cervantes, allegedly attempted to launder over a *billion* dollars. Far from being a bulwark against corruption, the military has shown itself as vulnerable to the seductions of the drug traffickers as any other institution. Instead of working to defeat the drug lords, the army has morphed into its own drug cartel.[96]

Mexico faces a crisis of legitimacy. In the face of a myriad of problems, its government, characterized by a weak presidency and a divided Congress, is unable to do much of anything. Making matters worse, drug traffickers have infiltrated every level of government, including the president's office, while drastically compromising law enforcement and the army. This is not a government that has earned the respect of the Mexican people, nor is it a government that is seen as exercising rightful power. For drug traffickers, none of this matters. They do not need an excuse to launch violent attacks against the leadership if they believe doing so will advance their interests. For others, however, the ineffectiveness and corruption of the government is central. By undermining respect for the government and the rule of law, the decision to resort to violence is becoming easier and easier to make. If grievances become sufficiently intense, the government increasingly will not have the cloak of legitimacy to protect it from the wrath of the people it was elected to serve.

PROSPECTS FOR THE SUCCESS OF VIOLENCE

The prospect of civil conflict in Mexico is so high because disaffected groups recognize they stand a good chance of achieving their interests by engaging in violence against the government. It is not so much that the groups are so powerful as it is that the ability of the Mexican government to suppress these groups is so weak. Few rebellions begin if there are no chances for victory. An ominous sign for Mexico is that various groups may believe, with reason, that violence will advance their goals. This does not mean that they are confident of toppling the government as the chances of any group overthrowing the regime are slight. Nevertheless, for some, either attacking the government or threatening to do so may be seen as an effective way to achieve what they seek. So long as the government cannot eradicate them, and so long as their potential for violence extracts concessions from the government, they win by not losing.

The overwhelming influence of drug lords in Mexican society stems from the recognition that in a confrontation with government forces, the drug traffickers are likely to emerge victorious. Large swaths of territory where governmental opposition has been minimal, including entire states such as Sinaloa and major cities such as Tijuana, Juarez, and Guadalajara, have been controlled by drug traffickers.[97] The drug lords maintain their own security forces, which in many cases are not only stronger than the forces deployed by the government, they *are* the forces deployed by the government, bought and paid for by the drug traffick-ers. Under the best of circumstances, the government might be able to defeat one or two of the drug organizations, but this would simply strengthen their rivals. The Mexican government simply lacks the power to take on all the drug cartels at the same time.[98]

The strength of the drug lords means that they do not have to attack the gov-ernment, because the knowledge they could do so is enough to achieve their aims. An accommodation has resulted, but it is achieved at a terrible cost, namely, allowing large illegal organizations to flourish within Mexican territory. This arrangement acknowledges that Mexico is unable to meet the basic attributes of a state, the exercise of supreme power within its territory. It also raises the possi-bility that at some point the drug traffickers or the government will no longer sup-port the status quo, with massive violence or even civil war as the outcome.

In addition to the drug traffickers, others may also believe they can advance their interests through violence or the threat of violence. Leftist supporters of the PRD might conclude the time is right to attack a government whose claim to rule is based, in their view, on electoral fraud. The Zapatistas achieved much through their 1994 rebellion. They secured massive aid for Chiapas while garnering na-tional and international recognition of their grievances. Despite government re-pression, the leadership and organization of the Zapatistas remain intact. More-over, the problems of poverty, discrimination, and landownership that gave rise to their initial attacks against the government have not gone away. Having shown that violence pays may well induce the Zapatistas to once again launch a rebel-lion against the government to get it to address their continuing concerns. Ex-tremist groups like the EPR and other fringe organizations in the poor states of Oaxaca and Guerrero may also see opportunities to advance their leftist political agendas, secure government aid, or simply be left alone through violent action. Other groups operating outside the law who may promote violence to achieve their ends include violent organizations such as Los Pancho Villas, who control sections of Mexico City, and land invaders seeking to seize farms from absentee landlords. What is especially ominous is that some of these groups have backing from elements of the PRI and PRD.[99]

Whatever their motivation, groups believe they can win through violence (or its threat) because Mexico's security forces are so weak. The police forces are rid-dled with corruption and do not pose a serious challenge to those who operate outside of the law. In addition to at times doing the bidding of the cartels, the army is underpaid, poorly trained, and hopelessly inept in counterinsurgency opera-tions. Moreover it resists assistance from the United States and refuses to learn from the experiences of other Latin American militaries.[100] Mexico's security forces have become a paper tiger unable and unwilling to protect the state from the forces arrayed against it. Nowhere was this made clearer than in the reaction to the 1994 Chiapas uprising. If a ragtag group of armed peasants can defy the might of the Mexican military, one shudders to think what a determined, organized revolt might accomplish. To the extent that the ability to defeat an adversary is an incentive to strike, the Mexican security forces do not offer much of a deterrent to would-be insurgents.

CATALYSTS TO VIOLENCE

All of the ingredients for civil unrest are found in Mexico. A wide range of groups, some of whom are armed, seethe with resentment and anger at a government they believe has done them wrong. The legitimacy of the Mexican leadership is fast eroding as the legacy of the 2006 elections, corruption and incompetence, take their toll. The Mexican army and police forces are increasingly seen as useless against criminal and insurgent threats. While Mexico seems to enjoy relative peace and stability, the good times can evaporate in an instant. All that is necessary to bring this about, to plunge Mexico into civil unrest, is a spark to ignite the antigovernmental forces. This prospect becomes all the more alarming given how likely it is that such a catalyst will emerge in the coming years.

A possible spark to widespread violence is economic collapse, similar to what occurred in 1994. An economic shock could unleash forces throughout Mexico that would shake the very foundations of Mexican society. The relative prosperity that Mexicans have experienced over the last decade ironically makes Mexico even more vulnerable to the effects of a precipitous economic downturn. Over the past years, people's hopes have risen about the kind of life they can expect. If instead of greater wealth they see their savings wiped out, jobs lost, and dreams for the future dashed, a violent reaction could occur. In the cities, unions, trade associations, and urban mobs may lash out at the system that failed them. In the countryside, it may be even worse. Mexico bought a tenuous peace in places like Chiapas by pouring money into troubled provinces. If the money is no longer there, a rebirth of rebellious activity cannot be far behind. Guerrilla groups remain intact and dangerous throughout rural areas in Mexico. Many are waiting for some major crisis to come out of hiding. An economic collapse would be just the signal they are seeking that the time is right to strike out at the Mexican government.

The chances of Mexico undergoing an economic collapse are so high because its financial health depends on factors that are beyond Mexico's control. Mexico's overwhelming dependence on the United States means that key decisions about Mexico's economy will depend on decisions made in Washington, not Mexico City. If the United States undergoes a recession or simply decides to change the direction of its trade away from Mexico, it will have a devastating impact on the Mexican economy. Similarly, an American decision to clamp down on cross-border traffic would remove a critical safety valve for Mexico's restive citizens, leaving the angriest and poorest Mexicans at home, primed to cause trouble. If nature takes its course and Mexico's oil wells run dry, the critical buffer provided by those plush revenues will disappear and with it the ability to keep the Mexican government functioning. Because drug trafficking is so critical to the Mexican economy, the decisions made by drug lords on what they do with their revenues also become critical to the Mexican economy. The removal of these funds, especially if done precipitously, could well bring about an economic breakdown, unleashing antigovernment protests.

Political developments can also serve as a catalyst for unrest. When President Fox tried to prevent then-mayor of Mexico City Lopez Obrador from running for president in 2006 by invoking a technical violation of the law, Lopez Obrador responded by mobilizing a massive march of more than 1 million of his supporters in Mexico City. This forced Fox to back down, while demonstrating Lopez Obrador's ability to bring about political change through the threat of violence. When Lopez Obrador subsequently lost the presidential election, his supporters again came out in force to protest what they believe was a stolen election. Although the initial crisis was defused, seething resentment remains. If Lopez Obrador's PRD again loses a close electoral contest, it is all too easy to imagine violent protests sweeping through Mexico's cities and the southern states, engulfing the country in widespread instability.

Civil conflict might emerge from something as simple as the death of a sitting Mexican president. Mexico has no vice president, leaving the selection of the president to the Congress in the event the president dies. A divided Congress might not be able to decide upon a successor, opening the door for extreme or extralegal solutions that might provoke civil unrest. If the president's death came about as a result of assassination, the resulting crisis would be all the worse. That drug traffickers have already been linked to several assassinations of high-ranking officials raises the possibility of drug lords either being involved in the killing of a president or playing a role in the naming of his successor — both outcomes that could precipitate widespread instability.[101]

A confrontation between drug cartels and the government could easily provoke a wider war. The shaky truce that has persisted between the government and the drug lords allowing for massive illegal drug dealing and only sporadic crackdowns may not survive long into the twenty-first century. It is easy to foresee the emergence of a Mexican leader who will not tolerate this growing state within a state and undertake a serious effort to rid Mexico once and for all of the drug cartels. Alternatively, the initiative for conflict might come from the drug lords themselves, unhappy with the policies of a given regime. In either case, so long as these powerful nonstate actors flourish in Mexico, the possibility of a massive clash cannot be discounted. If the government and the drug cartels engage in a Colombia-like war, there is little doubt it will involve virtually all sectors of Mexican society. Driven by the desire to defend the state, or, conversely, to bring it down, groups will choose their sides and the battle will be joined. Whichever side wins, Mexican stability would be the first casualty.

Mexico is very much a tale of two countries. In the past decade, economic liberalization has produced growth and prosperity, especially in the north. The PRI left power peacefully, following democratic elections. The countryside has been mostly quiet, as rebellions of the past fade into distant memory. But Mexico is also a country where the economy could collapse suddenly, rampant crime is worsening, drug dealers hold sway over large portions of the country, insurgent groups in the poverty-stricken south wait for signs of weakness, the government is unable to act decisively, and millions believe their votes do not count. It is this latter Mexico where the prospect of massive civil violence becomes thinkable in the coming years. It is a nightmare not only for the Mexican people, but for the United States, whose own economic health and sense of security is inextricably linked to the fate of its southern neighbor.

CHAPTER FIVE

China

Collapse of a Great Power

Most views of China foresee continued economic growth in a stable society, heralding the emergence of a new superpower for the twenty-first century. There is much to support this optimistic perspective. From its inception of economic reforms in 1978, in just 25 years China's gross domestic product grew eightfold, its per capita income went from $151 to $1,097, and its trade increased a staggering 41 times (making China the fourth largest trading country in the world).[1] China's military spending is second only to the United States', transforming what had been a ragtag Third World army into a highly professional fighting force. China is modernizing its nuclear weapons, giving it a capability of surviving a first strike with the means to retaliate anywhere in the world. China's international profile has been transformed from a country that was barely visible on the world stage into a diplomatic powerhouse, critical to the functioning of international institutions and global treaties. Visitors to China invariably comment on the rate and breadth of change, as private farms replace communes, vibrant skyscrapers make the old cities of China all but unrecognizable, and fashionable entrepreneurs crowd streets once filled with chanting Red Guards. It is difficult, if not impossible, to think of any country at any time that has accomplished so much so quickly.

Those who see China as a threat to the United States, and to the West more generally, point to its explosive growth as a source of concern. A stronger China, they argue, will be a more assertive China, which spells bad news for the United States, given the range of issues over which the two countries disagree. A wealthy, militarily strong China may no longer choose to accept the de facto independence of Taiwan, or it may compete aggressively to gain dominance over Asia, or replace American influence among the oil-rich states of the Middle East. Arguments over trade, human rights, and the environment may take a different tone when America is dealing with an adversary of equal or even greater strength. Whether because the United States and China each lead different civilizations, or simply because the rise of a competing hegemon typically creates trouble for the existing world leader, the prospect of a continued rise in China's power unsettles many in America.[2]

These fears may indeed be justified, but continued economic and military growth is not the only possible future for China. It is at least as likely that China in the coming years will fall victim to violent instability, bringing to a screeching halt its seemingly inexorable rise. Instability may come from those angry at not sharing the fruits of China's newfound prosperity, growing discrepancies of wealth in a state founded on principles of equality, mounting corruption by insensitive officials, incompetent governmental policies, and the absence of institutions to channel discontent. This anger matters because it is directed at a government whose "mandate of heaven" is increasingly shaky, since no one — including the leadership elite itself — believes in the Marxist-Leninist ideology that is trotted out to justify its rule. All of this takes place in an environment where the regime's ability to monitor and suppress antigovernment activity has never been lower. If economic growth can somehow continue its upward spiral producing enough benefits to coopt key groups, China may be able to avoid nationwide instability in the coming years. However, if as seems likely, the Chinese economy stalls and the escalating expectations of the Chinese people are no longer met, widespread civil conflict becomes all but certain.

While some American policymakers would greet the prospect of a China mired in internal conflict with relief, a crippled China presents its own threats to American interests, threats that are in many ways more dire than those posed by a rising China. American and Chinese economies have become closely intertwined with huge amounts of American investment in China and even larger Chinese purchases of American bonds. If domestic unrest undermines this relationship, any hope of China becoming prosperous would be dashed, while the American economy would be thrown into recession — or worse. China is a great power with a population of 1.3 billion people, bordering on 14 countries. Its collapse would threaten the stability of close American allies such as South Korea and Japan, create opportunities for mischief by Russia and North Korea, and produce a humanitarian catastrophe unprecedented in world history. Should China choose to stave off internal unrest through aggressive actions against Taiwan, prospects for a Sino-American military confrontation become all too real. Precisely because China needs good relations with its neighbors and the United States to continue on its path of economic growth, there is reason to hope that the Chinese leadership would not deliberately opt for bellicose policies. If China is wracked with instability, however, Chinese leaders may not be able to control what happens within and outside their borders, endangering key American concerns.

Understanding the consequences of a failing China for the United States requires first grasping why a stable China is so important to American concerns. As will be seen, China plays a central role in American economic and strategic interests. Why China, despite its seeming prosperity and progress, may fall victim to civil unrest is then examined. Unlike Pakistan, Saudi Arabia, and Mexico, China forces us to confront what the collapse of a great power would be like. Far from a welcome occurrence, the implications of such an event are potentially catastrophic for America, China's Asian neighbors, and the world community.

AMERICAN INTERESTS IN CHINA

The United States cares about what happens in China, because America's prosperity and well-being rests on China remaining stable. China is the second largest trading partner of the United States (after Canada), a relationship whose disruption would be disastrous for both countries. The low cost of Chinese exports has kept inflation down in the United States, while delighting consumers with $40 DVD players and $20 digital cameras. These benefits, while highly visible, pale in comparison to the critical role played by Chinese purchases of American securities. China holds over one *trillion* dollars in foreign reserves, one of the largest holders of such reserves in the world. Because China exports so much and imports so little, it accumulates huge amounts of dollars. This would normally cause the Chinese currency (yuan) to gain in value, thus reducing its exports and its mammoth reserves. To preserve its critical export sector, however, China has not allowed the yuan to float freely and instead has kept its value relatively constant by buying dollars to the tune of $20 billion per month, ensuring that its reserves will continue to grow. Approximately 70% of these reserves are in U.S. dollars, with the great majority in U.S. treasury bonds, widely seen as the most secure investment one can make, since they are backed in full by the American government. A major reason why interest rates in the United States have been kept low is because China buys so many of these bonds. These low interest rates are central to the health of the American economy, fostering economic expansion and high home prices. The housing market is especially critical, as it has been the major engine of growth for the American economy over the past several years, as homeowners (many of whom have saved little) borrow against the ever rising values of their houses, stimulating the economy with their robust consumer spending. If China stops buying American treasury bonds or dramatically slows down their purchase, American interest rates would need to increase in order to attract other buyers, making business expansion more costly, houses much more expensive, and dramatically cutting consumer spending.[3]

China displayed its economic clout the day after the Democrats won control over both houses of Congress in November 2006, when the head of China's central bank declared that the Bank would diversify more of its reserves into nondollar currencies. This prompted an immediate worldwide sell-off of American dollars, which dramatically cut the dollar's value. If such a seemingly benign announcement could produce this effect, one shudders to think of the impact of a major Chinese sell-off of American bonds on the United States.[4] Some have taken solace in the view that Chinese self-interest would prevent Beijing from acting in ways that would harm the American economy. If, for example, China halted its purchase of American securities, China too would suffer as the value of the bonds in its possession would also decrease. If China is convulsed with domestic disorder, however, it would be *unable* to purchase the American bonds, plunging the U.S. economy into crisis.

An unstable China also presents major strategic concerns for the United States. Since the death of Mao in 1976, China has largely cooperated with the United States on key foreign policy goals. China has been a prime player in talks with North Korea, striving to contain the damage done by Pyongyang's development of nuclear weapons. In part because of China's concerns about its own Islamic minority, Beijing has worked with Washington after 9/11 to confront terrorism. China has become a major international player in the United Nations, contributing more troops to peacekeeping missions around the world than any other Security Council member.[5] With Washington's endorsement, China joined the World Trade Organization, where it is expected to play a major role in lowering tariffs and establishing rules for free trade that the world (and it) will follow.

To be sure, the United States and China do not agree on everything. The United States is concerned about China's lack of democracy, overlooking of human rights abuses in Darfur and elsewhere, border disputes with its neighbors, close ties with Iran, and continuing claims to Taiwan. Nevertheless, in a world increasingly divided between those fostering terror and instability and those seeking to maintain order and enhance prosperity, China clearly belongs in the latter camp, much to America's relief. If China is beset by internal disorder, however, there is no telling what kind of regime might emerge in its wake. The brutal civil war in China in the late 1940s gave birth to an equally brutal government that made life miserable for its neighbors and America for decades. A twenty-first-century civil war could well bring about the emergence of a hostile, expansionist China that, armed with nuclear weapons and a strong economy, posed an even greater threat to American interests and world stability than its Maoist predecessor.

A strong China is necessary to preserve Asian stability, a vital interest of the United States. The prosperity of Asian nations is directly linked to the surging Chinese economy. In the 1990s, Asian nations produced goods largely for non-Asian countries, particularly the United States. By 2005, more than half of all regional exports were to other states in the region, with China the most likely destination. China is the number one trading partner of such Asian powerhouses as South Korea and Japan, both of which now provide more direct investment to China (over $5 billion per year) than even the United States.[6] Moreover, China has emerged as the major player in Asian multilateral organizations, including the Association of Southeast Asian Nations (ASEAN), the Shanghai Cooperation Organization (SCO), and the Asia-Pacific Economic Cooperation forum (APEC). None of these organizations could meet their goals of fostering economic and political interdependence without the active cooperation of China. Insofar as economic interdependence and international institutions promote peace and security, the continued economic growth and stability of China is essential for Asia.[7]

The importance of a stable China to American strategic interests is best seen by considering what might happen if China unraveled. One of the first consequences would be millions of refugees pouring from China's borders, unsettling its neighbors. The stability of key American allies such as Japan, South Korea, and Taiwan would be severely tested as they try to cope with this massive human flow along with the economic shockwaves of China's dissolution. Nor would the United States be immune, as many Chinese may take advantage of corrupt officials or professional human smugglers ("snakeheads") to make their way to America's shores.[8] North Korea, unpredictable under normal circumstances, may flex its military muscle along its borders with China and South Korea, with dreadful results. Ethnic minorities in provinces such as Tibet and Xinjiang might seize the moment to attempt to break away from Beijing's domination, fostering even greater instability. China's control of its more than 200 nuclear weapons, usually very secure, may be compromised, with the arms eventually falling into unknown hands. The territorial disputes that China has with Russia, Vietnam, India, and others could well degenerate into armed warfare as China loses control over its own military forces and its neighbors seek to take advantage of its internal strife.

As Chinese leader Deng Xiaoping remarked (following the 1989 Tiananmen demonstrations), the collapse of Chinese rule would have terrible effects that would go far beyond China's borders: "And if a civil war broke out, with blood flowing like a river, what 'human rights' would there be? If civil war broke out in China, with each faction dominating a region, production declining, transportation disrupted and not millions or tens of millions but hundreds of millions of refugees fleeing the country, it is the Asia-Pacific region, which is at present the most promising in the world, that would be the first affected. And that would lead to disaster on a world scale."[9] While Deng may have had reason to exaggerate the effects of the toppling of the Chinese regime, his concerns ring true.

American relations with China would be severely damaged in the wake of Chinese unrest. The Chinese regime might single out the United States as an enemy in order to stifle civil strife by fostering anti-American nationalism. If China violently suppressed protests, as it did during the 1989 Tiananmen demonstrations, the American Congress might retaliate with economic sanctions, further escalating tensions between China and the United States. Especially if China takes actions against groups favored by the United States, such as Chinese Christians, the American leadership is likely to react harshly against Beijing. Chinese leaders already worry about the United States exploiting internal unrest to remove them from power. Actual American support of insurgent groups even if it is confined to expressions of sympathy, could be taken as a sign that Washington had joined with the rebels, throwing Sino-American relations into crisis. China would very quickly turn from an erstwhile ally into a superpower adversary.[10]

The deterioration of the American relationship with China would be especially dangerous regarding Taiwan. Under the best of circumstances, Taiwan presents a flash point in the Chinese-American relationship. China's claims that Taiwan is a renegade province belonging to the People's Republic fly in the face of America's commitment to protect Taiwan, a democratic and prosperous ally. So long as Taiwan does not declare its independence, the United States and China can agree to disagree about Taiwan's future, but should internal unrest engulf China, this uneasy and informal accommodation could unravel. If China falls victim to widespread instability, the pressure to act against Taiwan would be enormous. It would give China the excuse to impose martial law, improving its abilities to suppress any budding revolt. China's claims to Taiwan enjoy near unanimous approval among the Chinese people. Acting against Taiwan would enable the Chinese leadership to fan the flames of nationalism, one of the few means at its disposal to rally support for an otherwise illegitimate regime.[11]

A Sino-Taiwanese confrontation could also come about inadvertently if the Chinese leadership decided to provoke a crisis over Taiwan only to find itself at war as popular emotions prevented a peaceful resolution of the crisis. If a Taiwanese leader decided to exploit Chinese unrest by declaring independence, the Chinese government might have no choice but to launch an attack. As the political scientist Susan Shirk argues, no Chinese regime can stand aside and allow Taiwan to announce its independence without going to war if it expects to survive in power.[12] Whether through miscalculation or brinksmanship, war with Taiwan producing a Sino-American confrontation could well be the unintended outcome of Chinese civil conflict.

China is well prepared to take forceful action against Taiwan if it decides to do so. China has been constantly upgrading its air and sea capabilities for a possible invasion across the Straits of Taiwan.[13] If China chooses not to invade, it could launch the hundreds of ballistic missiles deployed on its coast against Taiwan or it could blockade its two principal ports. Given that Taiwan is critically dependent on foreign trade (75% of its GDP) and imports of fuel for energy consumption (95% of its energy needs come from outside the country), either of these actions would cripple the island state.[14] It is difficult to see the United States remaining indifferent to a brutal assault against one of its allies.

Perhaps most worrisome, we simply do not know all of the effects that the collapse of China would bring. The prospect of civil unrest in China threatens an existing great power poised perhaps to become *the* major power of the twenty-first century. The impact of civil conflict in China cannot be isolated to one or a handful of consequences. As seen in the French Revolution of 1789–1799 and the Russian Civil War of 1918–1920, great powers do not suffer civil violence quietly, or alone. Given China's central role in the world economy, enormous population, nuclear arsenal, and growing international influence, the unraveling of China cannot help but be shattering for the world. Change can be beneficial, and the weakening of a prospective superpower competitor would be celebrated in some American quarters. Nevertheless, an uncontrolled, cataclysmic transformation in China would threaten American interests as much as, if not more than, the purposeful designs of Maoist China a generation ago.

An unstable China would be one in which widespread violence, lasting at least several months, proved too great for the government to suppress, calling into question the future viability of the state. In order to demonstrate the plausibility of this kind of violence erupting, it must be shown that there exist in China intense grievances against the regime, a belief in the right to rebel against the government, and a conviction by insurgents that violent action will advance their goals. Structural flaws in the Chinese economy, an illegitimate government run by a decaying party, and a fractured elite presiding over a security establishment reluctant to use force against insurgents are just some of the factors that suggest that these conditions are well on their way to being met. Insofar as the United States depends on a stable, cohesive China to safeguard its interests, there is much cause for concern.

ECONOMIC GRIEVANCES

It is ironic that the same economy that has made China into a wealthy world power also contains the seeds that threaten its continued stability. There are essentially two developments, which if they occur, spell trouble for the future of China. First is the prospect of growing inequality breeding resentment by those who believe they are not sharing fairly in the newfound wealth of the country. Second, a slowdown in Chinese economic growth would create anger among those whose expectations are not met, while depriving the government of the ability to buy off groups who would otherwise threaten its rule. Unfortunately for China — and the United States — the prospects for each of these occurring are not only plausible, but likely.

There is no question that along with economic growth, inequality in China has risen to alarming proportions. A commonly used measure of inequality, the Gini coefficient, where 0 is perfect equality (everyone has the same income) and 1 perfect inequality (where one person has all the wealth and everyone else has nothing), had China at a very egalitarian 0.15 in 1978 (just before economic reforms began), shooting up to a disturbing 0.45 in 2000 — with some saying the real figure is closer to 0.5 or 0.6.[15] Inequality is said to reach dangerous levels when the Gini coefficient reaches 0.4, so even the lower estimates place China in a precarious position, while the higher figures would include China among the most unequal countries in the world.[16] As multimillionaires and even billionaires become ever more present in Chinese society, some 222 million Chinese are said to be living in "extreme poverty," over 100 million Chinese live on less than $1 a day, and in 2003, for the first time since the post-Mao reforms began, the number of Chinese living in poverty increased.[17]

Income inequality is a problem for any country but is especially acute in China, where there is a strong tradition of egalitarianism.[18] The Chinese government is supposed to make sure that everyone does well, not foster an ever widening divide. The situation becomes even more dire upon examining just who is and is not getting wealthy. Seventy percent of China's population and the traditional bedrock of support for the Communist regime are workers and farmers, and yet in this critical group wages have fallen and job security has all but disappeared.[19] Incomes in cities are more than five times those in rural areas, with expectations the gap will widen in the coming years as China continues its policies of neglecting the countryside to support the cities.[20] The disparity between the coastal areas and the hinterlands continues to grow, encouraging separatist tendencies in poverty-stricken provinces such as Tibet and Xinjiang. The Chinese leadership recognizes the dangers created by growing income inequality but is at a loss in figuring out how to respond. The obvious solution would be to increase taxes on the newly rich, namely, the wealthy entrepreneurs who are so visible on the Chinese scene, and to distribute the revenues to the poor, especially those in the countryside. China, however, depends on these entrepreneurs to keep its economy growing. More than half of China's GDP is now produced in privately owned companies. If China stifles this sector, it cripples its economy while angering newly empowered groups it cannot afford to alienate.[21]

The Chinese regime is also constrained by the influence wealthy groups and individuals wield in the provinces, where they are protected by local officials. Even if the central government decided to soak the rich, it is not clear that local officials would permit it to do so. The widespread (and usually accurate) perception that many of those earned their fortune through ties with corrupt political officials increases anger directed at the regime. Chinese leaders are thus left in a terrible position. They recognize that increasing inequality will anger the workers and farmers who constitute the backbone of the regime, but are loathe to pursue policies of income redistribution that would infuriate their new allies among the nouveau riche. As a result, little is being done to diminish mounting income inequality despite the intense grievances it produces against the regime.

Nothing is more likely to cause civil conflict in China than an economic slowdown. Every threat to the Chinese leadership, from violence in the capital to minority unrest in far-off provinces, will worsen if the Chinese economy fails to grow at the rate it has maintained over the past few decades. The economy, more than anything else, lies at the center of what has gone right in China and is also central to what could go wrong. In this sense, China is not different from other states threatened with instability. Theorists of revolution such as Ted Robert Gurr have emphasized that civil unrest is most likely in those situations when a period of economic growth is followed by a sharp downturn. When this happens, the gap between what people expect and what they actually receive spikes, creating the conditions for violent unrest.[22] There is much to suggest that this is precisely what is happening in China.

The Chinese economy is not likely to continue its growth, because political changes necessary to sustain a rising economy have not kept pace with economic changes. China's move to private markets had been largely completed by 2000, with 90% of commodities, virtually all labor, and two-thirds of capital stock bought and sold in markets.[23] Nevertheless, China continues to be led by a one-party, Marxist-Leninist state as if it still lived in the Maoist era. Market economies can only survive when there is a rule of law and institutions to constrain government interference in the economy. In China, however, the government is largely above the law, leaving it free to take what it wants regardless of the economic consequences. China lacks the basic institutions necessary for the functioning of a free economy. There is little in place to protect property rights or place limits on state interference. Alone among the great powers of the world, China is without a modern legal system.[24]

China is also unable to regulate its increasingly complex economy. Chinese officials themselves estimate that about half the contracts signed in China each year are fraudulent, nearly half of the products made in the country are substandard, and that 80% of the private entrepreneurs avoid taxes.[25] The absence of legal checks and strong institutions on governmental rule means that there is nothing to curb the power of the regime. This creates what political scientist Minxin Pei calls a "predatory" state, that is, a ruling elite that loots the wealth of the country to serve its own selfish ends. Because it acts in its personal interest and not the national interest, resources needed for economic growth instead find their way into the pockets of corrupt government officials while investment is made not in productive enterprises but in those areas where it will do the most to enrich party cadres. Not surprisingly, predatory states, by distorting the market economy, make prolonged economic growth impossible.[26]

China's economic growth may already be slowing down. Using official Chinese statistics, China grew by 12% per year from 1990 to 1995 but only 8.3% from 1995 to 2000. What's more, these figures are widely believed to be exaggerated, with some analysts arguing gains in GDP are a full one-fifth lower than what was reported.[27] Especially alarming is a 2007 reassessment by the World Bank suggesting that China's economy was approximately 40% *smaller* than previously believed ($6 trillion instead of $10 trillion). China apparently is far less wealthy than many had thought.[28] Insofar as the Chinese economy has risen in the past years, it is far from certain that it will be able to maintain its growth. China's economy grew so quickly in part because it was able to transfer capital and labor away from agriculture as a result of the dismantling of the communes and the benefits it achieved through the privatization of the economy. According to the World Bank, gains from these moves were essentially one-time boosts, whose benefits will end around 2015. In order to continue its economic rise China will have to depend on other factors, especially technological innovation. China, however, like all authoritarian states, has traditionally lagged in developing new technology. Its best scientists and engineers often go abroad to live and work, depriving China of their intellectual capital.[29]

Moreover, China faces a crisis in taking care of its aging population. The percentage of those 60 and over is growing more quickly in China than in any other major country, doubling the number of retirees between 2005 and 2015. There will be only two workers supporting each retiree in 2040 (compared to a ratio of six to one in 2007) as China's one-child families assume the responsibility of taking care of their parents. Chinese society, to say nothing of its economy, is ill prepared to deal with this looming aging crisis.[30] As impressive as China's economic miracle may have been, signs suggest that the good times are coming to an end.

These signs are especially compelling when one examines the lynchpin of the Chinese economic system, its banks. While China has moved to a market economy, the banking system remains a creature of the state. This leads to several difficulties, all of which spell trouble for the continued health of China's economy. First, China's central bank, the People's Bank of China (PBC), is supposed to set monetary policy in a way that ensures growth and stability, but it is unable to do this because it must first answer to the Chinese government. Since the PBC is not autonomous, its goal of monetary stability (neither high inflation nor deflation) must be subordinate to the government's goal of high economic growth.[31] If the PBC seeks to curb inflation by restricting the money supply but the Chinese government demands continued high growth, it is to the Chinese government that the PBC must defer, despite the long-term damage inflicted on the economy. Moreover, the PBC is often not able to carry out monetary policy, even when it is determined to do so. A good deal of the power of the central Chinese government has devolved to the periphery and banking is no exception. Local officials typically pressure branches of the PBC to make loans for pet projects even when the PBC is trying to limit lending. The managers of local branches are forced to comply with the demands of government officials because their jobs depend on those officials. The result is spurts in inflation caused by spikes in the monetary supply, spikes the PBC is powerless to halt. So long as China's economy depends on a central bank that is unwilling or unable to implement macroeconomic policies it believes are necessary, the future health of China's economy cannot be secure.[32]

The staggering number of bad or nonperforming loans made by Chinese banks also poses a threat to the Chinese economy. Just as the PBC is forced to follow government dictates when making macroeconomic policies, state-owned banks are also forced to make loans not on the basis of good business sense, but rather on what the government demands. What the Chinese government wants most of all from the four large state-owned banks is for them to make loans to state-owned enterprises (SOEs) no matter how uncreditworthy they may be. The SOEs, for their part, feel no obligation to repay the loans, since they see the banks and themselves as all part of the same government. When loans become due, the state-owned enterprises simply secure new loans to repay the old ones. Not surprisingly, approximately 75% of the bad loans the state banks make go to SOEs and other collectively owned enterprises.[33]

Just how many bad loans there are is subject to some dispute, but even the low estimates are alarming. The Chinese government, using very loose criteria, admits to a 27% nonperforming loan rate, which is more than twice the level judged as safe by international authorities.[34] Standard & Poor's calculated that the real ratio of nonperforming loans was 45%, with other estimates even higher. As a result of these bad loans, all the major state banks, the centerpiece of the Chinese banking system, became technically insolvent in the mid-1990s.[35] While some steps have been taken to reform the banking sector, such as allowing foreign banks to partially own Chinese banks,[36] the future solvency of the banking system remains very much in doubt.

Since most of the problems with nonperforming loans revolve around the SOEs, it would seem to make sense to reform or eliminate them. Not only do they generate bad loans, they are a major drag on the Chinese economy, using up two-thirds of China's domestic capital — resources that would be far more productive in the private sector — while accounting for only one-third of China's GDP. That SOEs are monstrously inefficient should surprise no one. They are a creation of the Maoist era, a part of the "iron rice bowl" safety net designed as much to deliver social services, such as a lifetime job and housing, as they were to be economically productive.[37] The SOEs, like communes and Red Guards, should not have a place in the dynamic, privatizing economy of modern-day China. Nevertheless, despite some efforts to reduce their number, the Chinese government resists eliminating the SOEs because it fears the consequences of a surge of unemployed workers, lacking pensions and health insurance, unleashed in the cities.[38] If China's economy grew fast enough to absorb the newly unemployed, dismantling the SOEs would not pose a major threat, but such growth has not occurred over the past years. The SOEs then lumber on, distorting the Chinese economy while undermining the viability of the state banking system.

The third pillar of the banking system, the informal sector, is also deeply troubled. Fully half of the credit in the Chinese economy is believed to come from outside the banking system, in what political scientist Kellee Tsai calls "back-alley banking."[39] This includes private lending among individuals and businesses, pawn shops, and unlicensed private banks.[40] As the private sector explodes in China, entrepreneurs have to go somewhere for capital. With confidence in the state banks low and interest rates in the informal sector almost four times higher than what many government banks provide, it is not surprising that private institutions are so popular with the Chinese people.[41]

While they provide important services, they also create a major risk for the economy because they are completely unregulated. Since lending rates can run 20–30% per year, there is a danger that the private institutions will not be repaid. Unlike the government, the informal sector cannot print money, raising the risk that many of the institutions will fail. Any crisis among the private banks is likely to move to formal banks, as borrowers clean out their deposits in an effort to repay loans. With no deposit insurance in China, bank runs would likely ensue, destroying what little confidence the Chinese have in their banks. Some $25 billion already leaves China each year because of lack of faith in banks. If a run on bank deposits occurred, that figure would increase manyfold.[42] The likely response by the Chinese government would be a large infusion of cash by the central bank to cover the immediate shortfall, but this would cause inflation producing further withdrawals of savings deposits and a possible collapse of the entire system of credit.[43]

With an ineffective central bank, a state-run banking system drowning in loans that will never be repaid, and a growing informal financial sector without regulation, the Chinese economy is living on borrowed time.[44] Why doesn't China simply transform its banking system to keep pace with the explosive changes in its economy? The reason is that the Communist Party recognizes that it cannot change banking practices without jeopardizing its hold on power. The banking sphere is an enormous patronage machine run by the Party that provides 1.7 million jobs in 150,000 branches and untold billions of dollars to those who will support the regime. Allowing market-driven changes undermines the Party's control over these jobs and resources, reducing its overall power.[45] While economic logic demands liberalization, political survival dictates business as usual. With the needs of the Party taking precedence over the needs of the economy, China persists in keeping a banking system primed for failure.

China's reliance on foreign direct investment (FDI) also has the potential to do serious damage to the Chinese economy. Between 1985 and 2001, FDI rose from around $2 billion a year to over $20 billion (in constant 1995 dollars), making China the second largest recipient of foreign direct investment in the world. In addition to funds, FDI provides China with access to foreign managerial skill and the technology necessary for China to compete in the globalized market of the twenty-first century.[46] That FDI is central to Chinese economic growth is not in dispute. The problem for the Chinese economy lies in the fear that it cannot depend on robust FDI in the future. The logic of globalization is that money flows to places that provide a secure and profitable return on investment. If civil unrest breaks out in China, especially if it is sparked by concerns over the economy, foreign investors will move their assets elsewhere. Even short of widespread violence, something as basic as a major stock market scandal, a bank run, or bankruptcy could produce a massive exodus of foreign funds. A 50% decline in FDI, hardly unthinkable, would cut China's GDP growth by half.[47] This could not help but precipitate other crises in the Chinese economy, plunging the country into recession.

From the outside, China's economy certainly appears robust. Nevertheless, as political scientist Bruce Gilley notes, economic crises in authoritarian governments (such as in the former Soviet Union) are often only understood after they occur, at which point everyone wonders why the warning signs were not heeded.[48] Part of the reason why no one pays attention to impending dangers is that authoritarian regimes are very good at concealing weaknesses until it is too late. For all of China's economic progress, it cannot escape the contradiction of a single party seeking to rule over an increasingly complex, market-driven society. Whether that contradiction manifests itself in a massive bank failure or the collapse of foreign direct investment, its effects could deal a body blow to China's sense of stability.

CORRUPTION

While many of the problems of China's economy lie in the future, the Chinese people are angry now and getting angrier over time. In a remarkable release of official statistics, the Chinese government itself has recorded the growing fury of its citizenry. According to the Chinese government, there were 58,000 protests in 2003, 74,000 in 2004, and 87,000 in 2005. Many of these protests have tens of thousands of participants, with some possibly reaching the 100,000 mark.[49] Common to their grievances is resentment at a regime that is corrupt, incompetent, and unresponsive. This has led to a deterioration in the lives of many Chinese, which many believe will only worsen in the coming years.

The principal grievance of the Chinese, as attested to by a series of public opinion polls, is corruption.[50] Both the number of people accused of corruption and the amount of money involved in corrupt activities have steadily increased throughout the 1990s and into the twenty-first century.[51] The costs of corruption to the Chinese economy are enormous, with most estimates placing the damage at between 10% and 20% of China's GDP.[52] Many of these costs stem from distortions of investment, are money flows not into areas where it is most likely to be productive, but rather where it will pad the pockets of government cadres. These financial costs do not, of course, take into account the anger generated among the Chinese people as corruption increasingly has become a way of life. Government officials routinely take bribes, sell government offices, engage in insider trading, and even cooperate with organized crime.[53] For a Chinese wanting to get a better housing assignment, a promotion, a license to open a shop, or virtually anything that requires government approval, a payoff is often the price of doing business. The constant need to pay bribes, the spectacle of government officials enriching themselves at the cost of others, and the open flouting of rules in a society that still prides itself as adhering to socialist principles understandably breeds resentment against the regime that fosters this hypocrisy.

Making matters worse, there is every indication that corruption will continue to flourish in China. With the end of Mao's totalitarian rule it is less likely that a corrupt official will be caught and, if he is, that he will be punished severely. The monitoring system of the Maoist era, in which everyone watched everyone else and where mass campaigns exhorted the people to turn in crooked officials, is no more. As for the few who do get caught, according to a 1997 report by the Central Discipline Inspection Commission (CDIC), 82% of Communist Party members determined to have committed corrupt acts received virtually no punishment.[54] When highly publicized punishments for high-level officials do occur, they are more likely to stem from using corruption as an excuse for a political purge than as a sanction against corruption itself.

While the risks and penalties of corruption are negligible, the possibilities to attain wealth have exploded in recent years. Corruption thrives because a privatized economy has so many more opportunities to make money than one run under socialist precepts. The Chinese economy is flush with cash. Private entrepreneurs, foreign investors, and the Chinese government itself all seek an edge in getting the best return on their capital. With so much money sloshing around, it is not surprising that more than a little finds its way into the wallets of government officials. Corruption also stems from the devolution of power from the center to the provinces. As local cadres establish control in the countryside in the absence of central authorities, their word becomes law, creating temptations to use their power for personal enrichment. If someone seeks to establish a factory, takes over a peasant's land, or needs help resolving a criminal dispute, some government official will almost always need to be paid off. Moreover, because it is unclear as to just what is and is not legal, corruption exists because no one is certain just what corruption is.[55] It is virtually impossible to become rich in China without breaking some rule, written or implied. There is little doubt that corruption will continue to grow in China, hurting the economy and, even more important, the support of the Chinese people for government officials who enrich themselves at the expense of the citizens they are supposed to serve.

RURAL AND URBAN GRIEVANCES

Much of the rage directed against the Chinese government is rooted in the countryside. About 80% of the Chinese population, or some 850 million people, live in rural areas, and a great many are unhappy. Their anger stems from many sources but has in common the realization that the Chinese government has favored urban residents at the expense of peasants. Of particular concern is the government's seizure of rural land with little or no compensation.[56] China's *Economic Daily* has estimated that as many as 200 million farmers have been displaced by the conversion of agricultural land for everything from industrial zones to golf courses.[57]

Peasants are also furious about taxation. The government supposedly limits taxes for rural dwellers, but local cadres, anxious to build roads and schools and knowing that they can expect little support from the central government, routinely go well beyond any tax cap.[58] The declining income of peasants makes matters worse. Chinese peasants benefited from the ending of the Maoist communes in the late 1970s and the creation of private plots. Starting in the mid-1990s, however, farm income plummeted because of falling prices for grain and rising prices for farm tools and fertilizers. As China becomes more integrated into the world economy and assumes obligations of free trade, Chinese farmers are finding it increasingly difficult to compete with agribusinesses from other countries.[59] An increase in rural poverty and a widening income gap between those living in the countryside and the city is the outcome.

Chinese farmers are also unhappy because they are unhealthy. The World Health Organization estimates that some 80% of the Chinese health budget is spent in the cities, leaving less than 10% of Chinese peasants with health care protection (compared to 90% in the Maoist era).[60] Chinese peasants face political discrimination as well. Unlike workers, peasants do not have their own representative body and are counted as only one-quarter of a person in seats in the national parliament. Their lack of political clout may explain why in parts of the country-side the state is all but absent, with traditional clans or criminal gangs filling the vacuum.[61] Other complaints of Chinese peasants include birth control policies that limit the size of families, thus diminishing the pool of labor and caretakers for the elderly; a household registration system that inhibits migration to the cities; growing pollution; and abusive officials.[62] Not surprisingly violent protests in the countryside have increased markedly over the past decade.

As important as unrest in the countryside may become, the most serious threats to the Chinese leadership stem from the cities (which explains their pref-erential treatment). It is in the cities where the burgeoning middle class is located, the economy is centered, and the elite of the Communist Party lives. None of this bodes well for the Chinese leadership, because the city dwellers are just as en-raged, if not more so, than their counterparts in the countryside. Much of their anger stems from rising unemployment. The official urban unemployment rate is a low 3%, but rises to 10% if unregistered and temporarily laid-off workers are counted, and may reach an astonishing 20% in 2010. Nearly one-third of the over 4 million Chinese graduating from universities in 2005 still had not found jobs a year later.[63] Some 50 million unemployed Chinese living in cities come from failed state-owned enterprises, a number that is expected to increase as privatiza-tion continues.[64]

The urban unemployed also come from the countryside, as poverty-stricken peasants desperately seek work. Over the past decade, China has seen the largest migration of rural workers in the history of mankind. In just the past few years, Chinese cities have taken in some 114 million rural workers, with the expectation that they will have to assimilate between 300 and 400 million more in the com-ing decades. China's urbanization rate is projected to increase from 39% in 2002 to 60% in 2020, an unprecedented transformation for such a short time.[65] Many of the formerly rural peasants moving to the cities exist as a "floating population" with no jobs or fixed address. They come to cities seeking employment, health care, and education but often get nothing. Instead, they live on the fringes of society, as a sullen, alienated group of young men. The existence of large youth cohorts in cities, unemployed, with few job prospects and no safety net is a formula for vi-olent unrest.[66] As people pour into the cities, it is unclear where jobs are going to be found for all these new arrivals, especially if the Chinese economy falters. In the past, unemployed Chinese workers could, as a last resort, always return to the land, but no more. For the first time in Chinese history, large numbers of its citi-zens are both unemployed and landless, leaving them with few or no options.[67]

In the countryside and especially in the cities, crime has become a serious problem, adding to the grievances the Chinese people have against their government. Since the late 1970s, the crime rate has tripled, and since most crimes go unreported the situation is probably even worse than the official statistics indicate.[68] Under Mao, crime prevention worked because people were responsible for each other. Neighborhood organizations, work units, and millions of informers kept the population in line. This kind of surveillance no longer exists in China. Instead, with one officer for every thousand residents, China is one of the most underpoliced countries in the world.[69] Aside from lack of monitoring, China's crime rate stems from its capitalist economy and mounting inequality, presenting temptations and frustrations that did not exist during the Maoist era. Rural migrants are a particularly serious problem, accounting for as much as 90% of crime in some cities.[70]

Government efforts to stop the rising numbers of rapes, robberies, and murders are ineffectual at best. China executes approximately 15,000 people a year — 97% of the world's total — but that has not made a dent in the surging criminal activity. In some situations, government action has made matters worse, as prosecutors and judges often cooperate with the very criminals they are supposed to put behind bars.[71] When people wax nostalgic about the Maoist era, the memory of safe streets and lack of fear from fellow citizens is a major reason why. The inability or unwillingness of the regime to put a stop to crime cannot help but erode its support among the Chinese population.

GENDER IMBALANCES

Another major source of anger and instability in China lies in its large percentage of young, unmarried males. Normal sex ratios are between 105 and 107 male births for every 100 female births. In China, the ratio is 120 to 100, with some regions' ratios ranging from 131 to a staggering 400 males for every 100 females.[72] Most Chinese prefer to have boys, and with the introduction of ultrasound machines in the mid-1980s combined with the general availability of abortion on demand, they now are able to select the sex of their children.[73] Youth bulges historically have been associated with political instability, with most major revolutions occurring in developing countries that have a large youth cohort.[74] China's history bears out the revolutionary potential of youth, especially young men. Natural catastrophes that caused many deaths in China often produced spikes in female infanticide, creating disproportionate numbers of young men in the population. These male, youth bulges in turn helped bring about some of China's worst cases of civil strife.[75] In the nineteenth century, when sex ratios went over the 120 to 100 limit in some regions of China, gangs of young men replaced the local governments and imposed control over millions of people.[76]

What is new today is that technology has allowed these sex imbalances to exist not just in isolated regions but throughout the country, and that the sheer numbers of unattached men are far higher than they have ever been. Already there are tens of millions of surplus males, what Valerie Hudson and Andrea Den Boer call "bare branches," men who are unmarried, uneducated, and unemployed. Using the conservative ratio of 120 males to 100 females, their numbers will swell to 40 million by 2020.[77] If China is fortunate, these roving bands of youths will simply engage in criminal activity. Nevertheless, it is equally plausible that these young men, almost all of whom have no future to speak of, will engage in political violence, directly or indirectly challenging Communist rule.

SEPARATIST MOVEMENTS

Separatist movements provide another set of grievances against the Chinese government. China is a remarkably homogenous country, with some 94% of its population classified as Han Chinese. Nevertheless, minorities predominate in some areas and, given the huge population of China, even small percentages create a critical mass of dissidents that could cause trouble for the Chinese government. Of particular concern are the provinces of Xinjiang and Tibet, which became a part of China (along with Taiwan) in the late seventeenth and early eighteenth centuries during the Qing Dynasty. Xinjiang is China's westernmost and largest province, making up one-sixth of China's landmass. Half of its population are Uighurs, a Turkish-speaking Muslim people, with the remaining half Han Chinese. Many of the Uighurs, of whom there are about 8 million in Xinjiang, do not consider themselves to be Chinese. Instead, they see themselves as a distinct ethnic group with a common language, history, religion, and culture that has much more in common with the newly independent states of Central Asia (Kazakhstan, Kyrgyzstan, and Tajikistan) than with China.[78] The Uighurs resent the influx of Han Chinese (who made up only 6% of the population in 1949), many of whom do not speak their language, discriminate against the Uighur population, and snatch up the best jobs, contributing to rising Uighur unemployment.[79]

The efforts of the Chinese government to improve conditions by allowing Uighurs to have their own schools and practice their religion have backfired. The establishment of the schools has reinforced separatist identity and the more than 20,000 mosques built since the early 1980s (there were only 2,000 in 1978) fuel concerns about Islamic extremism. These worries are not unfounded, as some

Uighur exiles have become members of Al Qaeda, while Uighur separatist groups (one of which was declared a terrorist organization by the U.S. State Department) operate from bases in Central Asian states, where they openly seek independence for Xinjiang.[80] The Uighurs have even struck in Beijing, placing a bomb in a bus that wounded 30 in 1997.[81] Violent incidents, such as bombings, riots, and assassination attempts, have increased over the past decade (there were over 1,000 incidents in 2001 alone), producing brutally repressive tactics by the Chinese regime that have been condemned by Amnesty International.[82] Coping with the challenges presented by the Uighurs will not be easy for the Chinese leadership. To allow the Uighurs to practice their religion and customs risks accelerating their efforts to disengage from China and declare independence. Efforts to assimilate the Uighurs and colonize Xinjiang with influxes of Han Chinese have been met with increasingly violent resistance. So long as the Chinese government is unable to find a solution to Uighur discontent, their anger and violence will only intensify.

Grievances against the Chinese regime also arise in Tibet. When the Chinese Communists conquered Tibet in 1950, they promised that the Tibetans would be able to keep their way of life and manage their own affairs. Instead, the Chinese regime has worked systematically to destroy Tibetan culture, eviscerate its religion, and fully assimilate it into the People's Republic. The Chinese government has limited the teaching of Tibetan in schools, reduced the number of monks and nuns, closed religious schools, selected their own successor to the Dalai Lama (the Tibetan religious leader), and flooded Tibet with Han Chinese.[83] In response, the Tibetans launched a series of revolts against Chinese rule. A major rebellion failed in 1959, causing some 80,000 Tibetans and the Dalai Lama to flee to India. Following the abortive revolt, the Tibetans continued to wage guerrilla war against the Chinese government and even established their own regime in exile. Major demonstrations erupted in Tibet during the 1980s, causing the Chinese to declare martial law in 1989, and there were two days of rioting in Lhasa in May 1993.[84]

In March 2008, riots killed scores of Tibetans and Han Chinese in Lhasa as Tibetans violently protested Chinese rule. Chinese authorities eventually suppressed the violence, but the potential for unrest to erupt again is high. Young Tibetan emigrés lack the restraint of the Dalai Lama, both in tactics and goals. Tibet remains the poorest administrative unit in China, ranking last in per capita income, life expectancy, and literacy. Especially disturbing for the Chinese is American support for Tibetan resistance. Not only did the United States back Tibetan guerrillas from 1959 to 1971, Washington still supports Tibetan exiles through the

Tibetan Policy Act of 2002 and its appointment of a senior State Department official as special coordinator for Tibetan issues.[85]

No one expects that the Tibetans or the Uighurs on their own could bring down the Chinese government. The Tibetan and Uighur insurgents are far from the capital, too weak and disorganized to pose a serious threat to Chinese rule. Nevertheless, if the Chinese regime is weakened by other factors, such as a major downturn in the economy, dissidents in Xinjiang and Tibet are likely to exploit the situation, adding to the woes of China's leadership when it can least afford another challenge.

HEALTH CONCERNS

Another source of anger is the manner in which the Chinese government has reacted against the outbreak of serious diseases. With over a billion people living often in close proximity to one another and a history marked by horrific epidemics, it is not surprising that so many in China fear the spread of disease and look to their government for protection. Although the Maoist regime made impressive strides against several diseases such as syphilis and tuberculosis, the response to more contemporary outbreaks has left many Chinese frustrated and enraged. SARS (severe acute respiratory syndrome) first appeared in China in late 2002. While health officials quickly detected the virus, incompetence, censorship, and an ineffective health care system combined to make a bad situation worse. After the government took too long to even acknowledge that SARS existed in China, the response to its outbreak proved to be too little, too late. SARS wound up killing approximately 350 people in China while sickening some 5,000. These are not large numbers in such a huge population, but the disease's psychological and economic effects proved far greater. Because of the anger of the Chinese people at their government's tepid and inept response, even the normally quiescent media expressed outrage, resulting in the firing of several government officials. Tourism took a major hit, contributing to an economic slowdown that sliced at least one percentage point off of China's GDP.[86] Most important, the ineffectual response to SARS demonstrated the potential of far greater harm if China fails to respond adequately to a much greater health threat, namely, the outbreak of AIDS.

AIDS is an especially pernicious disease. As Nicholas Eberstadt notes, it kills large numbers, those who are afflicted tend to be the young and productive, and the victims take a long time to die, during which they require expensive medical treatment that can range from between $6,000 and $15,000 per year per person.[87]

While much of the attention has been focused on Africa, China's AIDS population has exploded, making it perhaps the world's leader in the number of AIDS victims. Estimates of just how many Chinese have AIDS vary greatly. The Chinese government declared that (in 2002) approximately 1 million had AIDS, while the United States calculated the number at between 1 and 2 million, and a UN official said it was 6 million.[88] Whatever the exact figure, all indications are that the disease will continue to grow due to illegal drug use, unsafe sex practices (especially among the 100 million floating migrants), and blood transfusions from HIV-tainted blood. China and UNAIDS (the Joint United Nations Program on HIV/AIDS) estimate the increase in AIDS victims at between 20% and 30% per year, meaning the number of those afflicted will double in 30 months.[89] By 2010, China could have as many as 20 million of its citizens with AIDS, and by 2020 that number could rise to as many as 80 million.[90]

Any country would be staggered by this calamity, but China, with an inadequate health system, is especially ill prepared. Despite the immense challenge posed by AIDS, the Chinese government has done relatively little. It has provided meager funding, failed to publicize the extent of the disease, and lagged in educating the public on prevention measures.[91] Anger against the Chinese government is virtually certain to rise, as increasing numbers of sick people (and their families) question why their government is not doing more to stem the tide of the epidemic. Moreover, the Chinese economy is likely to be severely hurt, as even a minor epidemic would cut productivity growth in half, while a more serious outbreak would eliminate productivity growth altogether.[92]

Growing concern about the environment is still another source of discontent against the Chinese government. China is one of the most polluted countries in the world and despite heroic efforts to make up for past transgressions, all indications are that conditions will worsen. Nine of the world's ten worst cities in air pollution are in China, contributing to a situation in which some 400 million Chinese live in areas with poor air quality.[93] It is not uncommon for people in some cities to wake up to an inch of coal dust on the ground, dust that chokes lungs, sickens the population, and turns day into night.[94] Since China depends on coal (much of which is dirty) to meet two-thirds of its energy needs, China's air pollution problem is likely to worsen in the coming years, and with many of the new factories spewing out smoke in the rural areas, the countryside will be especially hard hit.

Some 300 million Chinese, mostly in the north, lack access to clean drinking water.[95] Since 1978, the demand for water from cities and industry increased fivefold, while water supplies only increased by 100%, creating a situation in which more than half of China's major cities are short of water.[96] Seventy percent of the lakes and rivers are polluted and acid rain falls on one-third of the country.[97] Less rainfall and warmer temperatures have disrupted underground water channels, decreasing the flow into the Yellow River (China's second largest), raising concerns for its future and the scores of cities that depend on its water. Because the surface runoff of rivers is very small in north China, even small amounts of pollutants have had devastating effects, making increasing amounts of water unfit for drinking and irrigation.[98] Misuse of chemical fertilizers has dramatically reduced the production of scarce arable land (China has one of the lowest ratios of arable land per farmer in the world), while forests are being replaced by deserts that have already swallowed up 27% to 38% of China and threaten much more.[99]

China's deteriorating environment places the regime in a dilemma. Lessening China's environmental degradation requires slowing down the economy, but that would create more unemployment, adding to the threats to the government. Allowing the environment to continue its downward spiral endangers future economic growth while spurring ever greater numbers of mass protests. Whatever the regime decides, it is all but certain that environmental issues will only grow in importance, posing an increasing threat to China's stability.

FAILED INSTITUTIONS

What makes all these grievances so threatening to the Chinese leadership is that they have yet to develop institutions to respond to them. Samuel Huntington's classic, *Political Order in Changing Societies*, argued persuasively that the inability of a regime to meet rising demands through the creation of effective institutions undermines political stability.[100] Despite the turbulent changes taking place in Chinese society, China remains a one-party state. So long as the Chinese government is beholden to the Communist Party, critical state institutions, such as the courts, representative bodies, and the media, have not acquired the autonomy and adaptability needed to cope with the demands placed on them.[101]

The Chinese have made some efforts to make their government more accountable, but these have been halfhearted and have never compromised the Party's ultimate authority. Most villages, for example, hold elections with several competing candidates. Nevertheless, the Party exercises substantial control over these elections, making sure that no one wins who is opposed to its agenda.[102] Chinese citizens are allowed to petition (*xinfang*) the government to deal with their grievances, but they do so at the risk of being beaten by authorities for their audacity. Of those who make it through the process, only a tiny handful actually get their problems resolved.[103] The National People's Congress is supposed to represent the Chinese masses, but the Communist Party selects its key personnel and makes certain that its decisions do not conflict with the Party's goals. Similarly, the courts are instruments of the Party, which explains why very few get to sue the state and only a tiny number ever emerge victorious.[104] The media remain under the control of the Party, which severely limits the kinds of stories they can report. When courageous journalists nevertheless publicize stories the government opposes, such as *New York Times* researcher Zhao Yan, who broke the news about Jiang Zemin's retirement, they are imprisoned on trumped-up charges.[105] In sum, Chinese institutions exist not to respond to people's demands, but rather to keep the Communist Party in power. This strategy may work for a while, but by crippling the institutions that enable lawful demands to be made, the Party becomes vulnerable to some future explosion of festering unrest that it will be ill equipped to meet.

RIGHT TO REBEL

Mounting grievances in China matter because they are directed against a government that is rapidly losing its legitimacy. The Chinese Communist Party bases its right to govern on Marxist-Leninist ideology. Acceptance of the objective truths of communism as the best way for the Chinese to organize their society justifies the one-party rule that has existed since 1949. Virtually no one, however, including those in the Party itself, believes in Marxism-Leninism.[106] Surveys consistently show that fewer than 10% of Party *members* seek to bring communism to China. Instead, Chinese join the Communist Party to make money by putting them in a position to run companies or gain access to foreign investors.[107] While few believe in communism, many believe in God. According to one poll almost a third of the Chinese population — some 400 million people — are religious, further demonstrating the declining appeal of ideology in the People's Republic.[108] Central to communist ideology is the notion that contradictions in capitalism will bring about its demise. But what about the contradiction of an ostensibly socialist regime governing a capitalist, increasingly religious country that no longer even pays lip service to Marxist-Leninist dictates? As the former Soviet Union demonstrated, when the governing elite loses faith in the principles that justify its rule, regime collapse is a likely outcome. Whether China can forestall such an eventuality remains to be seen.

Aside from ideology, the Chinese government can earn the loyalty of its citizens by meeting their needs. The problem, however, is that the same Party rule that undermines ideological legitimacy also prevents the Chinese government from doing its job. Since the Party is the supreme power in the land, the government is constantly hobbled by Party interference. Education reform, rural reconstruction, economic investment, crime control, and virtually every other governmental policy or initiative is subject to Party veto. Inasmuch as the government lacks the power to enforce its decisions, it is not surprising that these decisions often are ignored. Moreover, effective governance is prevented by perpetual conflict between the center and the periphery. There is no tradition of federalism or shared power in Chinese Communist history, which raises questions of how far the central government's authority reaches. Over the past few years, this war is being won in the provinces, where local cadres routinely ignore or undermine dictates from Beijing.[109] When quick, effective governmental action is called for, the result instead is often paralysis.

Government dysfunction is everywhere. As discussed, basic economic responsibilities such as overseeing the banking system, enforcing contracts, and protecting property rights are left unmet. Corruption is rampant, further eroding the Chinese people's belief that the government has earned the right to rule over them. The state has also failed miserably in its regulation of the safety of the workplace. Coal mine accidents routinely kill thousands and do so at a rate 20 times greater than the world average and 100 times greater than in the United States.[110] Horror stories of horrendous working conditions, exploding fireworks factories, and illegal exploitation of workers abound. Because of poor roads, inadequate driving training, and mechanically suspect cars, a person is 30 times more likely to die in a car accident in China than in the United States.[111] Under Communist rule, even the very poor could count on medical treatment from government-sponsored "barefoot doctors." In the post-Mao era, those who cannot afford medical care are turned away from hospitals, while diseases such as cholera and schistosomiasis, thought to have ended in the 1950s through governmental action, are making a comeback. No wonder that the World Health Organization places China in the bottom quarter of countries in health care.[112] If the Chinese government cannot provide a better life for its people, and especially if the structural flaws in the Chinese economy produce a protracted slowdown, the already shaky legitimacy of the Communist leadership could well collapse.

If ideology and competence cannot bestow upon the Chinese regime its "mantle of heaven," what about appeals to Chinese nationalism? Chinese nationalism has in fact emerged as an important rallying force, as seen by the nationwide anger expressed at the Japanese for failing to apologize adequately for war crimes during World War II and at the United States for its support of Taiwan and efforts to contain Chinese influence in Asia. The Chinese government has skillfully manipulated these and other resentments to enhance its popularity. Nevertheless, fanning the flames of nationalism is very much a double-edged sword that, once unleashed, can undermine the very government that seeks to exploit it. As political scientist Peter Hays Gries convincingly argues, much of the "popular nationalism" of the Chinese masses is not directed by the regime, but instead is very much a bottom-up process. In incidents such as the 1999 American bombing of China's embassy in Belgrade (which the Chinese insisted was not an accident) and the 2001 collision of a Chinese aircraft with an American spy plane, the widespread fury displayed on the Chinese "street" was spontaneous, deeply felt, and beyond the control of the government. Rather than the regime creating and controlling nationalist anger to serve its ends, the Chinese leadership found its policy options constrained by having to appease an increasingly inconsolable citizenry.[113]

It is easy to see how this nationalist fury can get out of hand and turn on the regime itself if the Chinese leadership, for example, fails to reverse a Taiwanese declaration of independence. Even in the absence of a crisis, the growing tendency of Chinese nationalism to identify not with communism but with the Chinese motherland and race spells trouble for a government that still bases its right to rule on Communist ideology.[114] Appealing to nationalism may be the best hope of the Chinese regime to secure the support of its subjects, but it is an approach that is fraught with risks.

How long the Chinese government can maintain even a shred of legitimacy in the face of the bankruptcy of its ruling ideology, abysmal government performance, and uncontrollable nationalism remains uncertain. What is clear is that violence against the regime will not be halted either because people are satisfied with the policies of their government or because they believe the government has the right to rule over them. If the Chinese regime is to forestall collapse, it must convince groups that challenging the government cannot hope to succeed. Sadly, for China, there is good reason to believe that in the coming years it will not be up to meeting this vital task.

VIOLENCE PAYS

During the Maoist years, launching an insurgency against the ruling regime was unthinkable. Informers lurked everywhere, the secret police enmeshed itself in society, and everyone knew they were being watched by someone. With the enthusiastic support of the government demanded of every individual in countless campaigns, even *thinking* rebellious thoughts could be fatal. Contemporary

China is very different. The Chinese government's ability and willingness to crush dissent has been dramatically weakened. At the same time, antigovernment groups are much better equipped to link up with each other, raising the threat that localized protests will become national. There is also a growing sense that the Chinese are no longer afraid of their government, encouraging the belief that a successful challenge against the regime can be made.

At first impression, the suppression capabilities of the Chinese regime appear daunting. China's military forces include almost 2.5 million men and women in the army, navy, and air force, and about 4 million police and paramilitary troops.[115] Over time, the number of security personnel devoted to internal stability has increased, while the regular military has been reduced, suggesting that the Chinese leadership recognizes that its greatest threats come from within the country and not from outside attack. Using informants, surveillance, and rapid arrests, internal security forces have prevented the tens of thousands of protests erupting in China over the past decade from developing into a widespread revolt. The Chinese leadership has also done much to prevent violent protest from emerging in the first place. Although no longer a totalitarian society, China has achieved a large degree of control over information through censorship and the threat of punishment, stifling dissent before it can erupt. To deal with the threat posed by the Internet, the Ministry of Public Security has employed tens of thousands of monitors to ensure that threatening websites are not accessed and that chat rooms contain no antigovernmental activity. The regime has become skillful at coopting intellectuals and entrepreneurs, making it clear that promotions and access to wealth are dependent on toeing the party line.[116]

Despite these efforts, the Chinese leadership in the post-Mao era knows it is no longer secure from internal revolt. It knows this first because it has already confronted challenges that have shaken its rule, the most serious being the 1989 Tiananmen demonstrations. Begun by students in the spring of 1989 to encourage greater liberalization, the protests quickly spread throughout China, as tens of millions of Chinese, including workers and intellectuals, joined the student movement. While the government pondered how to respond, the demands of the protestors escalated, with some even calling for the establishment of democratic rule and the end of the Communist Party. Although some Chinese leaders, most notably Party head Zhao Ziyang, called for compromise with the students, they were overruled by Party elders led by the former head of China, Deng Xiaoping, who feared a civil war that would physically remove the leadership from power. With the students in control of Tiananmen Square in the heart of Beijing and some soldiers marching in support of their cause, the elders ordered a brutal crackdown. Elements of the People's Liberation Army (PLA), many brought in from far away provinces to ensure that they would obey the regime's orders, murderously suppressed the protest, killing hundreds of students and wounding thousands more in the process. The students' champion, Zhao Ziyang, also fell victim to the protest, ousted by the elders soon after the demonstrations were quelled.[117]

If another Tiananmen-style protest erupted today it might well succeed in toppling the government. The agonizing decision to use force was made by a group of aging Party leaders, veterans of the 1932 Long March, seeking to preserve the Communist rule they had established. None of these individuals are alive today to pressure a ruling elite whose commitment to socialist rule is far more tenuous. Even if the order to violently suppress a demonstration was given, it is far from certain that the PLA today would comply. The PLA has long prided itself on being the *people's* army, not a force that turns its weapons on its fellow Chinese. The PLA opposed using force in Tiananmen and only did so with the greatest reluctance. The PLA of the twenty-first century is a much more professional force, better integrated with society and less ideologically motivated than the military that acted in Tiananmen. Having lost its seat on the Standing Committee of the Politburo in 1997, the PLA will be less beholden to a regime that has tried to cripple its political power and would not want to side with a leadership it believes would crumble in the face of protest.[118] The police would also not be of much help in dealing with widespread disturbances. Many of the new recruits are the same rootless young men who are the source of much of the violence that wracks China. Ill educated and poorly trained, they lack the capability and perhaps the will to stifle major demonstrations, something not lost upon would-be insurgents.[119]

The inability of the Communist Party to monitor and control the Chinese people is another reason that insurgents can hold out hope of successfully confronting the regime. With only around 5% of the general population as Party members, numbers alone were never the principal source of Party influence. Rather, the Party relied on a variety of carrots and sticks to garner its support, many of which no longer exist. Adhering to the Party line may help in getting a good job, but decades of economic reform mean that private markets and local officials play a much larger role in providing benefits to individuals than some cadre in far-off Beijing. Because of post-Mao reforms, the Party no longer controls what people do for a living, where they reside, if they can travel outside the country, and how they get their news. For the vast majority of Chinese who live in rural areas, the Party barely functions. Made up of old men who have long ago stopped believing in communism, it must compete with feudal clans, many of whom engage in criminal activity that the Party is unable or unwilling to stop.[120]

In the cities, the Party has increased its proportion of entrepreneurs, even allowing "capitalists" to serve as members, but only at the cost of further diluting the Party's core principles. The result is a Communist Party that is a shell of its Maoist past. Barely functioning in most areas, ineffective and disrespected where it makes an appearance, the Party arouses resentment without being able to impose its will. As Lenin demonstrated, one-party rule can work only insofar as that Party instills fear and compels obedience. The Chinese Communist Party does neither, which cannot help but encourage those who seek to replace it.

Challenges to the regime also have a greater likelihood of success because it is much easier today to mobilize opposition throughout the country. The thousands of protests that have plagued China in the last several years have been mostly local and short-lived. The nightmare of the Chinese regime, and the hope for those seeking to replace it, is that this dispersed, inchoate discontent will be transformed into a nationwide movement.[121] There are signs that this may indeed occur. Since the Tiananmen protests, China has become a much more wired society, making communications among groups that much easier. Internet and mobile phones hardly existed in China in 1989, while in 2006 there were over 123 million Internet users and over 426 million Chinese with mobile phones.[122] How protestors might use this capability became apparent in April 1999, when more than 10,000 followers of the Falun Gong movement silently surrounded Zhongnanhai, the Chinese government compound. The protest demonstrated that an antigovernment group could organize itself and gather in the center of the capital, all without the Chinese government's knowledge. If the Falun Gong could use new technology to mobilize its supporters, more violent groups could do so as well. Protests anywhere, even in a remote village, instantly become news everywhere. Grievances thought to be parochial are now recognized as widespread. Insurgent leaders seeking to make contact with far-flung followers and like-minded groups have gained the means to do so quickly, cheaply, and beyond the control of the regime.

Encouraging the belief that antigovernment forces can win against the government is the realization that the Chinese leadership is itself divided. From the very beginnings of the Chinese Communist Party in 1921, factionalism, attempted coups, and purges have dominated its politics. In the case of Tiananmen the specter of a divided leadership spurred the demonstrators on, convincing them they had a chance to achieve their objectives and perhaps even topple a weakened regime. In the years after Tiananmen, factionalism and purges continued. After 20 years of relative consensus in support of market reforms, Marxist critics of the Western path taken by the Chinese economy are emerging, complaining of growing inequality, popular unrest, and corruption. There is even some evidence that these critics have supporters in the regime itself.[123]

Within the leadership, disputes have broken out over fundamental policies, such as how much control the Party should exercise over the economy and the political process.[124] At times, elite struggles break out into the open for all to see. During the leadership of Jiang Zemin (1989–2002), six politburo members were purged after being defeated in political struggles. In the fall of 2006, President Hu Jintao, facing dissent from high-ranking Chinese Communist Party members who opposed his efforts to slow down economic growth, purged a powerful Shanghai boss, the most influential leader removed from power since 1995. By firing the leader for "tolerating" corruption, as opposed to being personally corrupt, Hu laid the basis for additional purges.[125] To be sure, such purges might result in the strengthening of the Chinese regime, lessening the chances for rebellion. They could, however, signal to potential protestors that the government is divided and incapable of a forceful response, making widespread violence all the more likely.

Aside from being divided, the Chinese leadership encourages revolt by suggesting that if confronted it will not stand and fight. Chinese officials have already created safe havens to flee to if conditions deteriorate. Foreign passports are provided to family members who have established businesses in other countries funded by the ill-gotten gains of the government officials. Thousands have already left China with tens of billions of dollars of stolen money to escape prosecution for corruption.[126] The same preparations that enable officials to flee to avoid arrest can be used to escape a violent challenge to the regime. Almost all of the top leaders have children living and studying abroad. According to some estimates, China spends more than $4 billion per year to support overseas studies, much of which is devoted to the sons and daughters of senior officials.[127] In addition to providing a quality education to their sons and daughters, these officials are creating a safety net so that they and their children can live elsewhere should the regime collapse.

None of this is to suggest that the Chinese leadership is on the brink of collapse. Chinese officials want to hold on to the perks of power and recognize that dissension in their ranks will encourage those who seek to topple the regime. Nevertheless, they may not be able to control factionalism, despite their best efforts. Moreover, because the elites *can* leave, they are more likely to do so at the first sign of a serious challenge. Knowledge of this cannot help but encourage would-be insurgents to believe that if they press their cause strongly enough, there is a good chance they will be successful.

CATALYSTS

Those who might violently challenge the Chinese regime are not difficult to identify. In the cities, the most sensitive area of Communist control, armies of unemployed workers, destitute and without their "iron rice bowl" of benefits, might join with the swelling ranks of the "floating" population of tens of millions of migrants to protest their plight. In the countryside, millions of peasants, angry at losing their land, rising taxes, falling agricultural prices, and corrupt leadership, may take out their anger at the government that has increasingly failed them.[128] The Chinese military, still smarting over Tiananmen, with its status and ties to the Communist Party diminishing over the past years, could turn on a regime that has failed to provide it with the resources and respect it believes it deserves. The tens of thousands of protests that have wracked China in recent years show it to be ripe for internal conflict. Thus far, these demonstrations have been easily suppressed by government forces. Nevertheless, the development of technology to unite disparate forces, questions about the willingness and ability of the Chinese forces to suppress large-scale protest, and the growing demands of the Chinese people that the government provide them a better life will pose far more potent challenges to Communist rule in the future. With all the conditions present for large-scale instability, all that is needed is some spark to create what could become an uncontrollable conflagration.

Several possibilities threaten to ignite local disputes into nationwide chaos. Economic disaster precipitated by a collapse of the banking system or a crash of the credit markets would likely cause massive violent protest. The legitimacy of the Chinese government rests on performance, on providing the Chinese people with ever greater material benefits. If the hope of the Chinese people for a better life evaporates, so too will support for the Chinese regime. A major foreign policy setback, such as a failed attack on Taiwan, could also bring about challenges to government rule. A Chinese invasion of Taiwan or even lesser uses of force, such as missile attacks, may lead to international isolation and economic sanctions that could undermine the Chinese regime. It cannot be comforting to the Chinese leadership that the potentially catastrophic decision to use force against Taiwan may be driven by others, namely, the demands of an aroused public or declarations of independence emanating from Taipei.

Natural disasters often preceded the end of dynasties, both because they suggested the government had lost the "mandate of heaven" and because inept official responses inflamed the populace. The Chinese government may fail to respond adequately to hurricanes or floods, occurrences made more likely due to environmental degradation. Even more serious would be a mixed natural / man-made disaster, like the collapse of the mammoth Three Gorges Dam, which is located in an earthquake-prone area. It is easy to imagine the Chinese regime failing to contain the spread of AIDS or being unable to cope with a repeat of a SARS-like epidemic. Especially if it appeared that a failed government response resulted from corruption, such as placing unqualified officials in positions of power or lacking adequate resources because emergency funds had been diverted for personal use, anger could well morph into uncontrollable violence. A public and bitter leadership struggle might mobilize elements of the armed forces and even the citizenry into supporting competing factions, leading to something that looks a lot like civil war.

China has all the ingredients for a violent, nationwide revolt. Grievances against the government are widespread and growing. The regime lacks legitimacy and, so long as it clings to one-party rule, shows few signs of earning the people's support. The ability of the leadership to suppress violent protest and control dissent is in question at the same time that groups are more and more able to form nationwide links. The leadership itself is increasingly brittle, with exit strategies replacing efforts at a serious rethinking of the wisdom of Leninist rule over an increasingly complex civil society. As long as China continues to grow economically, these contradictions can be managed as dissidents are coopted and the angry are given hope for better times to come. However, if the economy falters — and there is much evidence to believe it might — the ties holding China's society together are likely to unravel, plunging China and the countries that depend on its stability into a nightmare of frightening proportions.

CHAPTER SIX

The Coming Storm

One of the greatest dangers the United States faces in the post–Cold War era is the prospect of civil conflicts tearing up countries that are critical to American interests. The perils raised by these conflicts are different from what American policymakers feared in the past. Historically, American leaders, like the leaders of other great powers, worried most about being attacked by other countries. Those times are gone. While it is too soon to declare international war obsolete, the decline of such conflicts, especially since the end of the Cold War, has been the most important change in international relations since the emergence of states themselves. In those few instances when leaders may choose to go to war, it is highly unlikely that they would do so against the United States. American military might is so overwhelming that any adversary or group of adversaries knows that to attack the United States would be suicidal. There has never been a time in American history when the United States has been as safe from aggression from other countries as it is today.

And yet, the United States cannot afford to be complacent, because the threat of wars *between* countries has been replaced by the threat of wars *within* countries. Civil conflict is so worrisome for two reasons. First, unlike international war, internal war is not going away. The overall number of civil wars has undergone a post–Cold War decline, but civil war still represents the most common form of armed conflict by far. There are few signs that the prevalence of civil conflict will change anytime soon. The causes of peace that played such an important role in virtually eliminating international war, such as the spread of democracy, the existence of nuclear weapons, and the growing belief that war does not pay, do not apply to civil conflicts. At the same time, the causes of civil war are very much with us. The world remains filled with groups nursing intense grievances against illegitimate governments driven by the belief that violence pays. Moreover, because it takes such a small group to plunge a country into violent disorder, the potential for civil conflict will never wholly disappear.

Internal war is also worrisome because its effects go beyond the country where it takes place, at times threatening the vital interests of the United States. America's well-being relies on certain countries maintaining order within their borders. If that order is shattered, so too are American interests. The American economy is dependent on the free access of imported oil at reasonable prices, and robust trade and investment. America's physical security relies on countries maintaining tight controls over their nuclear arsenals. The United States counts on its neighbors to police their borders and safeguard the lives of American citizens living and traveling in their countries. The safety of America's allies depends upon other great powers behaving responsibly.

Each of these interests is threatened by the prospect of civil unrest erupting in key countries. Civil war in Saudi Arabia might deny the United States and much of the rest of the world the oil necessary to keep the international economy afloat. Widespread violence in Pakistan could result in nuclear arms being transferred to terrorist groups, or launched by accident or without authorization. Instability in Mexico would threaten millions of Americans living and traveling there, the security of scores of American cities and towns, a critical economic relationship, and the ability of the United States to stem the flow of illegal immigration and drugs across its southern border. Massive violence throughout China would wreak havoc on America's efforts to finance its budget deficit while threatening the stability and security of America's Asian allies. Insofar as war poses a threat to American interests in the post–Cold War era, it is civil war — not international war — where the principal danger lies.

While the prospect of civil conflict in Saudi Arabia, Pakistan, Mexico, and China poses a deadly threat to the United States, the nature of the threat and the probability of it arising differ with each country. Pakistan is of greatest concern because the most horrific danger faced by the United States is the possibility of one or more of its cities being wiped out by nuclear weapons. A close second is Saudi Arabia and the economic calamity that would occur if the oil fields were ablaze. China and Mexico follow in order of concern, not because the possibilities of Asian instability, economic disruption, and disorder spreading across the American border are trivial, but because the other threats are so overwhelming.

What is noteworthy about all of the threats unleashed by civil war is that many would exist even in the absence of domestic disorder, raising the question of just how important these internal conflicts are to the United States. Civil strife is critically important first because it makes these threats against the United States much more likely to emerge. The argument that states would choose not to pursue policies that would harm America because they would hurt themselves even more by doing so carries little weight when the damage done to the United States is unintentional. It may be true that no Saudi leadership would willingly forgo the revenue from oil exports by launching another embargo, but that is scant comfort when the Saudi oil wells are engulfed in flame due to civil war. We are told that the leaders even of developing countries will act to prevent nuclear weapons accidents or unauthorized uses of nuclear bombs,[1] but that means little when civil disorder causes the government to lose control over its arsenal. It is in the interests of Mexico's government to protect Americans in Mexico while making sure that illegal immigration and drug smuggling does not get out of hand, but a Mexican government preoccupied with widespread unrest may lack the capacity to cope with these problems. Halting the purchase of American treasury notes and attacking Taiwan would be disastrous policies for China, but that is exactly what might happen if the People's Republic found itself convulsed in civil conflict. Effective governments will indeed safeguard American interests from a range of dire threats, but when civil war renders these governments powerless to control what goes on within their borders, the threats they held in check are likely to burst free with fearful consequences for the United States.

Civil conflict is also critical in making potential threats far worse. While a partial embargo of Saudi oil would cause tremendous harm to the world economy, the total loss of Saudi oil as a result of civil war would be even more devastating. A single nuclear weapon falling into the hands of a group like Al Qaeda would be terrible enough. If widespread disorder in Pakistan leads to several nuclear weapons falling under Al Qaeda's control, the horror would be virtually unimaginable. The half million or so illegal immigrants who successfully sneak into the United States each year from Mexico, the tons of illegal drugs smuggled across the border, and concerns over violence spreading to border towns and to Americans in Mexico have caused a great deal of American consternation even when Mexico is relatively stable. If Mexico plunges into civil conflict, all of these problems become much worse. A slowdown of Chinese purchases of American treasury notes would be cause for serious concern; a complete halt in their purchase combined with a rapid sell-off of existing securities would wreak untold havoc on the American economy. A more aggressive China would worry American policymakers, but not as much as a China out of control, pouring out refugees and engaging in diversionary wars. Both because they make threats to vital American interests more likely to occur and because they make these threats far more dangerous, the prospect of civil wars in key states cannot be ignored.

LIKELIHOOD OF UNREST

While each of the countries considered in this study is vulnerable to civil conflict, they differ in the likelihood of it coming about. Civil conflict is most likely to occur in Pakistan, followed by Saudi Arabia, China, and then Mexico. Created in 1947, Pakistan has never quite decided whether it is a state for Muslims, in which a persecuted minority can find safe refuge, or a Muslim state, that is, a country ruled according to Islamic precepts.[2] In part, because Pakistan's very reason for being remains mired in controversy, its governments have come and gone with alarming frequency, with no elected government ever succeeding another. Complicating matters are regional separatist movements (one of which tore the country in half in a brutal civil war in 1971), desperate poverty, wide swaths of territory where the government dares not show its face, increasing anger at leaders who flout democratic principles, and the growing influence of extremist Islamic forces, as befits a country that gave birth to both the Taliban and Al Qaeda. Post-9/11 governments will forever be walking a tightrope between accepting critical assistance from the United States while placating an increasingly anti-American citizenry. No one should be surprised if this balancing act totters, plunging Pakistan into violent disorder.

Saudi Arabia is ripe for internal unrest because the legitimacy of the royal family depends on being able to meet the escalating demands of a young, frustrated population while satisfying the increasingly impossible standards of its extremist Wahhabi clerics. Exacerbating the plight of the Saudi regime are the resentment of tribal minorities and a restive Shiite community, divisions in the military, no clear succession procedures, and terrorist attacks from Al Qaeda (backed by Saudi Arabia's most famous exile, Osama bin Laden). To be sure, the obituary for the Saudi regime has been written many times before and rising oil prices may yet give the Saudi rulers some breathing room. Nevertheless, religiously based monarchies are hardly the wave of the future and the present Saudi leadership shows few signs of being able to undertake meaningful reforms to meet the challenges it faces, especially when the price of oil falls. Saudi Arabia looks more and more like Iran in the late 1970s, and few should be surprised if the Saudi king went the way of the shah.

China's long-term stability is also very much in question. Even officials of the

Chinese government no longer believe in communism, raising doubts about the viability of a regime that rules under its mantle. The ability of the Chinese government to deliver double-digit growth rates each year is highly questionable, especially as it continues to foster wasteful state-owned enterprises and a dysfunctional banking system. As some Chinese become wealthy, the income divide between the rich and poor has grown to alarming proportions. Symptomatic of the unease gripping China is the skyrocketing growth in violent rural unrest, just now being acknowledged in official statistics. China's one-child policy has created a demographic nightmare as young men — who are most likely to engage in violence — make up an increasingly large portion of the population. Masses of unemployed youth roaming the countryside seeking work in hostile and alien cities adds to the unease gripping China. Regional resentments leading to separatist tendencies, environmental degradation, and an explosion in the use of the Internet contribute to the sense that the present order cannot long endure. China's rich history is marked by episodes of violent instability involving the entire country and producing millions of casualties. At this time of rapid economic and social change, China's tradition of insurgency and revolution may well continue into the twenty-first century.

Of the four countries, Mexico is least likely to experience violent unrest in the near future. Fresh from having successfully removed the 70-year reign by the PRI by democratic means and with a growing economy, there are few storm clouds on the immediate horizon. And yet, structural flaws in Mexico point to a very uncertain future. Mexican prosperity is underwritten by oil exports that may disappear in the coming decade, while drug trafficking and the corruption and crime it spawns continue to play a central role in the Mexican economy and society. While some have done well, the income disparities between a rich north and a poor south continue to grow. This divide worsened as a result of the 2006 elections, in which millions of "have nots" refused to accept the excruciatingly close victory of Felipe Calderon over their candidate, Andres Manuel Lopez Obrador, producing mass protests in its wake. To deal with these mounting problems, Mexico has a government in which lame-duck presidents preside over lame-duck, divided legislatures where paralysis is the rule. Making matters worse, Mexico does not control its own fate. Instead, decisions made in Washington on such matters as trade policy and immigration will determine Mexico's future. Mexico's collapse may not be imminent, but its long-term future is hardly secure.

Saudi Arabia, Pakistan, Mexico, and China are not the only countries where the prospect of civil conflict poses risks to the United States, raising the question of which other states warrant American concern and which can be safely ignored.

Determining this requires first identifying threats to American vital interests that might be unleashed by civil conflicts, deciding which states could conceivably pose such threats, and then assessing the likelihood of civil strife actually erupting in those countries. Countries capable of endangering vital American security interests are likely to be great powers themselves or countries that possess weapons of mass destruction, especially nuclear arms. Most great powers (aside from China) are allies of the United States and politically stable, diminishing any potential threat they pose to America's security. An exception is Russia, which if it devolved into civil conflict, raises the threat of both diversionary wars and loose nukes. So far, Russia's leadership and oil wealth have provided it with a surprising degree of stability. Nevertheless, given the potential for Russia unraveling and the horrendous harm that would cause, it is a country that bears close scrutiny. The threat of nuclear proliferation greatly expands the list of countries of concern. Aside from India and North Korea, which have already tested nuclear weapons, Iran, Syria, and Egypt (and Saudi Arabia) may acquire nuclear arms in the next decade or so, and all could fall victim to domestic conflict. The dangers that Pakistan faces of accidents, unauthorized launchings, and extremists gaining control of nuclear weapons would apply to all of these countries as well.

As far as economic threats to vital American interests, no country presents quite the danger posed by a cutoff of Saudi oil. Nevertheless, major oil producers vulnerable to protracted civil unrest include Russia, Venezuela, Nigeria, and of course Iraq. Already engulfed by civil war, Iraq has been able to maintain roughly prewar levels of production largely due to the presence of the American military. Once American forces depart, however, those levels might not be able to be sustained, raising difficulties for the United States and other oil importers, but even a total Iraqi cutoff would not cause nearly the damage of Saudi Arabia going offline. Regarding trade, the United States is fortunate in that, with the exception of Mexico and China, none of its top ten trading partners (accounting for well over half of American trade) are likely to experience serious civil conflict.

While countries such as Russia, North Korea, India, Venezuela, Nigeria, and many of the Middle Eastern states need to be watched as future sources of instability that could threaten key American concerns, even this list is not definitive. As discussed in chapter one, roughly half the world's countries are at risk to succumbing to major civil unrest. Any one of them could threaten vital American interests by endangering Americans living and traveling within their borders, by creating a "failed state" that serves as a sanctuary for terrorists, or by spilling over its violence to countries where American interests are engaged. Given the virtually limitless number of states that could conceivably harm America if engulfed in civil conflict, it makes sense for American policymakers to focus their efforts on Saudi Arabia, Pakistan, Mexico, and China, where the combination of risk of civil war and impact on American interests makes them the most dangerous places.

RESPONDING TO THREATS OF CIVIL CONFLICT

In the coming years, it is likely that Saudi Arabia, Pakistan, China, or Mexico will undergo massive civil strife, unleashing threats that endanger vital American interests. Responding to this challenge should be an American priority, but the United States is still caught up in a world where threats to American concerns come from the purposeful actions of other countries, not the unintended harm spun off by domestic strife. The 9/11 attacks demonstrate that it is very difficult to prepare for events that stem from new kinds of threats. This makes it all the more important that serious thought be given to just how the United States, and indeed the world community, can cope with the implications of civil conflict in key states.

The first approach worth considering to deal with threats stemming from civil violence is deterrence. Deterrence played a central role in the Cold War, when the United States and the Soviet Union protected themselves from nuclear attack by the mutual threat of massive retaliation. In the post–Cold War era, deterrence might be expected to play an equally central role in safeguarding American security, especially given America's extraordinary ability to punish those who might threaten its interests. Deterrence, however, is not very effective against unintended threats. If no one is actively behind the threat, if there is no defined "agency," then there is no one to be deterred. Nor is deterrence useful against terrorists who lack a "return address" and thus cannot be punished, or whose embrace of martyrdom makes no punishment costly enough to dissuade them from lashing out at the United States. These qualifications raise questions on the utility of deterrence to protect America from the threats unleashed from civil wars.

Assessing the effectiveness of deterrence for potential civil wars requires reviewing the principal threats to be deterred, who is behind the threats, and their motivations for acting as they do. For Saudi Arabia, America is most concerned about the loss of Saudi oil to the world market for six months or more. Those who would destroy the oil fields include a wide variety of groups, such as disgruntled members of the royal family, disaffected Shias, angry tribal members, and Islamists perhaps working with Al Qaeda. Their reasons for attacking the oil fields include toppling the Saudi regime by depriving it of its principal source of income, destroying the fields to harm the United States and the West, or simply as an act of vandalism when facing defeat. Oil production could also be seriously impaired by inadvertent destruction in the course of widespread fighting.

At best, American deterrence would play only a modest role in halting attacks on the oil fields. Once disorder erupted and it became clear that the Saudi regime was incapable of suppressing the challenges on its own, the United States could make it clear to the insurgents that any attack on the oil fields would prompt a devastating American retaliation. Such a threat would cost the United States little, and given the stakes involved, would be highly credible. Nevertheless, the threat would almost certainly not succeed in deterring the insurgents. Attacks against the Saudi regime might begin with assaults on key choke points in the oil fields, making deterrent threats too late to be effective. Even if the oil installations have not been attacked, the belief by insurgents that forestalling oil production for an appreciable amount of time would topple the hated Saudi regime may well be stronger than the inhibiting effect of any American deterrent threat. Insurgents facing defeat or caught up in the heat of battle would have little incentive to halt their attacks on the oil installations. Terrorist groups seeking to lash out against the United States or Islamist forces who see oil as the source of Saudi Arabia's impurity would similarly not be deterred by the threat of punishment. Nor will deterrence play any role if the oil fields are damaged in the course of fighting, with no deliberate effort to bring about their destruction. The rapidity in which attacks would likely be launched, the strong motivations of the attackers to wreak destruction, and the lack of control over the course of the attack make deterrence an ineffective policy to safeguard Saudi oil production.

Deterrence would similarly have little impact on stemming Mexican violence. If internal violence wracks Mexico, the United States faces threats from spreading disorder, an increase in drug trafficking and illegal immigration, harm done to the American economy as trade and investment suffer, and the prospect of millions of Americans being caught up in the ensuing chaos. What these threats have in common is the lack of any central authority who could be persuaded not to act in ways that would hurt American interests. With no one in charge, there is no one to respond to American threats, undermining the ability of deterrence to safeguard American concerns. This is especially the case with what would worry Washington most — the fate of Americans living and traveling in Mexico. Widespread violence that threatens the lives of these Americans would almost certainly be unpredictable and uncontrollable — not subject to the rational calculations of deterrence. At the margins, the United States could try to deter groups seeking to take advantage of the disorder in ways that would exacerbate the threats to the United States, such as drug cartels and criminal gangs profiting from illegal immigration. A warning that the United States would take harsh reprisals against these groups and their leaders might cause them to refrain from acting in ways inimical to American concerns. This kind of approach, however, is unlikely to be effective. Fear of the United States has had little deterrent effect on drug lords and the illegal immigration network when Mexico is stable. In the chaos of civil strife, it is difficult to believe that the United States would be able to identify those threatening American interests, much less persuade them to desist.

Deterrence would also not play any significant role in dealing with Chinese unrest. A China wracked with civil conflict threatens the United States by interfering with China's ability to support the American economy through the purchase of American treasury notes and by lessening the extensive trade that occurs between the two countries. Chinese unrest may also threaten American allies in Asia by encouraging the Chinese government to pursue an aggressive foreign policy, by unleashing a flood of refugees, and through the spillover of violence to neighboring states. Those behind the civil conflict might include ethnic minorities, jobless youth, regional separatists, rural workers, unemployed city dwellers, or angry military factions. Their motivations would range from sheer anger at the situation they find themselves in to a desire to topple the regime. Whatever the cause, it is difficult to see how American deterrence could work to end instability in China. As with the other possibilities of civil unrest, there is likely to be no clear, identifiable leadership upon whom a deterrent threat could be addressed. The sheer size and power of China would also make it very unlikely that any American deterrent threat would be credible, given the dangers Washington would face of becoming enmeshed in a Chinese civil war. Just as American deterrence played no role when China became engulfed in instability during its civil war in the late 1940s and the Cultural Revolution in the late 1960s, it is difficult to believe that American deterrence would be a factor in preventing China from once again falling victim to widespread disorder.

One area where deterrence might be able to play some role is in dissuading the Chinese leadership from dealing with civil unrest by pursuing a diversionary war, most likely against Taiwan. The Chinese leadership might calculate that an attack against Taiwan is just what they need to fire up nationalism to regain the support of a restive citizenry, given that appeals to ideology are likely to ring hollow. If Taiwan's leaders take advantage of Chinese unrest to declare independence, the Chinese leadership may believe it has no choice but to attack Taiwan in order to hold on to power against what would surely be an enraged populace. By warning China that striking out at Taiwan would provoke a fierce and forceful American response, the Chinese leadership might be convinced to refrain from taking forceful action. The Chinese regime, unlike rebellious Chinese groups, has a return address and is sensitive to costs, seemingly making it susceptible to deterrent threats. Nevertheless, if the Chinese leadership believes its survival depends on launching a diversionary war and/or questions America's willingness to follow through on threats that would endanger the security of the United States as well, then American deterrence is likely to fail.

The prospect of Pakistani nuclear weapons falling into the hands of those who would use them against American allies or the United States itself is the worst nightmare that civil unrest can bring about. Internal disorder, by creating chaos, diverting troops, and perhaps causing nuclear sites to be the targets of attacks, makes this horror all too likely. Groups who might seize Pakistani nuclear weapons include homegrown Islamists, members of Al Qaeda and the Taliban, and disgruntled Pakistani military and government officials. Their wide-ranging motivations could include toppling the Pakistani regime, settling scores with India, and punishing America for its policies in the Islamic world. Efforts at deterrence by the United States are unlikely to be effective. Deterrence would play no role in the event of accidents or unauthorized launchings. Accidents cannot be deterred, since the threat is unintended, and it is impossible to be confident of deterring every fanatic who might gain control of nuclear arms. It is troubling, given deterrence's failure in these instances, that the possibilities for accidents and unauthorized launchings rise so precipitously in times of civil conflict.

There are, however, certain limited instances where deterrence might be effective against nuclear threats from a Pakistan in turmoil. Ironically, deterrence would work best in the event of an insurgent success, rather than a protracted failure. If a rebel group succeeded in toppling the Pakistani regime and establishing a government of its own, the new leadership, no matter how odious, would still have a "return address." Since the new leaders presumably would seek to hold on to power and not commit suicide, they might be swayed by American threats of massive retaliation should they use their freshly gained nuclear arsenal. In this regard, deterrence can play a key role in protecting America against a nuclear attack. If, on the other hand, insurgents seized nuclear weapons, but did not gain power, the danger to the United States would become far worse. Cornered rebels with nothing to lose would be virtually undeterrable. If they retain the ability to strike out with nuclear arms, especially if they are driven by extreme beliefs, they are not likely to be dissuaded by fear of American punishment from doing so.

In the event that an international terrorist group such as Al Qaeda seized Pakistani nuclear arms in the midst of a civil conflict, deterring it from using them has little chance of success. As discussed, nonstate actors who welcome death are hardly candidates for successful policies of deterrence. Nevertheless, it is a mistake to believe that deterrence has no role to play when confronting terrorists. It is useful to think of terrorism as a chain, some links of which are more deterrable than others. The leadership of Al Qaeda, for example, may be more frightened with the prospect of death than its foot soldiers. There is a growing literature arguing that Al Qaeda, for all its murderous tactics, is led by rational leaders seeking well-defined goals, such as the creation of "truly" Islamic regimes in the Middle East and elsewhere.[3] In order to achieve their aims, the core leadership of Al Qaeda must survive. Osama bin Laden may be prepared to die for his cause, but it is noteworthy that he and his peers were not among the 19 hijackers flying into the World Trade Center and the Pentagon. A deterrent threat by the United States to wipe out Al Qaeda's sanctuaries on the Afghan-Pakistani border might be enough to deter an Al Qaeda nuclear strike of its own. Launching a major attack against terrorist bases in the remote Afghan-Pakistani region might seem fanciful today, but just as 9/11 changed thinking to make the invasion of Afghanistan (and Iraq) possible, so too might the seizure of nuclear arms by Al Qaeda make an American military intervention a likely response.

Even if Al Qaeda (or some similar extremist group) might not be deterred through the threat of retaliation, this does not mean that deterrence can play no role in halting a terrorist attack. Terrorist groups do not operate in a vacuum. Some measure of state support is often required for them to survive, and states, unlike groups, have territory, making them deterrable. Following the terrorist seizure of Pakistani nuclear arms, America would surely make it clear to other countries (such as Iran) that any support given to the extremists would make their country a target for American retaliation. In order to dissuade Pakistani nuclear technicians or military officials from transferring nuclear weapons to extremists, the United States may be able to convince them that it has the ability to trace the source of a nuclear explosion, thus deterring any contemplated "leakage."[4] The threat of targeted killing may also have some effect on deterring individuals who seek to assist the terrorists. Pakistanis thinking of cooperating with the terrorists by giving nuclear arms to extremist groups, individuals involved in the transport or concealment of the weapons, and those who would help in smuggling the weapons to the United States can all be warned that their assistance will result in their demise. For some, such a threat will have little effect. But, as the largely successful policy of Israeli targeted killing demonstrates, not everyone embraces martyrdom and deterrable elements exist in even in the most rabid groups.[5]

Despite these glimmers of hope, once extremist groups get hold of Pakistani nuclear weapons, it is highly unlikely they could be deterred. In the chaos of civil conflict it may not be known if any nuclear weapons had been seized, much less who did it, undermining any chance at successful deterrence. Even where a group could be identified, the absence of a state to retaliate against and the challenge of dissuading highly motivated militants would doom most deterrent efforts. If Al Qaeda or a similar group exploits Pakistani civil strife to acquire nuclear weapons, it will take more than deterrence to protect the United States and its allies from a horrific attack.

In sum, deterrence is not likely to be effective against the threats unleashed by civil disorder in Saudi Arabia, Mexico, China, and Pakistan. While deterrence offers some relief in certain situations, it offers little overall protection for the United States. Since vital American interests are at stake, American policymakers must look beyond deterrence to develop new approaches to respond to the emergence of these new threats.

PREVENTION

Just as it is easier to prevent a disease than to cure it, it would be far better to prevent civil strife from occurring at all than to try to cope with its consequences. Saudi Arabia, Mexico, Pakistan, and China are all at risk for internal conflict. If the United States, working with the international community, could promote substantive political development that addressed the causes of potential unrest, perhaps civil conflict could be averted. The problem, of course, is how do to this. As discussed in chapter one, political development, and especially the emergence of strong states, is a particularly difficult task for the countries of the developing world that have not had the time to create coherent national identities and strong governments. Where political development has been successful, as in Taiwan or South Korea, it has largely been the result of indigenous forces.[6] Moreover, creating strong governments to stop civil wars, even where feasible, may make a bad situation worse. According to R. J. Rummel, over 169 million people were killed by their own governments in the twentieth century, a figure that dwarfs the 38.5 million killed in international and civil wars during the same period.[7] Repressive governments not only commit atrocities on a wide scale, they also lay the basis for even greater internal violence in the future. Civil wars are indeed horrific, but in exceptional cases, they may be the lesser of two evils.

Nor will spreading democracy rescue America from the dangers of civil unrest. It is not at all clear that democracy can be transferred to other countries, especially liberal democracy, with its emphasis on basic liberties, such as freedom of the press and speech, an independent judiciary, and toleration of minorities. As

seen by the difficulties the United States encountered following its invasion of
Iraq, there is much evidence that certain societies are simply not ready for democracy due to religious and ethnic cleavages, lack of economic development, and
absence of a democratic tradition. In such cases, there is little the United States
or any outside power can do to hasten the process.[8]

The spread of democracy will be especially problematic for countries such as
Saudi Arabia, whose institutions and beliefs owe more to feudal times than the
twenty-first century. That Saudi Arabia is so far from adopting democratic practices may be for the best, as free and fair elections could well result in extremists
gaining power, catapulting the kingdom into civil war. China shows few signs of
moving in a democratic direction, and instead appears to be demonstrating that
economic development need not bring democracy in its wake.[9] Even where democratic rule is embraced, there is no guarantee that it will serve as a bulwark
against violent instability. The political scientists Edward Mansfield and Jack
Snyder's contention that democratizing societies are at the greatest risk of making
war, including civil war, is borne out by the experiences of Pakistan and Mexico.[10]
Pakistan's occasional embraces of democracy have exacerbated its regional, ethnic, and religious tensions, explaining why the periodic return to military rule has
been met with public enthusiasm. Mexico has achieved an impressive level of democracy, but that has done little to mitigate problems of crime, corruption, and
drug trafficking, and in some cases may have made the situation worse. The problems of civil strife will not be solved by democracy, either because democracy will
not be attained or because the transition to democracy will increase the prospects
of ruinous internal conflict.

Efforts to promote stability by the United States will be especially difficult
when the source of many of the country's problems lies with the existing regime.
Saudi Arabia, Pakistan, China, and Mexico have been and may in the future continue to be led by governments that are unwilling or unable to cope with the problems they face. Mired in the past, marked by corruption and resistance to reform,
the Saudi royal family is incapable of dealing with the religious and economic fer-
ment that is engulfing the kingdom. Pakistan's dictatorial leadership has incited
liberal reformers while proving unable — or unwilling — to defeat a growing Islamist insurgency. China's leadership remains tied to its totalitarian past, as seen
in its persecution of dissidents, widespread censorship, and continuing toleration
of a dysfunctional state sector. Mexico's inability to elect a united leadership al-
lows problems to fester, leading to a possible explosion that would destroy the ve-
neer of stability that has kept the country together over the past 75 years.

There is not much the United States can do when the regime, instead of addressing problems in its country, becomes the problem. The days of the United States easily toppling problematic leaders are long since gone. In the 1950s, the United States backed coups against governments it did not like with seeming ease, as seen in the removal of Iran's Mohammad Mossadegh and Guatemala's Jacobo Arbenz Guzman.[11] Since that time, however, casting aside unwanted governments has become much more difficult and costly for the United States. Instead of the relatively painless process of backing indigenous coups, it has become more and more apparent that the only sure way for the United States to remove regimes is through direct military action.[12]

Thus in the 1980s, the United States toppled regimes in Panama and Grenada by resorting to military intervention. Overthrowing Iraq's Saddam Hussein in 2003 necessitated a major American invasion followed by a protracted occupation. If toppling unwanted governments requires major American military involvement, including the deaths of American soldiers, such actions will be very rare and undertaken only in the most extreme circumstances. The governments of Saudi Arabia, Pakistan, China, and Mexico may at times frustrate and infuriate Washington, but none are close to reaching the level that would prompt a forceful American response to seek their removal. Where Washington has influence with the military, as in Pakistan, encouraging the departure of an unpopular and ineffective leader may bear fruit. In most cases, however, insofar as leaders make the potential for domestic strife worse, this is a problem that the United States will have to live with.

If it is impossible to bring risk-prone states up to the level where civil conflict is virtually unthinkable, the United States, working with other countries, can at least pursue policies that make domestic violence less likely in specific countries. There have been many proposals along these lines, including working with governments and nongovernmental organizations at the early stages of a crisis, undertaking preventive diplomacy through the United Nations or other institutions, the use of sanctions and inducements to prevent conflict from spreading, and the deployment of peacekeeping forces to impose order.[13] Organizations such as the International Crisis Group have been created precisely to nip conflict in the bud through early action. Nevertheless, as with promoting political development, focused efforts to prevent civil conflict often fail. Whatever steps might be taken by outsiders, civil wars will remain a feature of the global landscape for the foreseeable future.

LEARNING FROM NATURAL DISASTERS

How then can the United States respond to threats unleashed by civil wars? The elimination of deterrence and prevention as options suggests that American policymakers should rely less on traditional policies employed to deal with threats to national security and look elsewhere to determine how to meet the dangers stemming from civil wars. One source of valuable insights is the experience America (and others) have had in contending with natural disasters. Unlike dealing with threats to American security, coping with natural disasters requires policymakers to recognize that whatever they do, they cannot stop disasters from coming. Hurricanes, floods, and earthquakes — like most civil wars — cannot be deterred or prevented. Disaster-management teams ensconced within the Department of Homeland Security prepare the United States for these and other natural disasters by focusing not on stopping the unstoppable, but rather on what can be done before catastrophe hits so as to lessen the damage done and to accelerate recovery once the disaster has passed. By focusing on adaptation to an unpleasant reality rather than a futile effort at prevention, countries put themselves in a better position to deal with catastrophe once it strikes.[14]

Employing the natural disaster approach to civil wars means that American policymakers must assume that Saudi Arabia, Pakistan, Mexico, and China will at some time fall victim to internal conflict. As a result, the United States must take for granted that one day the Saudi oil fields will be destroyed, Pakistan will lose control over its nuclear weapons, waves of Mexican refugees will surge toward the American border while the lives of Americans in Mexico will be placed at risk, and China will no longer buy American treasury bonds and will adopt a reckless foreign policy. These disasters must be seen as unavoidable as a category five hurricane slamming into an American city. If it is assumed that some or all of this might happen in, say, the next ten years, American policymakers must determine what they need to do *now* to mitigate and contain the effects of these coming calamities.

SAUDI ARABIA

For Saudi Arabia, the threat to be prepared for is not civil war or even the destruction of the oil fields, but rather the harm done to the American economy because of the loss of Saudi oil. The key challenge for American policymakers, therefore, is not to stop a Saudi civil war (which may be impossible), but to be prepared to do without Saudi oil for several months or longer. As discussed in chapter two, this is a daunting challenge, but far from an impossible one. To deal with the immediate impact of the cutoff, the United States must first expand its Strategic Petroleum Reserve, which has barely two months' supply in storage.[15] The United States should have at least six months of oil available for use without having to depend on non-Saudi sources (most of which will be grabbed by other importers). This means pumping more oil into the reserve and not using it (as it has been) to defray momentary price spikes. When the destruction of the Saudi oil fields takes place, the United States will want to reassure the American public and the broader international community. Having a half year or more of oil before the devastation of the oil cutoff hits America's shores will do much to allow a calm and rational approach for dealing with the longer-term crisis.

Before any cutoff has occurred, the United States must also do better at what it is already doing to prepare for a world where there is no Saudi oil.[16] On the conservation side, the United States needs to do more in the transportation sector, which eats up two-thirds of American oil consumption.[17] Automobiles alone account for nearly 9 million of the 20 million barrels of oil the United States consumes each day. Controlling America's appetite for gasoline is not complicated. The United States should emulate its allies in Europe (where gasoline use has declined over the years) by increasing the tax on gasoline from its present level of around 40 cents to a dollar. A dramatically higher gasoline tax will use market forces to promote conservation while also providing an initiative to automakers to improve existing technologies and develop new ones to achieve much better gas mileage. To assist these market forces, the U.S. government has to get tougher on imposing mile-per-gallon standards on its automobiles. It makes no sense to exempt SUVs (because they are classified as light trucks) from Corporate Average Fuel Economy (CAFE) standards that impose mile-per-gallon averages. Simply maintaining a 27-miles-per-gallon standard on light trucks would save nearly a million barrels a day of oil in 7–10 years, while stiffening requirements for all cars and trucks would bring about even greater gains.[18]

On the supply side, the United States should open more federal lands for private gas and oil exploration without infringing upon sensitive areas such as the Arctic National Wilderness Reserve (ANWR). The United States only permits such exploration on 17% of federal lands (compared to 75% in the early 1980s), forgoing potentially huge deposits of oil and natural gas.[19] Nuclear energy, which already meets 20% of America's electrical needs and does not contribute to the "greenhouse effect," can be expanded to do much more. The United States is already the Saudi Arabia of coal. A far greater effort must be placed on gasification technologies that will enable the United States to burn coal more efficiently and cleanly. Oil shale development must be explored more vigorously as an alternative to imported oil.[20] Finally, incentives need to be given to oil companies to explore and develop new sources of oil, such as in the Caspian Sea, the Gulf of Mexico, and Canada. Government needs to play a key role in providing a safety net for companies, protecting them against the volatility of the market so that a passing drop in oil prices will not cripple a corporation that has invested in locating new oil deposits.

These recommendations, as important and familiar as they are, nevertheless leave the United States dependent on Saudi oil, albeit to a lesser degree. This may be acceptable so long as the United States and the rest of the world community have access to some Saudi oil. In the context of civil war that might destroy the oil fields or place in power a regime that refuses to export petroleum, however, virtually all Saudi oil may be gone from the world market at some point in the next decade. What can the United States do to prepare for such a catastrophe? At least two steps warrant serious consideration.

First, the United States needs to undertake a commitment on the order of the Manhattan Project, which developed the first atomic bomb, to achieve energy independence — or something close to it — in the next ten years. How this would be best achieved remains to be seen. It may be through the development of radically different technologies such as hydrogen fuel cells, or it may be through the better (and cleaner) use of existing technologies such as coal or nuclear energy. It could entail changes in the internal combustion engine, enabling cars to get 100 miles per gallon or more. It may be all of these things or something else. Undoubtedly, many of the projects receiving governmental funding would not be viable. Much money would be wasted, and there is even a chance that the United States would not succeed at gaining the energy independence it seeks. Nevertheless, far better to gamble on American ingenuity and entrepreneurial zeal to do what is necessary to lessen dependence on oil imports than on the continued stability of the Saudi kingdom.

The second way for the United States to cope with the loss of Saudi oil is to be prepared to take over the oil fields in the event of civil unrest. To be sure, such an operation would not be without difficulties. As discussed in chapter two, the oil fields are a target-rich environment filled with key choke points, the destruction of any one of which could cripple oil production for months. Nevertheless, the United States is in a much better position to defend the fields than it was in 1973, when the oil embargo first raised the issue of an American military intervention in Saudi Arabia.[21]

Unlike in the 1970s, when an American intervention to secure the oil would be undertaken against the Saudi government, any contemporary military intervention would presumably be at the request of and in support of a Saudi regime seeking to survive against the internal threats arrayed against it. Moreover, in the 1970s a critical concern about the United States intervening in Saudi Arabia was fear of a confrontation with the Soviet Union, a fear that has evaporated along with the Soviet state. The United States is also far better prepared militarily to intervene to defend the oil fields than was the case in the 1970s. With the Cold War over, the United States has many more military forces that could be assigned to a protective mission in Saudi Arabia. In the wake of the two wars with Iraq, America has dramatically improved its air and sealift capabilities, maintains troves of prepositioned military equipment in the Gulf, has a better sense of what it takes to fight in the desert, and has secured base agreements with many Gulf countries, including Kuwait and Bahrain, to assist any military effort.[22] A rapid American intervention should be able to forestall massive damage to the oil fields against attacks by what are likely to be ill-trained and -equipped insurgent forces. The United States can prepare to repair those facilities damaged in the fighting by stockpiling spare parts for critical equipment and providing skilled workers to get the oil production up to speed without too much of a delay.

Seizing and holding the oil fields will not be easy. Nevertheless, the costs and risks of doing so present less of a threat to American interests than absorbing a protracted cutoff of Saudi oil. Clearly, it is far better for the United States to be in a position where it does not need Saudi oil for its economy to survive. Until that stage is reached, however, the United States may have little choice in responding to an insurgent or terrorist attack on the oil fields but to go in itself to ensure that the oil keeps flowing. The only worse policy for the United States than intervening in the Saudi oil fields is not being prepared to do so when the need arises.

PAKISTAN

Pakistan lends itself well to the natural catastrophe paradigm, as there is little the United States can do to prevent civil war from once again engulfing this troubled state. As with Saudi Arabia, the threat comes not from the civil conflict itself, but from the threats that emerge in its wake. No threat is more terrifying than the specter of terrorists gaining control over Pakistani nuclear weapons. As discussed in chapter three, emphasis must be placed on making certain such a nightmare does not happen. Suggestions for doing so include getting Pakistan to store components of nuclear weapons in separate locations so the seizure of one site would be useless to the insurgents and encouraging Pakistan to deploy its arms in secure facilities and not in a mobile, "ready to strike" mode. Washington must also put aside its legal and secrecy concerns and agree to provide Pakistani nuclear weapons with American-made permissive action links that would be far more effective than what protects Pakistani arms today. All of these suggestions make sense, but they suffer from two drawbacks. First, they require the cooperation of the Pakistani leadership, which may not be forthcoming. Even more important, whatever Pakistan (or America) does, the possibility of insurgents seizing control of nuclear arms cannot be discounted. Instead of hoping that this day will never come, policymakers must assume that this nightmare will, in the not too distant future, become a reality. As such, preparations must be made before it happens to safeguard America for when it does.

What can the United States do if Pakistani extremists seize working nuclear weapons? Because the impact of a nuclear strike on American soil would be so devastating, emphasis must be on stopping the detonation of a nuclear bomb even after control of the nuclear weapons falls into insurgent hands. There are essentially two ways this can be done. First, the United States can rely on defense, that is, physically preventing the extremists from using their nuclear weapon against the United States or its allies. Defense holds out some, but not much, hope of dealing with a rogue Pakistani nuclear threat. While much attention has been placed on the pros and cons of ballistic missile defense, ballistic missiles are the *least* likely means of delivery of nuclear arms by some renegade group. Most countries (including Pakistan) do not have ballistic missiles with the range to hit the United States, and it would be enormously difficult to circumvent command and control safeguards to launch and retarget a ballistic missile even if access to the missile launching post could be achieved. Rather, if nuclear arms fell into the hands of anti-American zealots in Pakistan, the preferred means of delivery would probably be a cargo container or small ship, not an ICBM.

As detailed in chapter three, America's borders are frighteningly open. Nevertheless, more can and should be done to monitor those borders, including the development of better radiation detectors (especially important since Pakistani nuclear weapons are most likely to use highly enriched uranium, which is very difficult to detect), improved surveillance of American and foreign ports, greater use of devices that could see through cargo containers (such as exist in Hong Kong), and tighter control of America's borders.[23] The Department of Energy's NEST (Nuclear Emergency Support Teams), whose responsibility it is to detect and disarm hostile nuclear weapons, must be given special training to deal with "loose nukes" coming specifically from Pakistan. If resources need to be diverted from ballistic missile defense, so be it. America faces a far greater threat of being the victim of a Pakistani nuclear weapon from an anonymous, fanatical extremist than it does from a ballistic missile attack launched from a state. Policymakers need to ask themselves *now* what kind of border defenses they would want in place if Al Qaeda seized a Pakistani nuclear bomb, and then construct those defenses before that nightmare becomes a reality.

Since even a robust defense would be fallible, the United States also needs to be able to prevent extremist groups from getting their hands on Pakistani nuclear weapons in the event of civil conflict. This can be done in one of two ways. If the Pakistani military remains intact and open to cooperating with the United States, Washington could dispatch American forces to secure the nuclear weapon sites, protecting them from terrorist assault. Once order is restored, the United States could then depart, leaving the security of the nuclear arms again in Pakistani hands. If chaos continues to engulf Pakistan, Washington could spirit the nuclear arms out of the country, placing them in the United States for safekeeping or to be destroyed.

If the cooperation of the Pakistani military cannot be secured (perhaps because it has become enmeshed in the spreading disorder or because it has split into rival camps), the United States will have to be prepared to preempt the Pakistani nuclear capabilities. Preemption is a far more difficult strategy to pursue than deterrence. It requires the United States to know the location of all of Pakistan's nuclear weapons, including those that may be moved in the midst of domestic violence. The United States would need high confidence of destroying all the weapons, since leaving any of them in the hands of terrorists could be catastrophic. Another set of problems relates to timing. At what point would the United States launch a preemptive strike? If it acts too soon, it risks transforming what might have been a localized challenge within the ability of the Pakistani government to manage into widespread disorder that undermines the regime. The Pakistani government has already suffered because of its cooperation with the United States. A preemptive strike will kill innocent Pakistanis, inflaming an already vigorous anti-American sentiment. If the United States acts too late, when a rebellion has gotten underway, it not only risks saving the Pakistani regime but also faces the prospect that the nuclear arms will have already been seized. Obliterating nuclear sites does no good once the arms have already fallen into the hands of the extremists. Problems such as these have made preemption one of the rarest and least successful strategies in warfare.[24]

Despite these serious obstacles, the United States must be prepared to preempt Pakistan's nuclear arms in the wake of a Pakistani civil war. The Bush administration has already accepted preemption as one of its principal foreign policy instruments.[25] What needs to be done is to make certain that the United States has the capability to destroy Pakistan's arsenal quickly and completely. This means knowing where the Pakistani nuclear weapons are at any given time and maintaining the "real time" intelligence to determine if they are moved in the event of civil violence. It also means being able to launch conventional air strikes, cruise missile attacks, and assaults by commandos against the nuclear sites should they come under attack. Using nuclear weapons to eliminate Pakistan's arsenal remains a possibility, but because it would be so difficult for an American president to order the first use of nuclear arms, far better to have a conventional option that is more likely to be invoked. Moving from a deterrent mindset that emphasizes nuclear retaliation to one that emphasizes a first strike with conventional weapons flies in the face of 60 years of strategic planning. Nevertheless, given the possible consequences of a Pakistani civil war, it must be done.

Finally, the United States has to recognize that all of its efforts may fail, that civil war in Pakistan may result in a wayward nuclear weapon being detonated on American soil. Preparing to lessen the effects of such a nightmare must be undertaken before this happens. America will have to be prepared to deal with the public health consequences of a nuclear attack, including the psychological trauma that would ensue within the country at large. American policymakers should be thinking of the new laws that might follow such a detonation, including laws that affect civil liberties. Maintaining the continuity of government is especially critical, particularly if the target of the attack is Washington, DC. It also behooves scholars to think of ways in which international relations would be changed in the wake of this kind of attack. The terrorist attacks of 9/11 led to a greater willingness to engage in preventive war, as seen in American attacks on Afghanistan and Iraq. The destruction of an American city by a seized Pakistani bomb would surely make preemption, despite all its difficulties, a more attractive option. Whatever the specific impact of a nuclear attack might be, a new world will emerge in its wake. Considering what that new world will look like is as unpleasant as it is necessary.[26]

MEXICO

If mass violence erupted in Mexico in the near future the United States would have to act quickly to stem the catastrophic harm it would certainly produce. Most immediate would be acting to save the lives of Americans living and traveling in Mexico. In normal times, more than a million Americans are in Mexico, though it is possible many would have left in the wake of growing instability. Whatever the exact number might be, the U.S. government would be confronted with the challenge of moving large numbers of Americans to safety in a short period of time. Such a challenge would be similar to, but more difficult than, evacuating a city in advance of an approaching hurricane — a task that does not inspire confidence in the wake of Hurricane Katrina in 2005. Americans would have to be notified of the evacuation, brought together in assembly points, and spirited to safety all in the midst of what could well be a violently chaotic situation. Careful planning and preparation for this kind of disaster, including taking seriously the advance registration of American travelers and residents with the U.S. embassy, needs to be undertaken before disaster strikes.

Widespread Mexican disorder would also create concerns on the American side of the border. The United States will be worried about preventing violence from spilling over to American cities and towns, from large numbers of refugees flowing into the United States, and stemming the flow of drugs from a society that would lack even rudimentary police controls. The immediate response to these problems would be a deployment of the American military and National Guard along the border. Legal issues, such as suspending the Posse Comitatus Act (which prohibits the use of armed forces for domestic policing actions), and tactical concerns, such as deciding which units would go where, should be worked out in advance of the crisis erupting. In the event of spreading violence, the United States may also need to intervene militarily in Mexico. The past history of American interventions in Mexico during the years of World War I do not inspire confidence. Nevertheless, if Mexican violence threatens American lives and spreads to the American side of the border, military intervention to suppress the disorder may be necessary.

A key problem of any Mexican civil war will be dealing with an influx of refugees. Although related to America's broader problem of illegal immigration, in which some half million Mexicans cross the border illegally each year, the influx of Mexicans following civil violence presents a different challenge. The issue will be how to handle hundreds of thousands of Mexicans desperately fleeing to the United States over a period of weeks or even months. The primary concern would not be keeping Mexicans out of the United States, which would be impossible and inhumane. Rather it would be establishing control over the border so that the exodus could be managed and keeping track of the Mexicans once they arrived in America so that they could be repatriated once the violence subsides.

There is much the United States can do now to prepare itself for the possibility of a Mexican collapse. First, the United States has to get better control over its border. Fences in key areas are hardly a panacea, but they can work to give the United States some command over its southern frontier. After a 14-mile fence was built near San Diego, the number of illegal immigrants captured fell from around 200,000 in 1992 to only 9,000 in 2005.[27] Fences do not mean that Mexicans will be kept out, only that American authorities would have the ability to control who gets in. The 2006 law authorizing a 700-mile fence along portions of the border is a regrettable but justified move to regulate any mass surge of Mexicans seeking refuge in the United States. In addition to barriers, the United States should continue to improve its technological devices along the border to monitor traffic, including sensors, unmanned surveillance aircraft, and better lighting. More and better-trained border police would also make a difference. All of these steps would help not only to manage the aftermath of a Mexican meltdown, but also help stem the tide of illegal immigrants, potential terrorists, and drug traffic. To better keep track of Mexicans (and others) who enter the United States, a tamper-proof national identity card backed by a computer database needs to be established with severe penalties for employers who knowingly hire illegals. The purpose again would not be to prevent Mexicans from coming into the United States, but rather to be able to identify who is in America legally and who is not, so that when the civil conflict abates repatriation can be carried out. Finally, American authorities need to be prepared to provide humanitarian assistance — food, water, and shelter — to fleeing Mexicans.

The United States can also lessen the impact of a Mexican civil war by getting at the root of problems that afflict the two countries today. Illegal immigration will continue so long as Mexicans are paid much higher wages in the United States than they are at home. Helping Mexico improve its own economy and establishing a guest worker program that legalizes work while encouraging Mexicans to return home is the best approach for dealing with this contentious issue.[28] Drugs will continue to pour over the border so long as American demand produces gigantic profits for Mexican dealers. Only some form of decriminalization in the United States combined with expanded treatment programs for addicts will put a dent in the drug trade by curbing American demand.[29] By adopting sensible immigration and drug policies before civil violence wracks Mexico, the United States can better deal with ongoing problems while bracing itself for the horrendous effects a Mexican civil war would produce.

Even careful long-term planning will not insulate the United States from all the effects of Mexican internal conflict. If the violence continues for a long period of time and spreads throughout the country, America's economic ties with Mexico will take a beating. Moreover, if conflict morphs into something that looks like civil war with recognizable antagonists going at one another, the prospect of Mexican Americans being drawn into the conflict could well occur. There simply is not much that could be done to ameliorate these and other harmful effects. As with some terrible disease or wildly destructive hurricane, some of the damage caused by a Mexican civil conflict would simply have to be endured.

CHINA

Civil disorder gripping China would first threaten America's financial markets, particularly the sale of treasury securities. Blunting its impact requires the United States to be less dependent on Chinese purchases of its bonds, which in turn means doing more to erase the budget deficit. There are, of course, many reasons to reduce America's growing gap between what it earns and what it spends, but none is more compelling than lessening its dependence on foreign buyers who are also strategic rivals. Short of reducing the budget deficit, the United States could discourage the sale of securities to China by lowering the interest rate paid by the bonds. The problem is that the United States would also be discouraging the sale of securities to other countries as well, hurting the American economy in order to deal with a threat that may not come to pass. It is highly unlikely that such a decision would be made, nor should it. What the United States can do is develop contingency plans for what measures to take if the Chinese market plummets. Just as the logic of profit maximization cannot keep burnt Saudi oil wells pumping, so will it not keep the robust Sino-American economic relationship alive, however mutually beneficial it might be.

As for American foreign policy, the prospect of civil disorder in China strengthens the hands of those who opt for a wary approach toward the People's Republic. It is certainly true that the desire for economic growth and international reputation, under most circumstances, would inhibit China from adopting an aggressively expansionist policy toward its neighbors, particularly Taiwan. Nevertheless, as discussed in chapter five, the one glue that holds the Chinese state together is nationalism, a force that is likely to be especially volatile in times of civil unrest. A surge of nationalism unleashed during civil conflict could drive China to attack Taiwan or provoke the Taiwanese leadership to declare independence, producing a showdown with the United States. The lesson is clear: even in a globalized world where China seeks most to develop its economy, the unintended consequences of civil war could push both great powers to the brink of an unwanted confrontation. Thinking about how to deal with such an event before it arises, and having the military and diplomatic tools to cope with this kind of eventuality is the best safeguard for limiting the damage should China's relatively benign foreign policy fall victim to civil conflict.

CONCLUSION

A natural disaster approach to planning against strategically disruptive civil wars may be criticized on the ground that it would commit the United States to spend vast resources preparing for threats of unknown or low probability. This, however, is done anyway, and rightly so. It makes sense to plan for events of very high impact even if the probability of their occurring is low. What is more, many of the policies America should adopt make sense even if anticipated civil wars never occur. It is wise in any case to urge Pakistan to adopt safer deployment protocols for its nuclear weapons, to strive for energy independence, to prepare for an aggressive China, and to control America's border with Mexico. Since civil wars make these threats more likely and more harmful should they arise, all the more reason to prepare now for their coming.

The natural disaster approach may also raise concerns because it does not fit neatly into the paradigms developed during the Cold War. Some of the policies it suggests smack of containment, of insulating the United States from threats without seeking to remove them. These policies recognize that civil wars in key states will occur, the United States cannot do anything to stop the threats that will spin off from them, and so America should safeguard itself from the effects of these conflicts while staying out of them. Ending dependence on Saudi oil, diversifying purchasers of American treasury bonds, or better policing of the Mexican border fall into this category. Other approaches recognize that containment will not always work, that at times it will be impossible for the United States to insulate itself from the impact of civil wars, requiring more activist, interventionist policies to eliminate threats before they can take effect. Being prepared to preempt Pakistani nuclear weapons and seizing the Saudi oil fields are examples of this type of strategy. The mixture of responses reflects the diversity of challenges generated by civil wars today, as contrasted with the relative simplicity of the Soviet threat during the Cold War.

Just as international relations have undergone a fundamental change in the twenty-first century, so too have threats to the United States. The dramatic decline of interstate war means that countries have far less to fear from one another than at any point in recorded history. At the same time, oil and economic dependence, the prospect of extremist groups gaining control over weapons of mass destruction, and unguarded borders have created a situation in which the worst threats come from conflicts that erupt within states rather than between them. These threats are all the more dangerous because they are not intended by the leaders of countries and are sometimes not intended by anyone at all. Responding to these threats requires a different way of thinking about international politics and national security. Insights gained from natural catastrophes — threats that are also unintended and unstoppable — are useful in this regard. Whatever the response might be to civil conflict in key countries, it is imperative to recognize that the traditional world of international relations, with its focus on the fear of interstate war, is gone forever. Let us hope that it will not be missed.

Notes

CHAPTER ONE: A NEW KIND OF THREAT

1. There is a large literature warning of the hazards of America entangling itself in the problems of other states (be they civil wars or other issues). Two recent works are Stephen M. Walt, *Taming American Power: The Global Response to U.S. Primacy* (New York: Norton, 2005), and Robert J. Art, *A Grand Strategy for America* (Ithaca: Cornell University Press, 2003). For an earlier view that expresses why the United States should limit its involvement in the developing world, see Stephen Van Evera, "Why Europe Matters, Why the Third World Doesn't: America's Grand Strategy after the Cold War," *Journal of Strategic Studies* 13, no. 2 (June 1990): pp. 1–51.

2. The notion that the study of international relations is the study of great power conflict is put forth most strongly by the dean of "Realist" theorists, Kenneth Waltz. See Waltz, *Theory of International Politics* (Reading, MA: Addison-Wesley, 1979), p. 72.

3. For an optimistic view, see Francis Fukuyama, "The End of History?" *The National Interest* 16 (Summer 1989); for a view of international relations that sees never-ending great power wars, see John Mearsheimer, *The Tragedy of Great Power Politics* (New York: Norton, 2001).

4. John Lewis Gaddis, *The Long Peace: Inquiries into the History of the Cold War* (New York: Oxford University Press, 1987).

5. While the United States cannot be disarmed by a first strike against its nuclear forces, America's adversaries may not be as fortunate. For a persuasive account of why American nuclear dominance may also give it a disarming first-strike capability against Russia and China, see Keir A. Liber and Daryl G. Press, "The End of Mad?: The Nuclear Dimension of U.S. Primacy," *International Security* 30, no. 4 (Spring 2006): pp. 7–44.

6. Even the Department of Defense Report on China's military capabilities acknowledges that China has a long way to go before it can achieve superpower status; see "Annual Report to Congress: Military Power of the People's Republic of China, 2006," Office of the Department of Defense, May 2006, www.cfr.org/publication/10767/annual_report_to_congress.html (accessed August 2007).

7. *The Human Security Report 2005: War and Peace in the 21st Century* (New York: Oxford University Press, 2005), Andrew Mack director and editor in chief, published by the Human Security Centre, University of British Columbia, 2005, p. 148.

8. Marshall and Gurr make the point that Iraq accounted for all the international wars

in the post–Cold War era. They discount conflicts such as the Ethiopian-Eritrean conflict as more of a civil war than an international one. See Monty Marshall and Ted Robert Gurr, *Peace and Conflict 2005: A Global Survey of Armed Conflicts, Self-Determination Movements and Conflict Management* (College Park: University of Maryland, Center for International Development and Conflict Management, 2005), pp. 12, 13. Other sources list more international wars, but still many fewer than have been the case historically. E.g., Mikael Eriksson et al. argue that from 1989 to 2002, there were only seven interstate wars, and in some years (1993, 1994) there were none. Mikael Eriksson, Peter Wallensteen, and Margareta Sollenberg, "Armed Conflict, 1989–2002," *Journal of Peace Research* 40, no. 5 (September 2003): p. 594; see also Peter Wallensteen and Margareta Sollenberg, "The End of International War?: Armed Conflict 1989–1995," *Journal of Peace Research* 33, no. 3 (August 1996): pp. 353–370.

9. An excellent and concise description of the causes of peace can be found in Robert Jervis, "Theories of War in an Era of Leading-Power Peace (Presidential Address)," *American Political Science Review* 96, no. 1 (March 2002): pp. 1–14.

10. Karl W. Deutsch et al., *Political Community and the North Atlantic Area* (Princeton: Princeton University Press, 1957), pp. 5, 6.

11. For definitions of civil war and civil conflict, see Kristian Gleditsch, "A Revised List of Wars between and within Independent States, 1816–2002," *International Interactions* 30 (2004): pp. 231–262; Eriksson, Wallensteen, and Sollenberg, "Armed Conflict, 1989–2002," pp. 593–607; Nicholas Sambanis, "A Review of Recent Advances and Future Directions in the Quantitative Literature on Civil War," *Defence and Peace Economics* 13, no. 3 (2002): p. 218; Larry Diamond, "Slide Rules: What Civil War Looks Like," *The New Republic*, March 13, 2006, pp. 11–14. For a discussion of the definition of civil war and how it relates to America's intervention in Iraq, see Edward Wong, "A Matter of Definition: What Makes a Civil War, and Who Declares It So?" *New York Times*, November 26, 2006, p. A12.

12. The best analysis of the differences between ethnic and ideological civil wars is found in Chaim D. Kaufmann, "Possible and Impossible Solutions to Ethnic Conflict," *International Security* 20, no. 4 (Spring 1996): pp. 136–175. For an illustration of how a misunderstanding of this distinction has created a problem for the American intervention in Iraq, see Stephen Biddle, "Seeing Baghdad, Thinking Saigon," *Foreign Affairs* 85, no. 2 (March/April 2006): pp. 2–14.

13. Ted Robert Gurr, *Why Men Rebel* (Princeton: Princeton University Press, 1970), p. 11.

14. *The Human Security Report 2005*, p. 148.

15. Ibid., pp. 18–20; conflicts have at least 25 battle-related deaths per year; wars (both international and civil) have at least 1,000 battle-related deaths per year.

16. Marshall and Gurr, *Peace and Conflict 2005*, p. 13.

17. Ibid., p. 2.

18. On the difficulties of ending civil wars, see Roy Licklider, "The Consequences of Negotiated Settlements in Civil Wars, 1945–1993," *American Political Science Review* 89, no. 3 (September 1995): pp. 681–690; and Barbara Walter, "Designing Transitions from Civil War," in Barbara Walter and Jack Snyder, eds., *Civil Wars, Insecurity and Intervention* (New York: Columbia University Press, 1999), chap. 2.

19. On the wide range of causes of civil wars, see Steven R. David, "Internal War: Causes and Cures," *World Politics* 49, no. 4 (1997): pp. 552–576.

20. This concept borrows from K. J. Holsti's description of "vertical" and "horizontal" legitimacies. See Holsti, *The State, War, and the State of War* (Cambridge, UK: Cambridge University Press, 1996), pp. 84–90.

21. This view of the cause of civil conflict draws upon the ideas of many scholars, particularly Ted Robert Gurr's *Why Men Rebel*, esp. chaps. 1 and 2.

22. By the "developing world," I am referring to the countries in Asia (except Japan, the People's Republic of China, and Israel), Africa, and Latin America. For a rationale for lumping these states together, see Steven R. David, *Choosing Sides: Alignment and Realignment in the Third World* (Baltimore: The Johns Hopkins University Press, 1991), pp. 11–15.

23. The figure is from the World Bank, p. 1, of "PovertyNet," http://web.worldbank.org/WBSITE/EXTERNAL/TOPICS/EXTPOVERTY/0 (accessed March 2007).

24. For an argument that poverty, among other factors, is central to understanding the onset of civil war (and is more important than ethnic nationalism), see James D. Fearon and David D. Laitin, "Ethnicity, Insurgency and Civil War," *American Political Science Review* 97, no. 1 (February 2003): pp. 75–90.

25. Mohammed Ayoob, "Subaltern Realism: International Relations Theory Meets the Third World," in Stephanie Neuman, ed., *International Relations Theory and the Third World* (New York: St. Martin's Press, 1998), p. 44.

26. Freedom House, www.freedomhouse.org/template.cfm?page=363&%year=2007 (accessed August 2007).

27. Samuel P. Huntington, *Political Order in Changing Societies* (New Haven: Yale University Press, 1968).

28. On the absence of community in developing states, see Holsti, *The State, War, and the State of War*, esp. pp. 87–90; see also Robert Jackson, *Quasi-States: Sovereignty, International Relations, and the Third World* (New York: Cambridge University Press, 1990).

29. Ayoob, "Subaltern Realism," pp. 44–45.

30. Joel Migdal, *Strong Societies and Weak States: State-Society Relations and State Capabilities in the Third World* (Princeton: Princeton University Press, 1988), p. 274.

31. Charles Tilly, "Reflections on the History of European State-Making," in Charles Tilly, ed., *The Formation of National States in Western Europe* (Princeton: Princeton University Press, 1975), p. 15.

32. Migdal, *Strong Societies and Weak States*, pp. 273–274; see also Jeffrey Herbst, "War and the State in Africa," *International Security* 14, no. 4 (Spring 1990): pp. 117–139.

33. Michael C. Desch, "War and Strong States, Peace and Weak States," *International Organization* 50, no. 2 (Spring 1996): pp. 243–244.

34. John Mueller, *The Remnants of War* (Ithaca: Cornell University Press, 2004), esp. pp. 86–89, 106–107, 112. Mueller is an optimist. He is encouraged by the small number of rebels involved in civil conflicts, arguing that it makes it easier for effective governments to defeat them. The problem, however, is that effective governments are all too rare in the developing world, encouraging and empowering the few who seek to resist governmental rule. On natural resources and civil war, see Paul Collier and Anke Hoeffler, "Greed and

Grievance in Civil War," World Bank Policy Research Working Paper No. 2355, http://
ssrn.com/abstract=630727 (accessed July 2007).

35. The reversal of images is found in the work of several scholars focusing on developing states. See, e.g., Jackson, *Quasi-States*; Barry Buzan, *People, States and Fear: The National Security Problem in International Relations* (Chapel Hill: University of North Carolina Press, 1983); Mohammed Ayoob, "Security in the Third World: The Worm about to Turn," *International Affairs* 60 (Winter 1983–84): pp. 41–51.

36. One of the best accounts of how easy it would be for groups to get hold of and use nuclear weapons against the United States can be found in Graham Allison, *Nuclear Terrorism: The Ultimate Preventable Catastrophe* (New York: Times Books, 2004), esp. chaps. 2–4.

37. An excellent study of the background and future threat posed by biological weapons can be found in Jeanne Guillemin, *Biological Weapons: From the Invention of State-Sponsored Programs to Contemporary Bioterrorism* (New York: Columbia University Press, 2005).

38. Thomas Homer-Dixon makes a strong case for the term "disruption" over "destruction"; see "The Rise of Complex Terrorism," *Foreign Policy* no. 128 (January/February 2002): pp. 52–62.

39. On "dirty bombs," see Peter Zimmerman and Cheryl Loeb, "Dirty Bombs: The Threat Revisited," *Defense Horizons* no. 38 (January 2004); Chad Brown, *Transcendental Terrorism and Dirty Bombs*, Occasional Paper No. 54, Center for Strategy and Technology, Air University, Maxwell Air Force Base, February 2006.

40. On chemical weapons, see Jonathan B. Tucker, *War of Nerves: Chemical Warfare from World War I to al-Qaeda* (New York: Pantheon, 2006).

41. Even those who argue that terrorists can be deterred point only to very special circumstances where deterrence may work, providing very little reassurance to potential targets; see Robert F. Trager and Dessislava P. Zagorcheva, "Deterring Terrorism: It Can Be Done," *International Security* 30, no. 3 (Winter 2005/06): pp. 87–123.

42. Brian Jenkins, "Will Terrorists Go Nuclear?" *Orbis* 29, no. 3 (1985): p. 511; italics in the original.

43. "'Why We Fight America': Al Qa'ida Spokesman Explains September 11 and Declares Intentions to Kill 4 Million Americans with Weapons of Mass Destruction," The Middle East Media Research Institute, June 12, 2002; translated from Suleiman Abu Gheith, "In the Shadow of the Lances," Center for Islamic Research and Studies, cited in Allison, *Nuclear Terrorism*, pp. 12–13.

44. See, e.g., John F. Burns and Michael R. Gordon, "U.S. Says Iran Helped Iraqis Kill Five G.I.'s," *New York Times*, July 3, 2007, p. A1.

45. This is not to suggest that the United States should not take humanitarian issues seriously, or not take steps to halt mass murder or genocide, only that such concerns do not endanger America's vital interests of security and economic well-being, making a response more a matter of choice than necessity.

CHAPTER TWO: SAUDI ARABIA

1. Energy Information Administration, Country Analysis Briefs, "Saudi Arabia," August 2005, p. 1, www.eia.doe.gov/emeu/cabs/Saudi_Arabia/pdf.pdf (accessed March 2005); An-

thony H. Cordesman, *Saudi Arabia Enters the Twenty-First Century: The Political, Foreign Policy, Economic, and Energy Dimensions*, vol. 2 (Westport, CT: Praeger, 2003), pp. 467–475, 485; John Cassidy, "Pump Dreams," *The New Yorker*, October 11, 2004, p. 45.

2. "What If?" *The Economist*, May 27, 2004, p. 69.

3. Bhusan Bahree and Patrick Barta, "Awash in a Gusher of Cash, Oil Firms Are Reluctant Investors," *Wall Street Journal*, August 26, 2004, p. A1.

4. Steve Yetiv, *Crude Awakenings: Global Oil Security and American Foreign Policy* (Ithaca: Cornell University Press, 2004), p. 183; "What If?" *The Economist*, p. 70.

5. Energy Information Administration, *International Energy Outlook 2004*, "World Oil Markets," p. 28, http://tonto.eia.doe.gov/ftproot/forecasting/0484(2004).pdf (accessed November 2007). The EIA gives the figure of world energy use of 77 million barrels a day in 2001. In 2005, the figure is closer to 80 million barrels a day.

6. John Cassidy, "Pump Dreams," *The New Yorker*, October 11, 2004, p. 43.

7. Energy Information Administration, *International Energy Outlook 2004*, "World Oil Markets," pp. 31–33; Philip Andrews-Speed, Xuanli Liao, and Roland Dannreuther, *The Strategic Implications of China's Energy Needs*, Adelphi Papers, no. 346 (Oxford: Oxford University Press for the International Institute for Strategic Studies, 2002); Yetiv, *Crude Awakenings*, pp. 121–122; Daniel Yergin, "Ensuring Energy Security," *Foreign Affairs* 85, no. 2 (March/April 2006): p. 72.

8. Energy Information Administration, *International Energy Outlook 2004*, "World Oil Markets," pp. 31–33.

9. Cordesman, *Saudi Arabia Enters the Twenty-First Century*, vol. 2, pp. 483–485; Energy Information Administration, "Saudi Arabia," p. 1.

10. This is not to argue that oil price increases directly caused the recessions. The recessions came about largely due to the Federal Reserve's efforts to cope with inflation, which in turn was caused in part by the increase in the price of oil.

11. Khalid R. Al-Rodhan, "The Impact of the Abqaiq Attack on Saudi Energy Security," Center for Strategic and International Studies, February 27, 2006, p. 2, www.csis.org/media/csis/pubs/060227_abqaiqattack.pdf.

12. Robert Baer, *Sleeping with the Devil: How Washington Sold Our Soul for Saudi Crude* (New York: Crown, 2003), p. xxv.

13. Neil Adams, *Terrorism and Oil* (Tulsa, OK: Pennwell, 2003), p. 21.

14. For a gripping account of diplomacy during the oil embargo, see Daniel Yergin, *The Prize: The Epic Quest for Oil, Money and Power* (New York: Simon and Schuster, 1991), chap. 30.

15. One of the best accounts of why the Saudis would not launch another embargo can be found in Steve Yetiv, *Crude Awakenings*, esp. pp. 140–143.

16. Peter W. Wilson and Douglas F. Graham, *Saudi Arabia: The Coming Storm* (Armonk, NY: M. E. Sharpe, 1994), p. 58.

17. Osama bin Laden, "Depose the Tyrants" (December 2004), in Bruce Lawrence, ed., *Messages to the World: The Statements of Osama bin Laden* (London: Verso 2005), p. 272.

18. Anthony Cordesman and Nawaf Obaid, "Saudi Petroleum Security: Challenges & Responses," Center for Strategic and International Studies, Working Draft, November 30,

2004, pp. 16, 10, www.csis.org/media/csis/pubs/saudi_petroleumsecurity041129.pdf (accessed January 2007).

19. Baer, *Sleeping with the Devil*, pp. xvii–xix.

20. Al-Rodhan, "The Impact of the Abqaiq Attack," p. 5.

21. Cordesman and Obaid, "Saudi Petroleum Security," p. 10.

22. Energy Information Administration, "Saudi Arabia," p. 10.

23. Baer, *Sleeping with the Devil*, p. xxii.

24. Osama bin Laden, "A Muslim Bomb" (December 1998), in Lawrence, *Messages to the World*, p. 72. On Al Qaeda's efforts to acquire a nuclear weapon, see Graham Allison, *Nuclear Terrorism: The Ultimate Preventable Catastrophe* (New York: Times Books, 2004), pp. 27–28.

25. Charles D. Ferguson and William C. Potter, *The Four Faces of Nuclear Terrorism* (Monterey, CA: Center for Nonproliferation Studies, 2004), p. 260.

26. International Energy Agency, "Saudi Arabia," p. 1; Jad Mouawad, "Saudi Arabia Looks Past Oil," *New York Times*, December 13, 2005, p. C1.

27. International Energy Agency, "Saudi Arabia," p. 1.

28. Jeffrey D. Sachs and Andrew M. Warner, "The Curse of Natural Resources," *European Economic Review* 45 (2001): pp. 827–838; see also Paul Collier, *The Bottom Billion: Why the Poorest Countries Are Failing and What Can Be Done about It* (Oxford: Oxford University Press, 2007), chap. 3.

29. Cordesman, *Saudi Arabia Enters the Twenty-First Century*, vol. 2, p. 21.

30. Energy Information Administration, "Saudi Arabia," p. 2.

31. This is a major finding of Ted Robert Gurr; see *Why Men Rebel* (Princeton: Princeton University Press, 1970), esp. chap. 2.

32. For an excellent account of how the rentier status of Saudi Arabia can foster opposition, see Gwenn Okruhlik, "Rentier Wealth, Unruly Law and the Rise of Opposition: The Political Economy of Oil States," *Comparative Politics* 31, no. 3 (April 1999): pp. 295–315.

33. Cordesman, *Saudi Arabia Enters the Twenty-First Century*, vol. 2, p. 30.

34. John R. Bradley, *Saudi Arabia Exposed: Inside a Kingdom in Crisis* (New York: Palgrave Macmillan, 2005), p. 142.

35. J. E. Peterson, *Saudi Arabia and the Illusion of Security*, Adelphi Papers, no. 348 (New York: Oxford University Press for the International Institute for Strategic Studies, 2002), p. 45; Scott Wilson, "Saudis Fight Militancy with Jobs," *Washington Post*, August 31, 2004, p. A1.

36. F. Gregory Gause II, "Saudi Arabia over a Barrel," *Foreign Affairs* 70, no. 3 (May/June 2000): pp. 82–85.

37. Robert Baer, "The Fall of the House of Saud," *The Atlantic Monthly*, May 2003, p. 58.

38. Cordesman, *Saudi Arabia Enters the Twenty-First Century*, vol. 2, p. 141.

39. For a general view of the issues surrounding Saudi succession, see Simon Henderson, *After King Fahd: Succession in Saudi Arabia*, Policy Papers, no. 37 (Washington DC: The Washington Institute for Near East Policy, 1995); see also Cordesman, *Saudi Arabia Enters the Twenty-First Century*, vol. 2, pp. 136–141.

40. Michael Scott Doran, "The Saudi Paradox," *Foreign Affairs* 83, no. 1 (January/February 2004): pp. 36–38.

41. Peterson, *Saudi Arabia and the Illusion of Security*, pp. 29–30; Cordesman, *Saudi Arabia Enters the Twenty-First Century*, vol. 1, pp. 169, 170.

42. Doran, "The Saudi Paradox," p. 38; Cordesman, *Saudi Arabia Enters the Twenty-First Century*, vol. 2, p. 206. Doran puts the Shia population at between 10% and 15%, while Cordesman says it is only 5% of the Saudi population.

43. Bradley, *Saudi Arabia Exposed*, p. 78.

44. Doran, "The Saudi Paradox," pp. 36–38, 46.

45. Wilson and Graham, *Saudi Arabia*, pp. 251, 252.

46. One of the best accounts of the threats posed by Saudi tribes from which this account is drawn can be found in Bradley, *Saudi Arabia Exposed*, esp. pp. 9, 10, 39, 52, 55, 65.

47. See, e.g., bin Laden's message to Saudi cleric bin Baz, "The Betrayal of Palestine," in Lawrence, *Messages to the World*, esp. pp. 5–6.

48. For an insightful treatment of the marriage between religion and power that marked the origins of the Saudi state, see Nadav Safran, *Saudi Arabia: The Ceaseless Quest for Security* (Ithaca: Cornell University Press, 1988), esp. chap. 1.

49. Joshua Teitelbaum, *Holier Than Thou: Saudi Arabia's Islamic Opposition*, Policy Papers, no. 52 (Washington, DC: The Washington Institute for Near East Policy, 2000), pp. 10, 11.

50. Nadav Safran makes this point well; see Safran, *Saudi Arabia*, esp. pp. 54–56.

51. Wilson and Graham, *Saudi Arabia*, pp. 56–59.

52. Teitelbaum, *Holier Than Thou*, p. 21.

53. Fareed Zakaria, "The Saudi Trap," *Newsweek*, June 28, 2004, p. 31.

54. Teitelbaum, *Holier Than Thou*, pp. xiii, 35.

55. For background to this episode, see Bernard Lewis, "License to Kill: Usama bin Ladin's Declaration of Jihad," *Foreign Affairs* 77, no. 6 (November/December 1998): esp. pp. 14–16.

56. Peterson, *Saudi Arabia and the Illusion of Security*, p. 32.

57. Teitelbaum, *Holier Than Thou*, p. 33.

58. Ibid., p. 38.

59. Ibid., pp. 49–54.

60. Cordesman, *Saudi Arabia Enters the Twenty-First Century*, vol. 2, pp. 191, 192.

61. For an example of Qutb's philosophy, see Sayyid Qutb, *Milestones* (Beirut: Holy Koran Publishing House, 1978). On the specific point of *Jahiliyyah*, see Peter Bergen, *Holy War, Inc.: Inside the Secret World of Osama bin Laden* (New York: Free Press, 2001), p. 51.

62. Michael Doran, "Somebody Else's Civil War," *Foreign Affairs* 81, no. 1 (January/February 2002): p. 23.

63. It is difficult to find a reliable biography of the elusive bin Laden. A good place to start is with these two accounts: Jonathan Randal, *Osama: The Making of a Terrorist* (New York: Random House, 2004), and Peter L. Bergen, *The Osama bin Laden I Know: An Oral History of al Qaeda's Leader* (New York: Free Press, 2006).

64. This quote can be found in Rohan Gunaratna, *Inside Al-Qaeda: Global Network of Terror* (New York: Columbia University Press, 2002), p. 28.

65. Bin Laden, "The Betrayal of Palestine," in Lawrence, *Messages to the World*, p. 10.

66. Lewis, "License to Kill," pp. 14, 15.

67. For a list of terrorist incidents in Saudi Arabia post-9/11, see Anthony Cordesman and Nawaf Obaid, "Saudi Internal Security: A Risk Assessment," Center for Strategic and International Studies, Working Draft, May 30, 2004, pp. 9–13, www.csis.org/media/csis/pubs/sis_ariskassessment.pdf (accessed November 2007).

68. Daniel Benjamin and Steven Simon, *The Next Attack: The Failure of the War on Terror and a Strategy for Getting It Right* (New York: Times Books, 2005), pp. 100–102.

69. Lee Smith, "The Saudi Civil War," *Slate*, June 18, 2004.

70. Cordesman and Obaid, "Saudi Internal Security," p. 7.

71. Benjamin and Simon, *The Next Attack*, p. 103.

72. Cordesman, *Saudi Arabia Enters the Twenty-First Century*, vol. 1, pp. 169, 170.

73. Al-Rodhan, "The Impact of the Abqaiq Attack," p. 2; Cordesman, *Saudi Arabia Enters the Twenty-First Century*, vol. 1, chap. 5, esp. pp. 169, 170, 253, 261, 273; Wilson and Graham, *Saudi Arabia*, pp. 156–158.

74. Cordesman, *Saudi Arabia Enters the Twenty-First Century*, vol. 1, p. 259.

CHAPTER THREE: PAKISTAN

1. Graham Allison, *Nuclear Terrorism: The Ultimate Preventable Catastrophe* (New York: Times Books, 2004), p. 75; see also Institute for Science and International Security, www.isis-online.org/mapproject/country_pages/pakistan.html (accessed July 2007).

2. Cited in Samina Ahmed, "Pakistan's Nuclear Weapons Program: Turning Points and Nuclear Choices," *International Security* 23, no. 4 (Spring 1999): p. 183.

3. On Bhutto's efforts to build an atomic bomb, from his own perspective, see Zulfikar Ali Bhutto, *If I Am Assassinated* (New Delhi: Vikas, 1979), pp. 137, 138.

4. On Pakistan's development of nuclear weapons, see Ahmed, "Pakistan's Nuclear Weapons Program," pp. 178–204; George Perkovich, *India's Nuclear Bomb: The Impact on Global Proliferation* (Berkeley: University of California Press, 1999), esp. pp. 196–204; A. Q. Khan was later found to be directing a wide-ranging program to distribute nuclear weapons technology to several countries, including Iran, Libya, and North Korea. See International Institute for Strategic Studies, *Nuclear Black Markets: Pakistan, A. Q. Khan and the Rise of Proliferation Networks; A Net Assessment* (London: International Institute for Strategic Studies, 2007).

5. Although Pakistan has focused on the enrichment route for developing nuclear weapons, it is exploring ways to use plutonium to add to its arsenal. It has completed two plutonium production reactors and began building a third in 2007; see David Albright and Paul Brannan, "Chashma Nuclear Site in Pakistan with Possible Reprocessing Plant," Institute for Science and International Security, January 18, 2007, www.isis-online.org/publications/southasia/chashma.pdf (accessed August 2007); Jane Perlez, "U.S. Group Says Pakistan Is Building New Reactor," *New York Times*, June 23, 2007, p. A5.

6. For a list of Pakistani nuclear delivery capabilities, including missiles and aircraft, see "Nuclear Weapons Database: Pakistani Nuclear Delivery Systems," at www.cdi.org/issues/nukef&f/database/panukes.html (accessed February 2007).

7. This point is made vividly by Thomas C. Schelling; see his classic *Arms and Influence* (New Haven: Yale University Press, 1966), esp. pp. 19–20.

8. For a solid overview of Cold War strategies and anxieties, see Lawrence Freedman, *The Evolution of Nuclear Strategy* (New York: St. Martin's Press, 1989).

9. Kenneth N. Waltz, "More May Be Better," in Scott D. Sagan and Kenneth N. Waltz, *The Spread of Nuclear Weapons: A Debate Renewed* (New York: Norton, 2003).

10. The peace-inducing effects of nuclear weapons in South Asia are skillfully described by Devin T. Hagerty, "Nuclear Deterrence in South Asia: The 1990 Indo-Pakistani Crisis," *International Security* 20, no. 3 (Winter 1995–1996): pp. 79–114. For a view that nuclear arms make conventional war between India and Pakistan *more* likely (because they embolden Pakistan to attack knowing that India would restrain its retaliation), see Rodney W. Jones, "Pakistan's Nuclear Posture: Quest for Assured Nuclear Deterrence," in Charles H. Kenney, Kathleen McNeil, Carl Ernst, and David Gilmartin, eds., *Pakistan at the Millennium* (Oxford: Oxford University Press, 2003), p. 307. Even if nuclear possession increases the chance of conventional war, there would still be a mutual fear of escalating to nuclear conflict.

11. The key to identifying the source of a nuclear explosion is maintaining a library of nuclear samples to which the fallout from the explosion can be compared. The International Atomic Energy Agency (IAEA) and the United States have a wide range of nuclear samples that come from some — but not all — nuclear powers. On the ability to trace the source of a nuclear explosion, see National Academy of Sciences, Committee on International Security and Arms Control, *Monitoring Nuclear Weapons and Nuclear-Explosive Materials* (Washington, DC: National Academies Press, 2005); Michael May, Jay Davis, and Raymond Jeanloz, "Preparing for the Worst," *Nature* 443 (October 26, 2006): pp. 907, 908; William J. Broad, "New Team Plans to Identify Nuclear Attackers," *New York Times*, February 2, 2006, p. A17; David E. Sanger and Thom Shanker, "U.S. Debates Deterrence for Terrorist Nuclear Threat," *New York Times*, May 8, 2007, p. A10.

12. For a thoughtful account of how the United States might respond to the accidental use of nuclear weapons, see George H. Quester, *Nuclear First Strike: Consequences of Broken Taboo* (Baltimore: The Johns Hopkins University Press, 2006), esp. pp. 104–107.

13. This is a major argument of Kenneth Waltz in "More May Be Better," in Sagan and Waltz, *The Spread of Nuclear Weapons*, pp. 13–14.

14. Allison, *Nuclear Terrorism*, chap. 5, esp. pp. 112, 114, 119; see also Stephen Flynn, *America the Vulnerable: How Our Government Is Failing to Protect Us from Terrorism* (New York: HarperCollins, 2004), esp. chap. 5.

15. Seymour Hersh, "Watching the Warheads: The Risks to Pakistan's Nuclear Arsenal," *The New Yorker*, November 5, 2001, p. 54; see also Musharraf's attempt to allay American concerns in his memoir, *In the Line of Fire* (New York: Free Press, 2006), p. 291. On keeping Pakistani nuclear components separate, see Joseph Cirincione, *Deadly Arsenals: Tracking Weapons of Mass Destruction* (Washington, DC; Carnegie Endowment, 2002), p. 207.

16. Steven E. Miller, "Assistance to Newly Proliferating Nations," in Robert D. Blackwill and Albert Carnesale, eds., *New Nuclear Nations: Consequences for U.S. Policy* (New York: Council on Foreign Relations, 1993), p. 116.

17. Lewis A. Dunn, *Containing Nuclear Proliferation*, Adelphi Papers, no. 263 (London: International Institute for Strategic Studies, 1991), p. 20.

18. Scott D. Sagan, "More Will Be Worse," in Sagan and Waltz, *The Spread of Nuclear*

Weapons, p. 78. Sagan refers to the design of a proposed Iraqi nuclear weapon, but the principle of primitive weapons being subject to accidental detonation holds for wherever the bomb is made.

19. Subodh Atal, "Extremist, Nuclear Pakistan: An Emerging Threat?" CATO Institute Policy Analysis no. 472, March 5, 2003, www.cato.org/pubs/pas/pa472.pdf (accessed November 2007).

20. Excerpts from "The Terrorist Threat to the U.S. Homeland," a July 2007 National Intelligence Estimate. Excerpts are from the White House and can be accessed at www.whitehouse.gov/news/releases/2007/07/20070717–2.html (accessed July 2007).

21. Atal, "Extremist, Nuclear Pakistan," p. 5; Allison, *Nuclear Terrorism*, p. 28.

22. Allison, *Nuclear Terrorism*, pp. 91, 92; Scott D. Sagan, "Indian and Pakistani Nuclear Weapons," in Sagan and Waltz, *The Spread of Nuclear Weapons*, p. 103; David Albright, "Securing Pakistan's Nuclear Weapons Complex," Institute for Science and International Security, October 2001, p. 4, www.isis-online.org/publications/terrorism/stanley paper.html (accessed July 2007).

23. David E. Sanger and William J. Broad, "U.S. Secretly Aids Pakistan in Guarding Nuclear Arms," *New York Times*, November 18, 2007, p. A1.

24. Peter D. Feaver, "Command and Control in Emerging Nuclear Nations," *International Security* 17, no. 3 (Winter 1992/93): pp. 160–187. Feaver refers to the "always/never" dilemma rather than the reverse, but the meaning is the same. The following discussion of this dilemma as it pertains to Pakistan owes much to his analytical framework.

25. Sagan, "Indian and Pakistani Nuclear Weapons," p. 99.

26. Scott D. Sagan, "How to Keep the Bomb from Iran," *Foreign Affairs* 85, no. 5 (September/October 2006): p. 52.

27. Leonard S. Spector, *Going Nuclear* (Washington, DC: Carnegie Endowment for International Peace, 1987), pp. 25–30.

28. John W. Lewis and Xue Litai, *China Builds the Bomb* (Stanford: Stanford University Press, 1988), pp. 202, 203; Spector, *Going Nuclear*, pp. 32–37.

29. I am grateful to Scott Sagan for making this point.

30. Daniel Benjamin and Steven Simon, *The Next Attack: The Failure of the War on Terror and a Strategy for Getting It Right* (New York: Times Books, 2005), p. 105. Benjamin and Simon suggest that there may have been as many as six attempts on Musharraf's life since 2002.

31. For a discussion of how Indian nuclear doctrine may allow for a first or preemptive strike, see Syed Rifaat Hussain and Scott D. Sagan, "The Evolution of Pakistani and Indian Nuclear Doctrine," unpub. ms., pp. 35–43.

32. "Draft Report of National Security Advisory Board on Indian Nuclear Deterrence," p. 2, www.pugwash.org/reports/nw/nw7a.htm (accessed July 2007); see also Rodney Jones, "Pakistan's Nuclear Posture," p. 341.

33. Owen Bennet Jones, *Pakistan: Eye of the Storm* (New Haven: Yale University Press, 2002), p. xii. "A Survey of Pakistan," *The Economist*, July 8–14, 2006, p. 3.

34. *Human Development Report 2005* (New York: Oxford University Press, published for the United Nations Development Programme, 2005), p. 221.

35. Stephen P. Cohen, *The Idea of Pakistan* (Washington, DC: Brookings, 2004),

chap. 7, esp. pp. 232, 247. Although Cohen has hopes for Pakistan's future, even he acknowledges that over the long term, its prospects may become very grim.

36. Jones, *Pakistan*, p. 286.

37. Transparency International ranks Pakistan 138 out of 180 countries in its "Corruption Perceptions Index." Pakistan is given a 2.4 corruption rating on a scale that ranges from 10 (highly clean) to 0 (highly corrupt): www.transparency.org/policy_research/surveys_indices/cpi/2006 (accessed August 2007).

38. Jones, *Pakistan*, pp. 142, 143.

39. James Risen and David Rohde, "Mountains and Border Foil Quest for bin Laden," *New York Times*, December 13, 2004, p. A1.

40. Mary Anne Weaver, *Pakistan in the Shadow of Jihad and Afghanistan* (New York: Farrar, Straus and Giroux, 2002), p. 60; Cohen, *The Idea of Pakistan*, pp. 217–219.

41. Jane Perlez and Ismail Khan, "Taliban Pushing out of Frontier, Pakistani President Is Warned," *New York Times*, June 30, 2007, p. A1; see also Daniel Markey, "A False Choice in Pakistan," *Foreign Affairs* 86, no. 4 (Summer 2007): pp. 90–91.

42. Weaver, *Pakistan in the Shadow*, p. 95.

43. Cohen, *The Idea of Pakistan*, pp. 220–221; Jones, *Pakistan*, pp. 132–136.

44. For an eyewitness account of the fighting in Baluchistan, see Carlotta Gall, "In Remote Pakistan Province, a Civil War Festers," *New York Times*, April 2, 2006, p. A1.

45. Cohen, *The Idea of Pakistan*, pp. 214–215; Jones, *Pakistan*, p. 120.

46. Jones, *Pakistan*, p. 143.

47. Lawrence Ziring, *Pakistan in the Twentieth Century: A Political History* (Karachi: Oxford University Press, 1997), p. 425.

48. Ashutosh Misra, "Rise of Religious Parties in Pakistan: Causes and Prospects," *Strategic Analysis: A Monthly Journal of the IDSA* 27, no. 2 (April/June 2003): pp. 11–12; Stephen Cohen, "The Jihadist Threat to Pakistan," *The Washington Quarterly*, 26, no. 3 (2003): p. 10.

49. Cohen, "The Jihadist Threat to Pakistan," p. 17.

50. Misra, "Rise of Religious Parties in Pakistan," p. 1.

51. International Crisis Group, *Pakistan: The Mullahs and the Military*, Asia Report, no. 49 (Islamabad; Brussels: ICG, 2003), p. i.

52. International Crisis Group, *Unfulfilled Promises: Pakistan's Failure to Tackle Extremism*, Asia Report, no. 73 (Islamabad; Brussels: ICG, 2004), p. 18.

53. International Crisis Group, *Pakistan*, p. 1.

54. Jessica Stern, "Pakistan's Jihad Culture," *Foreign Affairs*, 79, no. 6 (November/December 2000): pp. 115, 116.

55. Weaver, *Pakistan in the Shadow*, p. 31.

56. Musharraf claims that while he gave in to most of America's demands, he refused to grant the United States blanket overflight rights over Pakistan or use of Pakistani ports and air bases; see his *In the Line of Fire*, pp. 205–206.

57. David Wood, "Crisis Raises Alarm over Arsenal," *Baltimore Sun*, November 8, 2007, p. 1A.

58. International Crisis Group, *Unfulfilled Promises*, pp. 1, 2; Misra, "Rise of Religious Parties in Pakistan," p. 3; "A Survey of Pakistan," *The Economist*, July 8–14, 2006, p. 8.

59. See, e.g., Mark Mazzetti, "Qaeda Rebuilding in Pakistan, Intelligence Chief Tells Panel," *New York Times*, February 28, 2007, p. A6; Mark Mazzetti and David E. Sanger, "Bush Advisers See a Failed Strategy against Al Qaeda," *New York Times*, July 18, 2007, p. A1.

60. The findings of the Pew report can be found in David Rohde, "Concern Rises in Pakistan of a War without End," *New York Times*, December 1, 2004, p. A10; see also Benjamin and Simon, *The Next Attack*, p. 107.

61. Benjamin and Simon, *The Next Attack*, p. 105. Stephen Cohen cites estimates of madrassas ranging from 10,000 to 45,000; see Cohen, *The Idea of Pakistan*, p. 182. For a less alarmist view of the number and impact of the madrassas, see Tahir Andrabi, Jishnu Das, Asim Ijaz Khuwaja, and Trislan Zajonc, "Religious School Enrollment in Pakistan: A Look at the Data," *Comparative Education Review* 50 (2006): pp. 446–477.

62. International Crisis Group, *Unfulfilled Promises*, esp. pp. i, ii; see also "Why They Hate Each Other," *Time*, March 8, 2007, p. 39; Carlotta Gall, "Behind a Siege in Pakistan, Rumblings of Wider Dissent," *New York Times*, July 8, 2007, p. A6.

63. These questions are addressed in detail in Cohen, *The Idea of Pakistan*, esp. pp. 34–38.

64. Lawrence Ziring provides a good account of Zia's policy of Islamization and its legacy. See Ziring, *Pakistan: At the Crosscurrent of History* (Oxford: Oneworld, 2003), esp. chap. 6.

65. Cohen, *The Idea of Pakistan*, p. 117.

66. Weaver, *Pakistan in the Shadow*, p. 32.

67. Cohen, *The Idea of Pakistan*, p. 112; Weaver, *Pakistan in the Shadow*, p. 31.

68. Jones, *Pakistan*, pp. 254, 255.

69. For a description of A. Q. Khan's activities, see International Institute for Strategic Studies, *Nuclear Black Markets*; see also Allison, *Nuclear Terrorism*, pp. 74–78.

70. Cohen, *The Idea of Pakistan*, p. 117.

71. Rohde, "Concern Rises in Pakistan," p. A10.

72. Jones makes this point convincingly, *Pakistan*, p. 251.

73. For similar points, see Cohen, *The Idea of Pakistan*, pp. 292–296.

74. The security dilemma that is created when governments collapse or weaken has emerged in many ethnic conflicts; see Barry Posen, "The Security Dilemma and Ethnic Conflict," *Survival* 35 (Spring 1993): pp. 27–47.

CHAPTER FOUR: MEXICO

1. "A Line in the Sand: Confronting the Threat at the Southwest Border," prepared by the Majority Staff of the House Committee on Homeland Security, Subcommittee on Investigations, p. 2, www.house.gov/mccaul/pdf/Investigaions-Border-Report.pdf (accessed August 2007).

2. Ibid., pp. 2, 3. John Mueller estimates that "hundreds" of Muslims from Muslim countries are apprehended along the Mexican border and acknowledges that "many more" probably make it through; see John Mueller, "Is There Still a Terrorist Threat?" *Foreign Affairs* 85, no. 5 (September/October 2006): p. 3; see also Susan Kaufman Purcell, "The

Changing Bilateral Relationship: A U.S. View," in Luis Rubio and Susan Kaufman Purcell, eds., *Mexico under Fox* (Boulder, CO: Lynne Rienner, 2004), p. 159. Purcell reports that a people-smuggling ring in Mexico specializing in Middle Easterners has brought record numbers into America since 9/11.

3. Jeffrey S. Passel, "Estimates of the Size and Characteristics of the Undocumented Population," *Pew Hispanic Center Report*, March 21, 2005, pp. 1, 2.

4. Samuel Huntington, *Who Are We?: The Challenges to America's National Identity* (New York: Simon and Schuster, 2004), pp. 225, 246.

5. John D. Eisenhower, *Intervention!: The United States and the Mexican Revolution, 1913–1917* (New York: Norton, 1993), pp. xv, xvi.

6. "A Line in the Sand," p. 4.

7. Ralph Blumenthal, "Texas Town Unnerved by Violence across Border," *New York Times*, August 11, 2005, p. A1.

8. For an intriguing look at this question, see Bill Masterson, "How Many Americans Live in Mexico?" at www.peoplesguide.com/1pages/retire/work/bil-maste/%23americans .html#Anchor-25583 (accessed March 2007).

9. Samuel Huntington, *Who Are We?* p. 223; Passel, "Estimates," p. 2.

10. Passel, "Estimates," p. 2.

11. Huntington, *Who Are We?* pp. 246, 247.

12. Washington Office on Latin America (WOLA), "Executive Summary," *Drug War Monitor*, December 2004, p. 7.

13. National Drug Intelligence Center, "National Drug Threat Assessment 2005," p. v, www.usdoj.gov/ndic/pubs11/12620/12620p.pdf (accessed July 2006).

14. Peter H. Smith, "Mexico," in Robert Chase, Emily Hill, and Paul Kennedy, eds., *The Pivotal States: A New Framework for U.S. Policy in the Developing World* (New York: Norton, 1999), p. 230.

15. U.S. Department of State, "International Narcotics Control Strategy Report 2005," released by the Bureau for International Narcotics and Law Enforcement Affairs, March 2005, p. 24.

16. National Drug Intelligence Center, "National Drug Threat Assessment 2005," p. vi.

17. Washington Office on Latin America, *Drug War Monitor*, pp. 4, 12, 17.

18. U.S. Chamber of Commerce, "Mexico," www.export.gov/articles/Mexico_MoM .asp (accessed July 2007).

19. U.S. Embassy, "Trade at a Glance," www.usembassy-mexico.gov/eng/trade_info .html (accessed March 2005); see also U.S. Chamber of Commerce, "Mexico," p. 1.

20. Smith, "Mexico," pp. 237–239.

21. U.S. Department of State, "Country Reports on Human Rights Practices 2004: Mexico," released by the Bureau of Democracy, Human Rights, and Labor, February 28, 2005, p. 1, www.state.gov/g/drl/rls/hrrpt/2004/41767.htm (accessed March 2005).

22. Timothy A. Wise and Kevin P. Gallagher, "NAFTA: A Cautionary Tale," *Foreign Policy In Focus*, October 24, 2002, p. 1, www.mindfully.org/WTO/NAFTA-Cautionary-Tale-FPIF24oct02.htm (accessed August 2007).

23. Juan Pardinas, "Fighting Poverty in Mexico: Policy Challenges," in Rubio and Purcell, *Mexico under Fox*, pp. 68, 69.

24. Jose Luis Velasco, *Insurgency, Authoritarianism, and Drug Trafficking in Mexico's "Democratization"* (New York: Routledge, 2005), p. 81.

25. For a description of the somewhat disappointing legacy produced by NAFTA for Mexico, see Joseph E. Stiglitz and Andrew Charlton, *Fair Trade for All: How Trade Can Promote Development* (New York: Oxford University Press, 2006), pp. 22–24.

26. Velasco, *Insurgency*, p. 101.

27. U.S. Department of State, "Country Reports on Human Rights Practices 2004: Mexico," p. 1. Figures refer to stranger kidnappings, not custody battles.

28. Ginger Thompson, "In Mexico's Murders, Fury Is Aimed at the Police," *New York Times*, September 26, 2005, p. A1.

29. Sara Miller Llana, "With Calderon In, a New War on Mexico's Mighty Drug Cartels," *The Christian Science Monitor*, January 22, 2007.

30. "Righting the Scales," *The Economist*, October 8, 2005, p. 45.

31. Robert S. Leiken, "Mexico: The Crisis Next Door," *Commentary* 106, no. 4 (October 1998): p. 38.

32. Llana, "With Calderon In, a New War on Mexico's Mighty Drug Cartels."

33. M. Delal Baer, "Mexico at an Impasse," *Foreign Affairs* 83, no. 1 (January/February 2004): p. 108.

34. Some of these "good news" points are made by Baer, "Mexico at an Impasse," p. 90. As Delal's title suggests, however, he was not optimistic about Mexico being able to sustain its progress.

35. Luis Rubio and Jeffrey Davidow, "Mexico's Disputed Election," *Foreign Affairs* 85, no. 5 (September/October 2006): pp. 75–80.

36. Christian Stracke, "Mexico—The Sick Man of NAFTA," *World Policy Journal* (Summer 2003): pp. 30–32.

37. Baer, "Mexico at an Impasse," p. 108.

38. Andres Oppenheimer, *Bordering on Chaos: Guerrillas, Stockbrokers, Politicians, and Mexico's Road to Prosperity* (New York: Little, Brown, 1996), p. 323.

39. Ibid., pp. 5, 313, 323; Stracke, "Mexico—The Sick Man of NAFTA," p. 30.

40. Purcell, "The Changing Bilateral Relationship," p. 150; Karin Brulliard, "Migrants Sent Home $300 Billion in 2006; Study Says Money Sent to Families Has Potential to Aid Development in Poor Countries," *Washington Post*, October 18, 2007, p. A20.

41. Donald E. Schulz, "Through a Glass Darkly: On the Challenges and Enigmas of Mexico's Future," *Mexican Studies/Estudios Mexicanos* 12, no. 1 (Winter 1996): p. 140.

42. "Into Deep Water," *The Economist*, February 26, 2005, p. 36.

43. Geri Smith, "Beating the Oil Curse," *Business Week*, June 4, 2007, p. 48.

44. "Is Pemex Nearly Bankrupt?" *Business Latin America* 39, no. 20 (2004): p. 3.

45. "Into Deep Water," *The Economist*, p. 36.

46. Purcell, "The Changing Bilateral Relationship," p. 153.

47. For the high figure, see Peter Andreas, "The Paradox of Integration: Liberalizing and Criminalizing Flows across the U.S.-Mexican Border," in Carol Wise, ed., *The Post-NAFTA Political Economy: Mexico and the Western Hemisphere* (University Park: The Pennsylvania State University Press, 1998), p. 129; for the lower range, see Velasco, *Insurgency*, p. 96.

48. Luis Astorga, *Drug Trafficking in Mexico: A First General Assessment,* Discussion Paper, no. 36 (Paris: Most Programme [UNESCO], 1999), p. 20.

49. Matt Levitch, "Cartels Lash Out at Mexican Crackdown on Drug Trafficking," *The Christian Science Monitor,* May 16, 2007.

50. Smith, "Mexico," pp. 225–227.

51. Velasco, *Insurgency,* p. 109.

52. Smith, "Mexico," p. 229.

53. "A Line in the Sand," p. 22.

54. In 1994, the PRI presidential candidate Luis Donaldo Colosio was assassinated. Some believe the assassination was carried out by drug traffickers angered at Mexican president Salinas's decision to crack down on drug dealers in an effort to please the United States and ensure the passage of NAFTA; see Oppenheimer, *Bordering on Chaos,* pp. 305, 306. More recently, in May 2007, a top intelligence official in the attorney general's office in Mexico City, Jose Nemesio Lugo Felix, was assassinated by what are believed to be drug dealers angry at President Felipe Calderon's efforts to suppress them; see Levitch, "Cartels Lash Out."

55. Francisco E. Thoumi, "Illegal Drugs in Colombia," in *The Political Economy of the Drug Industry: Latin America and the International System,* ed. Menno Vellinga (Gainesville: University Press of Florida, 2004), p. 78; Randy Willoughby, "Crouching Fox, Hidden Eagle: Drug Trafficking and Transnational Security—A Perspective from the Tijuana–San Diego Border," *Crime, Law and Social Change* 40 (2003): p. 116.

56. Marcos Pablo Moloeznik, "The Military Dimensions of the War on Drugs in Mexico and Colombia," *Crime, Law and Social Change* 40 (2003): pp. 108, 109.

57. Velasco, *Insurgency,* pp. 4–6.

58. U.S. Department of State, "Country Reports on Human Rights Practices 2004: Mexico."

59. Velasco, *Insurgency,* p. 57.

60. Oppenheimer, *Bordering on Chaos,* pp. 40–41.

61. Ibid., p. 36.

62. Schulz, "Through a Glass Darkly," p. 139.

63. Guillermo Trejo Osorio, "Indigenous Insurgency: Protest, Rebellion and the Politicization of Ethnicity in 20th Century Mexico," vol. 1 (PhD diss., University of Chicago, 2004), p. 2.

64. Velasco, *Insurgency,* p. 52.

65. Neil Harvey, *The Chiapas Rebellion: The Struggle for Land and Democracy* (Durham: Duke University Press, 1998): pp. 183, 184.

66. Philip N. Howard and Thomas Homer-Dixon, *Environmental Scarcity and Violent Conflict: The Case of Chiapas, Mexico,* Occasional Paper, Project on Environment, Population and Security (Washington, DC: American Association for the Advancement of Science and the University of Toronto, 1996), p. 5.

67. Oppenheimer, *Bordering on Chaos,* p. 52.

68. Harvey, *The Chiapas Rebellion,* pp. 187–190.

69. Oppenheimer, *Bordering on Chaos,* p. 50.

70. Ibid., pp. 244–245.

71. Osorio, "Indigenous Insurgency," vol. 1, p. 318.

72. On the role of the 2006 elections in promoting the north-south divide, see Rubio and Davidow, "Mexico's Disputed Election," pp. 75–78; see also James C. McKinley Jr.'s thoughtful commentary, "Mexico Faces Its Own Red-Blue Standoff," *New York Times,* July 9, 2006, p. 4.

73. Luis Rubio, "Democratic Politics in Mexico: New Complexities," in Rubio and Purcell, *Mexico under Fox,* p. 7.

74. Ibid., pp. 22, 23.

75. Baer, "Mexico at an Impasse," p. 102.

76. Rubio, "Democratic Politics in Mexico," p. 24.

77. Edna Jaime, "Fox's Economic Agenda: An Incomplete Transition," in Rubio and Purcell, *Mexico under Fox,* p. 51.

78. For an insightful look at Mexico's 2006 election, see Rubio and Davidow, "Mexico's Disputed Election," pp. 75–85.

79. Astorga, *Drug Trafficking in Mexico,* p. 26.

80. Smith, "Mexico," p. 226.

81. Louise Shelley, "Corruption and Organized Crime in Mexico in the Post-PRI Transition," *Journal of Contemporary Criminal Justice* 17, no. 3 (August 2001): p. 215.

82. Smith, "Mexico," p. 227.

83. Christian M. Allen, *An Industrial Geography of Cocaine* (New York: Routledge, 2005), p. 82.

84. Ibid., pp. 82, 83. Oppenheimer, *Bordering on Chaos,* pp. 193, 194, 201.

85. Velasco, *Insurgency,* pp. 111–114; U.S. Department of State, "Country Reports on Human Rights Practices 2004: Mexico."

86. Shelley, "Corruption and Organized Crime," p. 220.

87. Chappel Lawson, "Fox's Mexico at Midterm," *Journal of Democracy* 15, no. 1 (2004): pp. 139, 140.

88. Velasco, *Insurgency,* pp. 111–112.

89. Thompson, "In Mexico's Murders, Fury Is Aimed at the Police."

90. Allen, *An Industrial Geography of Cocaine,* p. 81.

91. James McKinley Jr., "Scandals Shake Mexico's Confidence in Elite Drug Police," *New York Times,* December 28, 2005, p. A3.

92. Patrick O'Day, "The Mexican Army as Cartel," *Journal of Contemporary Criminal Justice* 17, no. 3 (August 2001): pp. 278, 279.

93. Allen, *An Industrial Geography of Cocaine,* p. 81.

94. Julia Preston and Samuel Dillon, *Opening Mexico: The Making of a Democracy* (New York: Farrar, Straus and Giroux, 2004), p. 324.

95. David R. Mares, "U.S. Drug Policy and Mexican Civil-Military Relations: A Challenge for the Mutually Desirable Democratization Process," *Crime, Law and Social Change* 40 (2003): p. 70.

96. O'Day, "The Mexican Army as Cartel," p. 280.

97. Michael Radu, "The Looming Mexican Crisis," *Washington Quarterly* 20, no. 4 (1997): p. 124.

98. Shelley, "Corruption and Organized Crime," p. 214.

99. Rubio, "Democratic Politics in Mexico," p. 28.

100. Radu, "The Looming Mexican Crisis," p. 124.

101. M. Delal Baer, "Mexico's Coming Backlash," *Foreign Affairs* 78, no. 4 (July/August 1999): p. 95.

CHAPTER FIVE: CHINA

1. Minxin Pei, *China's Trapped Transition: The Limits of Developmental Autocracy* (Cambridge, MA: Harvard University Press, 2006), pp. 2, 3.

2. For views that see China in a threatening light, see Richard Bernstein and Ross H. Munro, *The Coming Conflict with China* (New York: Knopf, 1997); Aaron L. Friedberg, "The Future of U.S.-China Relations: Is Conflict Inevitable?" *International Security* 30, no. 2 (Fall 2005): esp. pp. 16–24; and Samuel P. Huntington, *The Clash of Civilizations and the Remaking of the World Order* (New York: Simon and Schuster, 1996), esp. pp. 218–243, 312–315.

3. For statistics showing the growing economic relationship between the United States and China, see US-China Business Council, "US-China Trade Statistics and China's World Trade Statistics," www.uschina.org/statistics/tradetable.html (accessed June 2006). For an insightful analysis of American vulnerability regarding China's purchase of American bonds, see Andrew Browne, "China's Reserves Near Milestone, Underscoring Its Financial Clout," *Wall Street Journal*, October 17, 2006, p. A1.

4. Susan Shirk, *China: Fragile Superpower* (New York: Oxford University Press, 2007), p. 249.

5. David M. Lampton, "The Faces of Chinese Power," *Foreign Affairs* 86, no. 1 (January/February 2007): p. 119.

6. Thomas J. Christensen, "Fostering Stability or Creating a Monster: The Rise of China and U.S. Policy toward East Asia," *International Security* 31, no. 1 (Summer 2006): pp. 89–91.

7. On how the Chinese role in international institutions fosters peace in Asia, see Friedberg, "The Future of U.S.-China Relations," esp. pp. 13–14.

8. Ko-lin Chin and Roy Godson, "Organized Crime and the Political-Criminal Nexus in China," *Trends in Organized Crime* 9, no. 3 (Spring 2006): p. 29.

9. Deng Xiaoping, *Selected Works*, vol. 3, 1982–1992 (Beijing: Foreign Languages Press, 1994), p. 347, cited in Bruce Gilley, *China's Democratic Future: How It Will Happen and Where It Will Lead* (New York: Columbia University Press, 2004), p. 139.

10. See, e.g., the alleged comments of Party elder, Bo Yibo, during the Tiananmen demonstrations, when he is reported to have remarked, "The whole imperialist Western world wants to make socialist countries leave the socialist road and become satellites in the system of international monopoly capitalism. The people with ulterior motives who are behind this student movement have support from the United States and Europe and from the KMT [Kuomintang]." Quoted in "The Tiananmen Papers," introduced by Andrew J. Nathan, *Foreign Affairs* 80, no. 1 (January/February 2001): p. 24.

11. Gilley, *China's Democratic Future*, p. 114.

12. Shirk, *China*, pp. 2, 254.

13. On China's efforts to modernize its forces, see David Shambaugh, *Modernizing China's Military: Progress, Problems and Prospects* (Berkeley: University of California Press, 2002).

14. Charles Wolf Jr., K. C. Yeh, Benjamin Zycher, Nicholas Eberstadt, and Sung-Ho Lee, *Fault Lines in China's Economic Terrain* (Santa Monica, CA: Rand, 2003), pp. 162–163.

15. Gilley, *China's Democratic Future*, p. 38.

16. June Teufel Dreyer, "The Limits to China's Growth," *Orbis* 48, no. 2 (Spring 2004): p. 237.

17. Shirk, *China*, p. 17; Pei, *China's Trapped Transition*, pp. 174, 175.

18. An Chen, "The New Inequality," *Journal of Democracy* 14, no. 1 (January 2003): p. 56.

19. Gilley, *China's Democratic Future*, p. 38.

20. Dreyer, "The Limits to China's Growth," p. 236.

21. Chen, "The New Inequality," p. 58; Pei, "Contradictory Trends and Confusing Signals," *Journal of Democracy* 14, no. 1 (January 2003): p. 80.

22. Ted Robert Gurr, *Why Men Rebel* (Princeton: Princeton University Press, 1970), esp. chap. 2.

23. Gilley, *China's Democratic Future*, p. 63.

24. Pei, *China's Trapped Transition*, pp. 7, 28.

25. Gilley, *China's Democratic Future*, p. 41.

26. Pei, *China's Trapped Transition*, pp. 38, 39.

27. Gilley, *China's Democratic Future*, p. 37.

28. Eduardo Porter, "China Shrinks," *New York Times*, December 9, 2006, p. 9 (section 4).

29. Gilley, *China's Democratic Future*, pp. 37, 40.

30. Howard W. French, "China Scrambles for Stability as Its Workers Age," *New York Times*, March 22, 2007, p. A1.

31. Nicholas Lardy, "Sources of Macroeconomic Instability in China," in David Shambaugh, *Is China Unstable?* (Armonk, NY: M. E. Sharpe, 2000), p. 57.

32. Wolf et al., *Fault Lines*, pp. 120–123.

33. Ibid., p. 128.

34. Dreyer, "The Limits to China's Growth," p. 241.

35. Pei, *China's Trapped Transition*, p. 110; Gordon C. Chang, *The Coming Collapse of China* (New York: Random House, 2001), pp. 124, 131.

36. Shirk, *China*, p. 28.

37. Chang, *The Coming Collapse of China*, p. 47.

38. Steven F. Jackson, "Introduction: A Typology for Stability and Instability in China," in Shambaugh, *Is China Unstable?* pp. 6, 7.

39. Kellee S. Tsai, *Back-Alley Banking: Private Entrepreneurs in China* (Ithaca: Cornell University Press, 2002).

40. Wolf et al., *Fault Lines*, p. 134.

41. Ibid.

42. Gilley, *China's Democratic Future*, p. 43.

43. Lardy, "Sources of Macroeconomic Instability," p. 61; Wolf et al., *Fault Lines*, p. 136.

44. Wolf et al., *Fault Lines*, p. 135.

45. Pei, *China's Trapped Transition*, p. 120.

46. Wolf et al., *Fault Lines*, p. 151.

47. Charles Wolf Jr., "Uncertain Times for Foreign Investment in China," *Financial Times*, June 24, 2002, cited in Gilley, *China's Democratic Future*, p. 104.

48. Gilley, *China's Democratic Future*, p. 105.

49. Gordon C. Chang, "Halfway to China's Collapse," *Far Eastern Economic Review* 169, no. 5 (June 2006): p. 27.

50. Yan Sun, *Corruption and Market in Contemporary China* (Ithaca: Cornell University Press, 2004), p. 2.

51. Pei, *China's Trapped Transition*, p. 133.

52. Gilley, *China's Democratic Future*, p. 38; Dreyer, "The Limits to China's Growth," p. 243.

53. Chin and Godson, "Organized Crime," pp. 5, 6; Pei, *China's Trapped Transition*, p. 12.

54. Pei, *China's Trapped Transition*, p. 141.

55. Ibid., pp. 147, 148, 12.

56. Lianjiang Li, "Driven to Protest: China's Rural Unrest," *Current History*, September 2006, p. 250.

57. Mary E. Gallagher, "China in 2004: Stability Above All," *Asian Survey* 14 (January/February 2005): p. 23.

58. Wolf et al., *Fault Lines*, pp. 17–18.

59. Dreyer, "The Limits to China's Growth," pp. 241, 243.

60. Gilley, *China's Democratic Future*, p. 39.

61. Shaoguang Wang, "The Problems of State Weakness," *Journal of Democracy* 14, no. 1 (January 2003): p. 41.

62. Thomas P. Bernstein, "Instability in Rural China," in Shambaugh, *Is China Unstable?* pp. 95, 96.

63. French, "China Scrambles for Stability"; see also Shirk, *China*, p. 30.

64. Chen, "The New Inequality," p. 54.

65. Cheng Li, "China in 2020: Three Political Scenarios," p. 20, www.nbr.org/publications/asia_policy/AP4/AP4%20China%20RT.pdf (accessed April 2006).

66. Jack A. Goldstone, "Population and Security: How Demographic Change Can Lead to Violent Conflict," *Journal of International Affairs* 56, no. 1 (Fall 2002): p. 14.

67. Gallagher, "China in 2004," p. 24.

68. Gilley, *China's Democratic Future*, p. 49.

69. Wang, "The Problems of State Weakness," p. 38.

70. Valerie M. Hudson and Andrea Den Boer, "A Surplus of Men, a Deficit of Peace," *International Security* 26, no. 4 (Spring 2002): p. 31.

71. Chin and Godson, "Organized Crime," p. 6.

72. Hudson and Den Boer, "A Surplus of Men," pp. 6, 10.

73. Martin Walker, "The Geopolitics of Sexual Frustration," *Foreign Policy* no. 153 (March/April 2006): p. 60.

74. Goldstone, "Population and Security," pp. 10, 11.

75. Hudson and Den Boer, "A Surplus of Men," p. 17.

76. Walker, "The Geopolitics of Sexual Frustration," p. 61.

77. Hudson and Den Boer, "A Surplus of Men," pp. 11, 12.

78. Herbert S. Yee, "Ethnic Relations in Xinjiang: A Survey of Uygur-Han Relations in Urumqi," *Journal of Contemporary China* 12, no. 36 (August 2003): pp. 439, 448; Rowan Callick, "Beijing Targets Hearts and Minds to Beat al-Qa'ida's Push," *The Australian*, February 26, 2007, p. 12.

79. Yee, "Ethnic Relations in Xinjiang," p. 450.

80. Ibid., p. 452.

81. Shirk, *China*, p. 58.

82. Nicholas Becquelin, "Xinjiang in the Nineties," *The China Journal* 44 (2000), pp. 86–88; Susan Shirk, *China*, p. 58.

83. June Teufel Dreyer, "Economic Development in Tibet under the People's Republic of China," *Journal of Contemporary China* 12, no. 36 (August 2003): p. 418.

84. Shirk, *China*, p. 58.

85. Barry Sautman, "China's Strategic Vulnerability to Minority Separatism in Tibet," *Asian Affairs, An American Review* 32, no. 2 (Summer 2005): pp. 89, 90, 95.

86. Gilley, *China's Democratic Future*, p. 249.

87. Nicholas Eberstadt, "The Future of AIDS," *Foreign Affairs* 81, no. 6 (November/ December 2002): pp. 38, 44.

88. Wolf et al., *Fault Lines*, p. 56.

89. Ibid.; Eberstadt, "The Future of AIDS," p. 30.

90. Gilley, *China's Democratic Future*, p. 47; Wolf et al., *Fault Lines*, pp. 171, 172.

91. United Nations, "HIV/AIDS: China's Titanic Peril," *Executive Summary of the Joint United Nations Program on HIV/AIDS* (New York: United Nations, 2002), cited in Pei, *China's Trapped Transition*, p. 174.

92. Eberstadt, "The Future of AIDS," pp. 40, 41.

93. Dreyer, "The Limits to China's Growth," pp. 243, 244; Li, "China in 2020," p. 7.

94. Jim Yardley, "China's Path to Modernity Mirrored in a Troubled River," *New York Times*, November 19, 2006, p. A1.

95. Li, "China in 2020," p. 26.

96. Wolf et al., *Fault Lines*, p. 87.

97. Shirk, *China*, p. 33.

98. Wolf et al., *Fault Lines*, p. 79.

99. Qinglian He, "A Volcanic Stability," *Journal of Democracy* 14, no. 1 (January 2003): p. 67; Jack A. Goldstone, "The Coming China Collapse," *Foreign Policy* no. 99 (Summer 1995): p. 36; Michael Sheridan, "Dust Clouds Threaten to Bury Silk Road Treasures as Deserts Creep Even Closer," *The Australian*, November 12, 2007, p. 14.

100. Samuel P. Huntington, *Political Order in Changing Societies* (New Haven: Yale University Press, 1968).

101. Minxin Pei, "Contradictory Trends and Confusing Signals," *Journal of Democracy* 14, no. 1 (January 2003): p. 81.

102. Li, "Driven to Protest," pp. 252, 253.

103. Pei, *China's Trapped Transition*, p. 202. A study found that only two out of a thousand petitioners found relief through *xinfang*.

104. Only 20% of plaintiffs get any judicial satisfaction through the courts, a figure that appears to be much lower for rural cases; see Pei, *China's Trapped Transition*, p. 202.

105. Shirk, *China*, p. 39.

106. One of the best examinations of the decline of the belief in communism in contemporary China can be found in Yan Sun, *The Chinese Reassessment of Socialism, 1976–1992* (Princeton: Princeton University Press, 1995).

107. Gilley, *China's Democratic Future*, p. 87.

108. Howard W. French, "Religious Surge in Once Atheist China Surprises Leaders," *New York Times*, March 4, 2007, p. A3. The article reports on a poll taken by the East China Normal University that estimated that 31.4% of the Chinese 16 years and older (400 million people) are religious. Official figures place the number of religious at 100 million, but their publication of the higher estimate may suggest they put credence in the poll's results.

109. Gilley, *China's Democratic Future*, p. 58.

110. Wang, "The Problems of State Weakness," p. 40.

111. Gilley, *China's Democratic Future*, p. 42.

112. Cited in Pei, *China's Trapped Transition*, p. 172.

113. Peter Hays Gries, *China's New Nationalism: Pride, Politics, and Diplomacy* (Berkeley: University of California Press, 2002), pp. 119, 128–129.

114. Ibid., p. 131.

115. *The Military Balance 2005–2006*, vol. 105, no. 1 (London: International Institute for Strategic Studies, 2006), p. 270.

116. Pei, *China's Trapped Transition*, pp. 83, 86–88; see also pp. 88–95 for a broad description of China's efforts to coopt key groups.

117. For a firsthand look at the Tiananmen demonstrations (albeit with some concerns over authenticity), see "The Tiananmen Papers," pp. 2–48.

118. Gilley, *China's Democratic Future*, pp. 111–112.

119. Hudson and Den Boer, "A Surplus of Men," p. 33.

120. Bruce Dickson, "Threats to Party Supremacy," *Journal of Democracy* 14, no. 1 (January 2003): p. 30; Bruce Dickson, "Political Instability at the Middle and Lower Levels," in Shambaugh, *Is China Unstable?* p. 42.

121. Bruce Gilley makes this point forcefully; *China's Democratic Future*, pp. 106, 107.

122. Li, "China in 2020," p. 21.

123. Shirk, *China*, p. 51.

124. Goldstone, "The Coming China Collapse," pp. 41–42.

125. Joseph Kahn, "In Graft Inquiry, Chinese See a Coming Shake-Up," *New York Times*, October 4, 2006, p. A1.

126. Pei, *China's Trapped Transition*, p. 155.

127. He, "A Volcanic Stability," p. 71.

128. Wolf et al., *Fault Lines*; see pp. 18–19 for a similar depiction of the potential of unrest in China.

CHAPTER SIX: THE COMING STORM

1. Kenneth Waltz makes these points forcefully in "Waltz Responds to Sagan," in Scott D. Sagan and Kenneth N. Waltz, *The Spread of Nuclear Weapons: A Debate Renewed* (New York: Norton, 2003), pp. 131–133.

2. This is a major theme of Stephen P. Cohen's works; see *The Idea of Pakistan* (Washington, DC: Brookings, 2004), esp. chaps. 1 and 2.

3. On the rationality of terrorists, especially suicide bombers, see Robert Pape, *Dying to Win: The Strategic Logic of Suicide Terrorism* (New York: Random House, 2005). On how Al Qaeda rationally seeks to counter American foreign policies, see Anonymous, *Through Our Enemies' Eyes: Osama bin Laden, Radical Islam and the Future of America* (Washington, DC: Brassey's, 2002), esp. chaps. 2, 15.

4. On efforts to trace the source of nuclear explosions, see National Academy of Sciences, Committee on International Security and Arms Control, *Monitoring Nuclear Weapons and Nuclear-Explosive Materials* (Washington, DC: National Academies Press, 2005).

5. Steven R. David, "Israel's Policy of Targeted Killing," *Ethics and International Affairs* 17, no. 1 (2003): pp. 111–126; see also, Robert F. Trager and Dessislava P. Zagorcheva, "Deterring Terrorism: It Can Be Done," *International Security* 30, no. 3 (Winter 2005/2006): pp. 87–123.

6. On the problems of state building, see the still-relevant work, Karl W. Deutsch and William J. Foltz, eds., *Nation-Building* (New York: Atherton, 1966). For a more contemporary analysis, see Francis Fukuyama, ed., *Nation-Building: Beyond Afghanistan and Iraq* (Baltimore: The Johns Hopkins University Press, 2006).

7. R. J. Rummel, *Death by Government* (New Brunswick, NJ: Transaction, 1994), chap. 1.

8. One of the best examinations of the problems and prospects for spreading democracy is Samuel Huntington, *The Third Wave: Democratization in the Late Twentieth Century* (Norman: University of Oklahoma Press, 1991).

9. For a different view, one that argues that China is on the democratic path, see the excellent work by Bruce Gilley, *China's Democratic Future: How It Will Happen and Where It Will Lead* (New York: Columbia University Press, 2004).

10. Edward D. Mansfield and Jack Snyder, *Electing to Fight: Why Emerging Democracies Go to War* (Cambridge, MA: MIT Press, 2005). Their book focuses on external war but also considers democracy's role in producing "turbulent transitions."

11. For an account of past American efforts to remove hostile regimes, see Steven R. David, *Third World Coups d'Etat and International Security* (Baltimore: The Johns Hopkins University Press, 1987).

12. For an argument that external invasions are the only reliable means of removing foreign governments, see Stephen T. Hosmer, *Operations against Enemy Leaders* (Santa Monica, CA: Rand, 2001).

13. On the value of prevention for dealing with the consequences of civil conflict, see *Preventing Deadly Conflict* (New York: Carnegie Commission, 1997).

14. There is, of course, a vast literature on responding to natural catastrophes. Two in-

triguing views include Richard A. Posner, *Catastrophe: Risk and Response* (New York: Oxford University Press, 2004), and William E. Easterling III, Brian H. Hurd, and Joel B. Smith, "Coping with Global Climate Change: The Role of Adaptation in the United States," Pew Center on Global Climate Change, June 2004, www.pewclimate.org/docUploads/ Adaptation.pdf (accessed August 2007).

15. The Strategic Petroleum Reserve was set up by President Ford in 1975 and stores oil in a number of sites in Louisiana and Texas. At full capacity it has 727 million barrels. In 2007, it had reserves that would last the United States only 56 days. See U.S. Department of Energy, "Strategic Petroleum Reserve," www.fossil.energy.gov/programs/reserves/spr/ spr-facts.html (accessed August 2007).

16. A good summary of steps to take to lessen America's dependence on outside sources of oil can be found in *Strategic Energy Policy: Challenges for the 21st Century; Report of an Independent Task Force Cosponsored by the James A. Baker III Institute for Public Policy of Rice University and the Council on Foreign Relations*, Edward L. Morse, chair, Amy Jaffe, project editor (New York: Council on Foreign Relations, 2001).

17. U.S. Department of Energy, Energy Information Administration, "Basic Petroleum Statistics," www.eia.doe.gov/ (accessed November 2007).

18. Edward L. Morse and Amy Jaffe, *Strategic Energy Policy Update: Update by the Chair and Project Editor of an Independent Task Force on Strategic Energy Policy—Challenges for the 21st Century* (New York: Council on Foreign Relations, 2001), p. 12.

19. Ibid., p. 13.

20. James T. Bartis, Tom LaTourrette, Lloyd Dixon, D. J. Peterson, and Gary Cecchine, *Oil Shale Development in the United States: Prospects and Policy Issues* (Santa Monica, CA: Rand, 2005); Morse and Jaffe, *Strategic Energy Policy Update*, p. 15.

21. For an account supportive of seizing the oil fields, see Robert W. Tucker, "Oil: The Issue of American Intervention," *Commentary* 59, no. 1 (January 1975): pp. 21–31. For a study casting doubt on the ability to seize the oil fields, see Special Subcommittee on Investigations of the Committee on International Relations, "Oil Fields as Military Objectives: A Feasibility Study," August 21, 1975, 94th Cong., 1st sess.

22. Steve Yetiv, *Crude Awakenings: Global Oil Security and American Foreign Policy* (Ithaca: Cornell University Press, 2004), pp. 66–72.

23. One of the best accounts of America's vulnerability to a smuggled nuclear device can be found in Stephen Flynn, *America the Vulnerable: How Our Government Is Failing to Protect Us from Terrorism* (New York: HarperCollins, 2004), esp. chap. 5.

24. Dan Reiter, "Exploding the Powder Keg Myth: Preemptive Wars Almost Never Happen," *International Security* 20, no. 2 (Fall 1995): pp. 5–34; see also Richard Betts, "Striking First: A History of Thankfully Lost Opportunities," *Ethics and International Affairs* 17, no. 1 (March 2003): pp. 17–24.

25. See section 5 of *The National Security Strategy of the United States of America*, September 2002, www.whitehouse.gov/nsc/nss.html (accessed March 2007).

26. An exception to this refusal to think about the unthinkable is George H. Quester, *Nuclear First Strike: Consequences of a Broken Taboo* (Baltimore: The Johns Hopkins University Press, 2006). On steps to take now to prepare for the nightmare of an American city falling victim to a nuclear detonation, see the thoughtful study from the Preventive De-

fense Project at Harvard and Stanford universities, Ashton B. Carter, William J. Perry, and Michael M. May, *The Day After: Action in the 24 Hours Following a Nuclear Blast in an American City*, http://bcsia.ksg.harvard.edu/publication.cfm?program=CORE&ctype= book&item_id=521 (accessed June 2007).

27. Rachel L. Swarns, "House Republicans Will Push for 700 Miles of Fencing on Mexico Border," *New York Times*, September 14, 2006, p. A18. Figures come from House Republicans.

28. For a persuasive view on steps to take to deal with illegal immigration that would also help in the event of a Mexican civil conflict, see Tamar Jacoby, "Immigration Nation," *Foreign Affairs* 85, no. 6 (November/December 2006): pp. 50–66.

29. For a balanced view on this controversial topic, see James A. Inciardi, ed., *The Drug Legalization Debate* (Thousand Oaks, CA: Sage Publications, 1999).

Index

Abdullah (king), 34, 48

Abqaiq oil complex, 25, 28–29, 45

Afghanistan, 1, 17, 52, 67, 68, 78

Afghan Saudis, 45

AFI (Federal Investigation Agency), 109

aging population: of China, 125; of Mexico, 92

AIDS, in China, 135–36

Al Qaeda: deterrence policy and, 157; dirty bombs and, 30; Pakistan and, 19, 50, 58–59, 64, 67–68, 73–74; Saudi Arabia and, 18; Saudi oil and, 28–29, 29; WMD and, 14–15. *See also* bin Laden, Osama

Al Qaeda of the Arabian Peninsula (QAP), 44–45

American citizens in Mexico, 84, 85, 167–68

americium, 30

anthrax, 13, 30

Arab oil embargo, 24, 25, 26

Arab states, 5

Arellano brothers, 107

armed forces. *See* military

Asia, stability in, 119

Asia-Pacific Economic Cooperation forum, 119

Asiri tribe, 36

Association of Southeast Asian Nations, 119

Astorga, Luis, 106

Baer, Robert, 28

Bahrain, 164

Balkans, 1, 81

ballistic missile defense, 165

Baluchistan, 68–69, 71–72

banking system, in China, 125–27

Bhutto, Benazir, 72, 75

Bhutto, Zulfikar Ali, 51–52, 68–69

Biafra, 6

bin Laden, Osama: Pakistan and, 58, 73; Saudi Arabia and, 27, 29, 40, 41, 42–45

biological weapons, 13, 30, 53

bonds. *See* treasury securities

border issues: Al Qaeda and, 58, 64, 73, 78; Mexico and, 83–84, 93–94, 98, 168–69; nuclear weapons and, 165; overview of, 17

Brazil, 12

budget deficit, 170

Bush administration, 166

CAFE (Corporate Average Fuel Economy) standards, 162

Calderon, Felipe, 90, 97, 102, 105, 109

Cali cartel, 108

Cantarell oil field, 94

Catholic Church, in Mexico, 101–2

Cervantes, Enrique, 109

Chad, 9

Chechnya, 11

chemical weapons, 13, 29–30, 53

Chiapas, Mexico, uprising, 82, 99–101, 111, 112

China: corruption in, 123, 128–30, 144; democratic practices and, 159; deterrence of, 155–56; domestic strife in, 8; economy of, 20, 115, 122–25, 127–28, 129; gender imbalances in, 132–33; grievances of people of, 122–28, 128–33; growth of, 115–16; health concerns in, 135–37, 139; instability in, 116–22; institutions in, 124, 125–27, 137–38; legitimacy of government of, 138–40; military power of, 4, 115, 141, 142; nuclear weapons of, 54, 62; overview of, x, 148–50; Pakistan and, 52; as petroleum importer, 21, 24; preparing for threats from, 170; as principal creditor, 16, 116, 117–18, 170; prospect of civil war in, 19–20, 119–21, 145–46,

China *(cont.)*
150–51; prospects for success of violence in, 140–44; revolution in, 1, 62; separatist movements in, 133–35; U.S. interests in, 117–22
Ciudad Juarez, Mexico, 108–9
civil conflicts / civil wars: causes of, 8–12, 101, 148; as chronic, 7; in Colombia, 98; conventional wisdom on, 1; definition of, 5–6, 7; democracy and, 159; deterrence of, 153–58; ignoring, 1–2; manipulation of, 17; natural disaster approach to, 160–61; in post–Cold War era, 12–17; prevention of, 158–60; primacy of, 7–8; responding to threats of, 153–58; threats of, x, 2, 147–48, 149–53; types of, 6–7; U.S. interests and, 17–18; as weakening government control, 3, 7
civil wars, prospect of: in China, 119–21, 145–46, 150–51; in Mexico, 87–88, 112–14, 151; overview of, 18–20; in Pakistan, 61–65, 69–70, 79–81, 150; in Saudi Arabia, 30–31, 36, 48–49, 150
Clinton, Bill, 92
cobalt, radioactive, 30
Cold War: deterrence during, 20; end of, 1; international relations theories and, ix; natural disaster approach and, 171; nuclear weapons and, 53–54. *See also* post–Cold War era
Colombia, 11, 19, 97–98
Colosio, Luis Donaldo, 187n54
Columbus, New Mexico, 84, 85
Committee for the Defense of Legitimate Rights, 41
Communist Party (China), 127, 129, 137–39, 140, 141–44
community, sense of, in countries, 10
Congo, 6
Congress: of China, 138; of Mexico, 104–5, 113
conservation of oil, 162
conspiracy, 7
containment, policy of, 171
conventional assault, 4
Corporate Average Fuel Economy (CAFE) standards, 162
corruption: in China, 123, 128–30, 144; grievances of people and, 9, 10; in Mexico, 106–10
Costa Rica, 12
costs of war: as deterrence, 3; between states, ix, 4–5; within states, 8

coups, backing of, by U.S., 160
crime: in China, 131–32, 133; in Mexico, 84–85, 89, 90, 96–97. *See also* drugs, illegal
Cuban Missile Crisis, 54
currency: of China, 117; of Mexico, 92

Dalai Lama, 134
Darfur, 118
Davidow, Jeffrey, 91
decapitating attack, 60, 63
democracy: civil wars and, 8; interstate war and, 5; legitimacy of government and, 9–10; in Mexico, 82, 99, 103–4, 106, 108, 159; in Pakistan, 66, 75, 159; in Saudi Arabia, 48, 159; spread of, 158–59
Democratic Revolutionary Party (PRD, Mexico), 82, 95, 104–6
Den Boer, Andrea, 133
Deng Xiaoping, 120, 141
Department of Energy Nuclear Emergency Support Team (NEST), 165
dependence: on imported natural resources, 16; on imported oil, 16, 21, 24–25, 26; of Mexico on U.S., 113
Desch, Michael, 11
deterrence, policy of: civil conflict and, 8, 153–58; during Cold War, 20; history of, 3; nuclear weapons and, 14, 54–55; terrorists and, 14–15, 56–57; unintended threats and, 3
detonation, accidental, 56, 58, 60
Deutsch, Karl, 5
developing status of states, 10–11, 12
dirty bombs, 13, 30, 53
disarming strike, 60, 63
disruption of Saudi oil production, 27–31
diversionary war, by China, 156–57
domestic violence. *See* civil conflicts / civil wars
Doran, Michael, 34
drugs, illegal: decriminalization of, 169; Mexico and, 19, 86–87, 96–97, 106–11, 113–14

Eberstadt, Nicholas, 135
economy: of China, 20, 115, 122–25, 127–28, 129; of Mexico, 84, 89, 91–97, 101, 102, 112–13, 169; of Pakistan, 65–66; of Saudi Arabia, 31–33; of Taiwan, 121; of U.S., 25, 29, 87, 93–94
education: in China, 133; in Mexico, 91; in Pakistan, 65, 74; in Saudi Arabia, 33

Egypt, 18, 26, 152
El Salvador, 1, 84
energy independence, 163
environmental standards: in China, 136–37; in
    Mexico, 87
EPR (Popular Revolutionary Army, Mexico),
    99, 102
Eritrean-Ethiopian civil war, 6
ethnic conflicts, 6
extremist ideologies: government weakness
    and, 9, 10; in Pakistan, 18–19; WMD and,
    14–15. *See also* Al Qaeda; terrorist groups
EZLN (Zapatistas), 99, 100–101, 102, 111

Fahd (king), 34, 41, 43
Falun Gong movement, 143
Faysal (king), 38–39
Feaver, Peter, 59
Federal Investigation Agency (AFI), 109
financial sector, in China, 125–27
first-strike capability, and disarming nuclear
    forces, 173n5
foreign direct investment: China and, 127–28;
    Mexico and, 90–91
Fox, Vicente: Chiapas and, 100; drug traffick-
    ing and, 107–8, 109; election of, 82, 103, 104;
    Lopez Obrador and, 113; oil industry and, 95;
    policies of, 91
France, 1, 26, 52, 61–62, 121
fuel efficiency standards, 162
Fuentes, Armado Carrillo, 109

Gaddis, John Lewis, 2
Garcia Abrego, Juan, 107
gender imbalances, in China, 132–33
Ghawar oil field, 28
Gilley, Bruce, 128
globalization, civil wars and, 8
government control: challenges to, 11–12; civil
    wars as weakening, 3, 7; grievances of people
    and, 9, 10; incompetent and corrupt regimes,
    9; international support and, 11; loss of, and
    civil conflicts, 12–13; in Mexico, 90, 102–6,
    110–12; in Pakistan, 66, 67, 75–76; repressive,
    158; in Saudi Arabia, 39–42; weaknesses in,
    10–12; of WMD, 14. *See also* legitimacy of
    government
Grand Mosque in Mecca, 38–39, 45–46, 47

great power competition, 17
great power war, ix, 2, 3–5, 147
Greece, 6
Grenada, 160
Gries, Peter Hays, 140
grievances, intensity of: in China, 122–28,
    128–33; likelihood of civil wars and, 8–9; in
    Mexico, 88–91, 97–102; in Pakistan, 65–66,
    70–74; in Saudi Arabia, 31–37
Guerrero, Mexico, 102, 111
Guillen, Rafael Sebastian, 101
Gulf War, 23, 33, 39–40
Gurr, Ted Robert, 6–7, 123
Gutierrez Rebollo, Jesus, 109
Guzman, Jacobo Arbenz, 160
Guzman Loera, Joaquin, 108

Haiti, 9
Hamas, 48
Han Chinese, 133
health issues, in China, 130, 135–37, 139
Hejazi tribe, 36
Hezbollah, 83–84
Hispanic bloc, in U.S., 83, 85–86
Hudson, Valerie, 133
Hu Jintao, 144
Huntington, Samuel, 10, 84, 137
Hussein, Saddam, 8, 27, 47, 49, 55, 160
hydrogen sulfide gas, 28

Ibn Saud, 38
ideological conflicts, 6
Ikhwan, 38, 39, 40
immigrants to U.S.: from Mexico, 83–84,
    85–86, 93, 169; from Middle East, 184n2
income inequality. *See* wealth, distribution of
India: China and, 119; domestic strife in, 8, 18;
    nuclear weapons and, 15, 54–55; Pakistan
    and, 5, 51, 61, 63–64, 66, 72–73; as petroleum
    importer, 21, 24
individual use of weapons of mass destruction,
    14, 53, 56
Indonesia, 18
Institutional Revolutionary Party (PRI, Mex-
    ico): corruption and, 107; end of reign of, 82,
    99, 108; government paralysis and, 103–5;
    Zapatistas and, 100

institutions: in China, 124, 125–27, 137–38; internal conflict and, 10; international, and interstate war, 5; in Mexico, 91–92, 107. *See also* judicial system; military; police force

insurgents: in Iraq, 29; in Mexico, 99–102; in Pakistan, 156; from Saudi Arabia, 42–46, 47–48; weak governments and, 10, 11–12

interest rates, 117–18

internal conflicts. *See* civil conflicts / civil wars

International Atomic Energy Agency, 181n11

International Crisis Group, 160

International Energy Agency, 25

international relations theory, ix–x, 12

international war, ix, 2, 3–5, 147

Internet, in China, 141, 143

Inter-Services Intelligence Directorate, 77

interstate war. *See* international war

investment: by China, in U.S., 16, 116, 117–18, 170; in oil and gas production, 23, 94–95, 162–63. *See also* foreign direct investment

investment and trade policies, threat to, 16

Iran: China and, 118; Iraq and, 17; Khan and, 78; Khomeini and, 35, 80; nuclear weapons and, 15, 152; oil of, 16; revolution in, 1

Iran-Iraq War, 25, 33

Iraq: civil conflicts in, 1, 9; Gulf War and, 23; Hussein and, 8, 160; Kuwait and, 4; loyalty in, 10; military intervention in, 160; oil of, 22, 29, 152; Saudis and, 36, 45; terrorists and, 15

"iron rice bowl" safety net, 126

Islam: in China, 20, 118, 133–34; in Iraq, 9; in Pakistan, 63–64, 68, 70–74, 75, 77; in Saudi Arabia, 27, 34, 35, 37–42, 48; Saudi jihadists and, 42–46. *See also* Wahhabism

Israel, 5, 8, 18, 26, 27

Japan, 5, 16, 19, 24, 119

Jenkins, Brian, 15

Jiang Zemin, 144

jihadists, 42–46, 47–48

judicial system: in China, 138; in Mexico, 90–91

Kahn, Abdul Qadeer (A. Q.), 52, 78

Kargil campaign, 61, 77

Kashmir, 51, 72–73, 77

Khadaffi, Muammar, 16

Khobar barracks attack, 41

Khomeini, Ayatollah, 35, 80

kidnapping, in Mexico, 84, 90

Korea, 1, 17. *See also* North Korea; South Korea

Kurds, in Iraq, 8

Kuwait, 4, 8, 23, 27, 49, 164

Lal Masjid mosque, 74

land issues: in China, 130, 137; in Mexico, 101

legitimacy of government: of China, 138–40; of Mexico, 102–3, 110; of Pakistan, 75–76; right to rebel and, 9–10

liberalism, classical, 5

Libya, 16, 78

locks, on nuclear weapons, 59, 164–65

"long peace," 2

Lopez Obrador, Andres Manuel, 102, 105–6, 113

Los Pancho Villas, 111

Lugo Felix, Jose Nemesio, 187n54

madrassas, 74, 77

Mansfield, Edward, 159

maquiladoras, 87

Marcos, Subcommander, 101

Marshall, Monty, 7

Marxist-Leninist ideology, 116, 124, 138

Mecca, 37, 38–39, 40

Medina, 37, 40

Mexican Revolution, 97

Mexico: corruption in, 106–10; crime in, 84–85, 89, 90, 96–97; democracy and, 82, 99, 103–4, 106, 108, 159; deterrence policy and, 154–55; economy of, 84, 89, 91–97, 101, 102, 112–13, 169; government of, 90, 102–6, 110–12; grievances of people of, 88–91, 97–102; illegal drugs and, 19, 86–87, 96–97, 106–11, 113–14; instability in, 82–83, 88; institutions in, 91–92, 107; insurgents in, 99–102; military of, 109–10, 111–12; oil exports from, 94–95; overview of, x, 148–49; preparing for threat from, 167–70; prospect of civil war in, 19, 87–88, 112–14, 151; prospects for success of violence in, 110–12; U.S. interests in, 83–88, 93–94, 113

Middle Easterners, as illegal immigrants, 184n2

military: in China, 4, 115, 141, 142; in Mexico, 109–10, 111–12; in Pakistan, 63, 64–65, 66, 71, 76–80; in Saudi Arabia, 34–35, 46–47; of U.S., 3, 4 military intervention by U.S.: at Mexican border, 168; in Mexico, 84, 168; in Pakistan, 166; in Saudi oil fields, 163–64

missiles, long-range, 4–5

MMA (Muttahida Majlis-e-Amal), 71–72

Mossadegh, Mohammad, 160

Mueller, John, 11

Musharraf, Pervez: assassination attempts on, 62–63, 73–74; Baluchistan and, 69; democracy and, 75, 78; Islamist parties and, 70; MMA and, 72; nuclear weapons and, 57–58, 61; terrorists and, 78; U.S. and, 73

Muttahida Majlis-e-Amal (MMA), 71–72

NAFTA (North American Free Trade Agreement), 82, 87, 89

narcotics industry in Mexico, 19. *See also* drugs, illegal: Mexico and

National Action Party (PAN, Mexico), 82, 104–6

national identity card, 169

nationalism: in China, 120, 139–40, 170; in Pakistan, 67

NATO (North Atlantic Treaty Organization), 26

natural disasters: China and, 145–46; lessons from, 160–61, 171

natural resources, 11, 16, 69. *See also* oil

Nayef (prince), 34, 47

Nepal, 6

never/always dilemma, 59–61

Nicaragua, 1, 17

Nigeria, 6, 10, 18, 23, 152

9/11: events of, 15, 36, 42, 167; Pakistan and, 67–68, 73

North American Free Trade Agreement (NAFTA), 82, 87, 89

North Atlantic Treaty Organization (NATO), 26

North Korea, 5, 15, 18, 118, 152

North-West Frontier Province (NWFP), 67–68, 71–72

nuclear attack: preparing for public health consequences of, 167; source of, 53–54; threat of, 13, 14, 50, 53; against U.S., 4

nuclear attribution, 55

Nuclear Emergency Support Team (NEST), 165

nuclear energy, 162

nuclear weapons: in China, 54, 62; civil wars and, 61–64; countries of concern with, 152;

defense against, 165–66; government control of, 14; inadvertent use of, 55–56, 58, 60, 61; in Iran, 15, 152; locks on, 59, 164–65; in Pakistan, 51–53, 57–61, 78; prospect of terrorists gaining control of, 56–57, 58–59, 62–63; securing, 166; use of without government authorization, 56, 62. *See also* nuclear attack

Nuevo Laredo, 85, 108

NWFP (North-West Frontier Province), 67–68, 71–72

Oaxaca, Mexico, 102, 111

oil: Arab embargo of, 24, 25, 26; Baluchistan and, 69; countries of concern producing, 152; Mexico and, 19, 87, 94–95; Persian Gulf and, 22, 29; preparation for cutoff of, 161–64; Saudi Arabia and, 18, 21–25, 27–31, 35, 49; U.S. dependence on, 16, 21, 24–25, 26; world demand for, 24

oil fields: attacks on, 27–28, 29–30; Cantarell, 94; deterrence policy and, 153–54; protection of, 46–47; U.S. takeover of, 163–64

oil terminals, in Saudi Arabia, 29

Organization of Petroleum Exporting Countries (OPEC), 23

Pakistan: democracy and, 66, 75, 159; deterrence policy and, 156–57; domestic strife in, 8; economy of, 65–66; government of, 66, 67, 75–76; grievances of people of, 65–66, 70–74; impact of civil war in, 61–64; India and, 5, 51, 61, 63–64, 66, 72–73; insurgents in, 156; military of, 63, 64–65, 66, 71, 76–80; nuclear weapons of, 15, 51–53, 55–61; overview of, x, 148–49; pacifying effect of nuclear weapons on, 54–55; preparing for threat from, 164–67; prospect of civil war in, 18–19, 61–65, 69–70, 79–81, 150; prospects for success of violence in, 76–79; separatist movements in, 64, 66–70, 80; threat to U.S. interests by, 50–51, 53–55, 81

Palestine, 8, 15, 48

PALs (permissive action links), 59

Panama, 160

PAN (National Action Party, Mexico), 82, 104–6

Pashtuns, 67

peace, international, reasons for, 4–5

Pei, Minxin, 124
PEMEX, 94–95
People's Bank of China (PBC), 125–26
People's Liberation Army, 142
People's Republic of China. *See* China
permissive action links (PALs), 59
Persian Gulf, oil in, 22, 29
Persian Gulf War, 23, 33, 39–40
poison gas, 13
police force: in China, 132; in Mexico, 85, 90, 108–9
political development, 158
Political Order in Changing Societies (Huntington), 137
political parties. *See specific parties*
political violence, 6–7
pollution, of air and water: in China, 136–37; in Mexico, 87
Popular Revolutionary Army (EPR, Mexico), 99, 102
population: of China, 125, 130, 133, 142; of Mexican Americans, 83, 85–86; of Mexico, 92, 99, 101; of Pakistan, 65; of Saudi Arabia, 32; of Xianjiang, 133
Posse Comitatus Act, 168
post–Cold War era: civil conflicts in, 2, 12–17; international war, decline of in, 3–5, 147; security community in, 5
poverty, 9. *See also* wealth, distribution of
PRD (Democratic Revolutionary Party, Mexico), 82, 95, 104–6
predatory states, 124
preemption, policy of, 3, 166–67
preparation for dealing with threats: challenges of, x; from China, 170; from Mexico, 167–70; from Pakistan, 164–67; from Saudi Arabia, 161–64
prevention of civil conflicts, 158–60
PRI (Institutional Revolutionary Party, Mexico): corruption and, 107; end of reign of, 82, 99, 108; government paralysis and, 103–5; Zapatistas and, 100
psychological effects of weapons, 13
Punjabis, 67

QAP (Al Qaeda of the Arabian Peninsula), 44–45
Qutb, Sayyid, 42

radiological weapons, 13, 30, 53
Ras al-Ju'aymah oil terminal, 29
rebellions, numbers involved in, 11
refugees: preparation for, 168; Taiwan and, 119
religion: in China, 138; in Mexico, 101–2; in Pakistan, 63, 68, 70–74, 75, 77; regimes and, 10; in Saudi Arabia, 34, 37–42, 48. *See also* Islam
remittances to Mexico, 86, 93
"rentier" state, Saudi Arabia as, 31
repressive governments, 158
retaliation, threat of, 154, 155–56, 157
Richardson, Bill, 85
right to rebel/attack: as cause of war, 8, 9–10; in China, 138–40; in Mexico, 102–3; in Pakistan, 75–76; in Saudi Arabia, 37–42
royal family of Saudi Arabia: bin Laden and, 43; citizens and, 26–27; succession issue in, 33–34, 48; tribal grievances against, 36; U.S. troop presence and, 40–41
Rubio, Luis, 91
Ruiz Massieu, Jose Francisco, 107
Ruiz Massieu, Mario, 107
Rummel, R. J., 158
rural grievances: in China, 123, 130–31; in Mexico, 89, 99–102
Russia: Chechen conflict in, 11; China and, 119; civil conflict in, 8, 12, 18, 121, 152; oil reserves of, 22, 24; revolution in, 1, 6. *See also* Soviet Union
Rwanda, 6, 11

Sachs, Jeffrey, 31
Salafiyya, 42
Salinas, Carlos, 91, 101, 107
Salinas, Raul, 107
SARS (severe acute respiratory syndrome), 135
Saud, Muhammad ibn, 37–38
Saudi Arabia: armed forces of, 34–35, 46–47; democratic practices and, 48, 159; deterrence policy and, 153–54; economy of, 31–33; government of, 39–42; grievances of people of, 31–37; jihadists in, 42–46, 47–48; oil of, 18, 21–25, 27–31, 35, 49; overview of, x, 148–49; preparing for threat from, 161–64; prospect of civil war in, 18, 30–31, 36, 48–49, 150; prospects for success of violence in, 46–48;

religion in, 34, 37–42; Shiite population of, 32, 35; U.S. troops in, 39–40, 43–44. *See also* royal family of Saudi Arabia

security community, 5

security forces. *See* military

security issues: border control and, 83–84; travel abroad and, 17

self-defense, policy of, 3

separatist movements: in China, 133–35; in Pakistan, 64, 66–70, 80

September 11. *See* 9/11

severe acute respiratory syndrome (SARS), 135

Shanghai Cooperation Organization, 119

Sharif, Nawaz, 72

Shiite population: of Iraq, 9; of Pakistan, 71; of Saudi Arabia, 32, 35

Shirk, Susan, 121

Sierra Leone, 6

Sindh, 69

smallpox, 13, 30

smuggling of nuclear weapons, 57

Snyder, Jack, 159

Somalia, 1

South Africa, 8

South Korea, 5, 12, 19, 21, 24, 119

Soviet Union, 1, 17, 52, 53–54. *See also* Russia

state-owned enterprises, in China, 126

Strategic Petroleum Reserve, 161–62

strong countries, creation of, by war, 11

succession issue in Saudi Arabia, 33–34, 48

Sunnis: of Iraq, 9; of Pakistan, 71

swing producer of oil, Saudi Arabia as, 23

Syria, 26, 152

Taiwan: Chinese-U.S. relations and, 116, 120–21; civil conflict in, 12; deterrence policy and, 155–56; independence of, 115; potential invasion of, 145; refugees and, 119; trade with China by, 19

Taliban: madrassas and, 74; Pakistan and, 19, 50, 68, 77, 78; Pashtuns in, 67

targeted killing, threat of, 157

technology sector, in China, 125

Teitelbaum, Joshua, 40

territorial issues, 4–5

terrorist groups: border with Mexico and, 83–84; defense against, 165–66; deterrence

policy and, 14–15, 156–58; nuclear weapons and, 55, 56–57, 62–63; in Pakistan, 58–59, 72–73; prevention and, 166. *See also* Al Qaeda

threats to United States: characteristics of, x; civil wars as, 2–3, 148–50; dependence on imported natural resources, 16; investment and trade policies, 16–17; overview of, ix–x; responding to, 153–58; as unintended, 3, 171–72; WMD, 13–15. *See also* preparation for dealing with threats

Tiananmen demonstrations, 120, 141–42, 143

Tibet, 119, 123, 133, 134–35

Tilly, Charles, 11

trade: interstate war and, 5; Taiwan and, 121; between U.S. and Mexico, 82, 87, 89, 93

treasury securities, 16, 19–20, 116, 117–18, 170

tribes: in Pakistan, 58, 67; in Saudi Arabia, 35–36

Tsai, Kellee, 127

Turkey, 18

turmoil, definition of, 6–7

Uighurs, 133–34

unemployment: in China, 131; in Mexico, 91, 92; in Pakistan, 65–66; in Saudi Arabia, 32

unintended threats, x, 3, 171–72

United Nations, 10, 118

United States: China and, 117–22; civil war in, 6, 8; dependence on oil by, 16, 21, 24–25, 26; deployment of troops in Saudi Arabia by, 39–40, 43–44; economy of, 25, 29, 87, 93–94; Mexico and, 83–88, 93–94, 113; military power of, 3, 4; MMA and, 72; national debt of, held by foreigners, 16; oil reserves of, 22; promotion of stability by, 159–60; as safe from foreign aggression, 147; security community and, 5; Tibet and, 134–35. *See also* immigrants to U.S.; military intervention by U.S.

uranium, reprocessing and enrichment of, 52

urban grievances, in China, 131

Valle Espinosa, Eduardo, 98

Venezuela, 18, 23, 152

Vietnam, 1, 6, 17, 119

Villa, Pancho, 84
violence: in China, 140–44; gain from, 8–9; in
  Mexico, 84–85, 99–101, 102, 110–12; in Pakistan, 74, 76–79; political, 6–7; in Saudi Arabia, 41–42, 44–45, 46–48; in Xianjiang, 134

Wahhabism, 34, 35, 36–39, 45–46, 48
Waltz, Kenneth, 54, 173n1
Warner, Andrew, 31
wealth, distribution of: in China, 122–23; in
  Mexico, 89, 99, 101; in Saudi Arabia, 32
weapons of mass destruction (WMD): attacks
  on oil fields using, 29–30; individual use of,
  14, 53, 56; Pakistan and, 18–19; threat of,
  13–15. *See also specific types of weapons*

Western Europe, 5
Why Men Rebel (Gurr), 6–7
World Trade Organization, China and, 118
World War II, ix, 2

Xinjiang, 119, 123, 133–34

Yemen, 9
youth cohort, male, in China, 132–33
Yugoslavia, 12

Zapatistas, 99, 100–101, 102, 111
Zedillo, Ernesto, 107, 108
Zhao Ziyang, 141, 142
Zia-ul-Haq, Mohammad, 52, 69, 70–71, 77